The Letters *of an* Unexpected Mystic

The Letters *of an* Unexpected Mystic

Encountering the Mystical Theology in First and Second Peter

ROBERT D. FLANAGAN

Foreword by Yvonne Dohna Schlobitten

WIPF & STOCK · Eugene, Oregon

THE LETTERS OF AN UNEXPECTED MYSTIC
Encountering the Mystical Theology in First and Second Peter

Copyright © 2022 Robert D. Flanagan. All rights reserved. Except for brief quotations in critical publications or reviews, no part of this book may be reproduced in any manner without prior written permission from the publisher. Write: Permissions, Wipf and Stock Publishers, 199 W. 8th Ave., Suite 3, Eugene, OR 97401.

Wipf & Stock
An Imprint of Wipf and Stock Publishers
199 W. 8th Ave., Suite 3
Eugene, OR 97401

www.wipfandstock.com

PAPERBACK ISBN: 978-1-6667-0505-8
HARDCOVER ISBN: 978-1-6667-0506-5
EBOOK ISBN: 978-1-6667-0507-2

JULY 14, 2022 10:19 AM

Unless otherwise indicated, Scripture quotations are taken from the New Revised Standard Version Bible, copyright © 1989 the Division of Christian Education of the National Council of the Churches of Christ in the United States of America. Used by permission. All rights reserved.

Scripture from the New King James Version® is copyright © 1982 Thomas Nelson. Used by permission. All rights reserved.

To Lanie,
my Chief Encouragement Officer (CEO)

Like living stones, let yourselves be built into a spiritual house, to be a holy priesthood, to offer spiritual sacrifices acceptable to God through Jesus Christ.

1 Pet 2:5

Contents

Foreword by Yvonne Dohna Schlobitten | ix
Acknowledgments | xxiii
Scripture Abbreviations | xxiv

1. Mystic and Mysticism | 1
2. Threefold Seeing | 20
3. Dianoia | 35
4. The Unexpected Mystic | 45
5. The Mystical Theology of First Peter | 59
6. The Mystical Theology of Second Peter | 88
7. Metanoia | 107
8. Petrine Mystical Theology | 118
9. Petrine Mysticism and the Twenty-first Century | 138
10. The Threefold Rose | 151

Bibliography | 155
Subject Index | 163
Scripture Index | 171

Foreword

THE WORK OF ART AND THE ORIGIN OF KNOWLEDGE[1]

ROMANO GUARDINI, who wrote about figures (*Gestalten*) from theology, philosophy, ethics, art and literature, spirituality and psychology, pedagogy and natural science, expresses in his thinking a deep connection between comprehension and contemplation in the process of creative work.[2] Guardini uses the relationship between the artist, the work of art, and the beholder—that is, the contemplator (*Betrachter*)—which relate to each other in a dynamic triangle, to weave together the central categories of image and figure, form and fullness, formation (*Formung*) and figuration (*Gestaltung*),

---

1. This new understanding of Guardini's thinking was developed by me and justified by the new sources in the archives, systematically developed and elaborated by Helmut Zenz. I have agreed with him that in future translations of Guardini into other languages, we will pay more attention to the German language of the texts. Where the target language allows fewer variations, but the associated loan or foreign words are too one-sided, this means that related words in German (*Sein, Dasein, Wesen*) are all three translated with the same English term "being" (provided with the German term in parentheses) instead of using the philosophical loanwords "existence" and "essence" with their one-sided connotations. The use of these words in English would lead to a rendering with *Existenz* and *Essenz* when translated back, but in German philosophical discourse, they lead to a dialectic of existentialism and essentialism, while in Guardini, *Sein/Dasein* and *Wesen* have no such dialectic relation. Also, in the English translation for *Gestalt* and *Gestaltung*, we use the formula "figure" (*Gestalt*) and "(con)figuration" (*Gestaltung*), because the translations with "form" or "design" are incorrect. We would also like to point out that Guardini uses the terms *Anschauung, Betrachtung*, and *Kontemplation* largely synonymously, so that the *Anschauende* or *Betrachter* of a work of art in the English translation is best identified with "beholder" and "contemplator," but not with "observer" or "spectator." Finally, we believe that Guardini's quoted *Blick Christi* is unhappily translated as "the gaze of Christ." We are aware that the more literal "the look of Christ" is also weak in English. Therefore, we usually dodge the rendering with "the threefold seeing" (*Blick Christi*).

2. Dohna Schlobitten, "Lasciarsi Guardare."

and transformation and transfiguration.³ He looks on figures, regardless of whether they are artists, works of art, or beholders of works of art, with the "look of Christ" (*Blick Christi*), which is the look of the Trinitarian God on the whole of the world.

His approach to art and knowledge of art becomes the foundation of his trinitarian approach and the knowledge of the trinitarian knowledge itself as the origin of the structure of the individual disciplines.

The secret of Guardini's comprehension of art and knowledge of art lies in their connection to self-realization, namely, the realization of self as a creative part of the world and the realization of self as an image of God (*Ebenbild Gottes*), as a creative artistic process that has taken on the form of the being (*Dasein*) in the work of art. My research focuses on the analysis and revival of Guardini's contribution on the nature of the work of art and his reflections on art appreciation and art knowledge (*Kunsterkenntnis*) as the origin of his "Catholic comprehension of the world" (*katholische Weltanschauung*).⁴

Guardini goes beyond this, which is about a "world" that is born in every work of art, a world that reveals itself through our seeing and perception.

This deals with two different conceptions of the world, the "world of first degree" (nature) and the "world of second degree" (culture). In the latter, a work of art, according to Guardini´s eschatological conception, builds a bridge to the coming world. In autobiographical notes that have not yet been published, Guardini says that he developed this eschatological conviction very early on during his student days in Munich and Berlin.⁵

Every true work of art is an authentic world: an ordered and filled space in which we have access to the very Other (God), the created object, and myself through looking, listening, and walking. With the threefold seeing (*Blick Christi*) of a work of art, a space of knowledge opens into which man can enter, and, in this opening, an urgent task is revealed.

To best understand the space to which Guardini refers, we must explore each aspect of the triadic relationship and, in each, the threefold seeing (*Blick Christi*), which for Guardini seems similar to the seeing of the artist who is like a child or a prophet.

---

3. Dohna Schlobitten and Gerhards, *Lotta di Giacobbe*, 17–75, 99–103, and Dohna Schlobitten, "Forma dell'immagine."

4. Dohna Schlobitten, "Romano Guardini e la Weltanschauung."

5. Guardini, "Report on My Life," 152.

THE ARTIST

The first aspect of Guardini's triangle is the artist. Through an intimate encounter, the artist sees the "whole" and is able to realize his comprehension in the work of art, so that we can see the "whole" in it.

Knowledge is an act of an encounter in love, says Guardini.[6] The artist, through a personal threefold knowledge (theoretical knowledge, knowledge of experience, and contemplative knowledge [*katholische Weltanschauung*]), shows the sense of the thing and, in so doing, shows the sense of himself. In this way, the artist's creativity is subordinated to a task: to serve being (*es dient dem Dasein*).[7]

The artist himself must become a work of art to reveal the being of the encounter with things and events through the figure (*Gestalt*), and each artist works according to his own talent and perspective.[8] By encountering the "thing," the artist (the painter) clarifies his own self-realization and the realization of the work of art as a "trace of the trinitarian God" (*vestigium Trinitatis*/*Spurbild des dreifaltigen Gottes*).[9]

By grasping the being of things, he grasps himself in truth; by becoming aware of the being of the thing, the artist increases his self-awareness, the awareness of both the Other and the other, leading to what Guardini calls the "encounter," which leads to a kind of awakening and penetration in a threefold way. It is in this threefold relation that a great work of art is configured creatively (*wird kreativ gestaltet*).

To better understand this idea, one must see that this is truly an encounter, as opposed to an accidental meeting or crossing of paths or simply clashing into each other. Rather, although each representation is focused on a fragment of the world, the artist perceives and processes it, creating something mysterious, creating the whole. Guardini's threefold seeing (*Blick Christi*) is able to see the whole and the fragment, the concrete reality

---

6. Guardini, *Gestalten*, 17.

7. Guardini, *Vita come opera d'arte*, 5 and 88; also in Guardini, *Wurzeln eines großen Lebenswerks*, 3:338.

8. Guardini's own approach to the knowledge of art began with the publication of a selection of eighty poems and thirty-four letters by Michelangelo, as well as a further five letters from Vittoria Colonna to Michelangelo. Guardini translated all the letters into German himself. This collection, published in 1907, is characteristic of his artistic way of thinking.

9. Guardini, *Wurzeln eines großen Lebenswerks*, 1:12.

and the abstract, at the same time and is able to give sense to the being as a whole *(Dasein als Ganzes)*.

In doing so, the artist enters an extraordinary dimension, for not only does he show how truth touches humans, but the artist, who understands properly, also succeeds in extrapolating this truth and using it to show various aspects of human nature in their generality, giving the experience depicted a profound anthropological-theological sense.

Thus, the great works are unsurpassed messages about human nature, emerging from an idiosyncratic and intimate comprehension of the individual to reveal the secrets of the soul of each of us. They are images that have a saving and illuminating effect on the spirit and creativity of the artist himself, on his way to realizing himself as a work of art.

THE WORK OF ART

To understand the fundamental reflections on the being of art, Guardini places Van Gogh's chair at the center of his explanations, knowing in it the *power* the work of art has as a whole of being (*das Ganze des Daseins*) that becomes present. For Guardini, a genuine work of art is not, like every directly perceived appearance, a mere section of what exists but a whole. The chair in front of him, for example, is in a context that extends in all directions. As soon as he takes a picture of it with the photographic apparatus, the character of the detail comes into sharp focus.[10]

Guardini further explains that he never sees this whole directly before his eyes. He himself sees only as a tiny part of an incalculable context, such that every object he encounters is likewise; and thus he understands his life is always only a relationship from fragment to fragment.[11]

Everything we encounter is therefore seen only in a "fragment-fragment" relationship. Yet something special happens in the process of the artistic creative work: each aspect that emerges from the thing and the beholder (*Betrachter*) perceiving the part that emerges then generates a kind of force. Around this force, the whole of being becomes present and the whole thing—the whole of nature, man, and history—lives in one. But when Vincent van Gogh sees it, a peculiar process already begins in his seeing. Guardini says that the chair becomes the center around which everything else in the room gathers; at the same time, it forms itself in such a

---

10. Guardini, *Vita come opera d'arte*, 98.
11. Guardini, *Vita come opera d'arte*, 99.

way that its parts arrange themselves around its own center in its own being (*Dasein*).

Around it, the whole *(das Ganze)* of this being becomes present in nature, which is the whole of things (*das All der Dinge*), and in history, which is the whole of human life (*das All des Menschenlebens*), both alive in One. Therefore, this whole (*All*) is catholic in the old Greek sense of *katholikos* (all-embracing, all encompassing). In this way: "Around him resounds the sound of the whole (*All*)."[12]

This all-embracing dimension of the work of art is paradoxically based on the unconscious impulses of the artist that act upon his thought and creative act. Equally, the images receive a redemptive and illuminating effect on the mind and creativity of the artist himself, becoming unsurpassed images that ultimately reveal the secrets of the soul of the thing in the beholder (*Betrachter*).

Guardini describes the transformation of texts, especially biblical texts, into images through the following process. The artist perceives the fragment and processes it, creating something mysterious—in Guardini's words, a "power"—which sees each fragment and, at the same time, sees the whole, which does not mean to see a unity of the fragments or a synthesis but the ability to see the "in between" and thus give sense to the whole of the being (*das Ganze des Daseins*).[13]

However, religious artwork has a different reality from the biblical text. In the creative act, through a process in which the core of the work has penetrated the intimacy of the artist, the artwork is given a sophisticated character. What this creative act reveals cannot be otherwise. For every artist reveals "his encounter" with the biblical text but in a "ciphered" way. For the work of art is not a mere detail like some optical appearance but represents a whole (*das Ganze*). By making the text of the Bible present in its universality, the artist encounters the being of the work explicitly and becomes it. In this way, the artist creates something that touches himself and, as such, could touch all people. In the work of art, however, we not only know how the artist looks at the biblical text and how he transforms it, but we can also see the encounter, the process of knowing, in light of the biblical context.

---

12. Guardini, *Vita come opera d'arte*, 99.

13. Guardini, *Vita come opera d'arte*, 99; also in Guardini, *Über das Wesen* (2005), 16, 346.

Thus, the work of art is a place where one can enter with one's senses to perceive one's own sense of the being (*Dasein*). As a literary work, for Guardini, the Bible is itself also a work of art and thus a space into which one can enter with one's senses. Beyond that, however, it is also a direct, historically authenticated self-revelation of God in the incarnation of God. Therefore, the Bible itself is able to "penetrate into the soul of the beholder" (*Betrachter*) and to experience the actual "sense of being" (*Dasein*) to reveal the biblical text.

In addition, however, the work of art also has the power to convey a theological, biblical message, at least in the form of the inherent promise and the inherent trace of the Trinity.

For Guardini, every work of art contains this eschatological promise, but in no way does every work of art "reinforce" a theological message. Many works of art—including many devotional and cult images—make the theological message of the Bible less clear (e.g., kitsch); images and works of art with non-biblical motifs, on the other hand, can sometimes reinforce the theological message of the Bible through the "sincerity" of the promise, without having any direct biblical reference.

The more truthful and intimate the process of the artist, in dealing with and elaborating the biblical text, the more sincere and powerful the message. However, according to the Bible, we should love ourselves, the other, and God with all our thoughts or with all our mind, as a reflection of a universal light that conducts figures (*Gestalten*) to arrive at the truth of being (*Wahrheit des Seins*) and the knowledge (*Erkenntnis*) of man in his spiritual and existential dimension.

THE BEHOLDER (*BETRACHTER*)

In his attempt to explain the being of the work of art and its perception, Guardini first writes about the "perception" of the artist.

The contemplating of the painter becomes a figure (*Gestalt*) in the work of art. In the re-contemplating of the beholder (*Betrachter*) of this outer structure of the lines and colors of the canvas can appear this figure (*Gestalt*). A work of art opens up to something in advance that is not yet there. It is not clear how and when it will arise; nevertheless, one feels it in the innermost promise.[14]

---

14. Guardini, *Über das Wesen* (1959), 25: "Man spürt die Verheissung."

Guardini writes that the painter has formed the thing by looking, that is, by contemplatively knowing the whole (*Ganze*) of the being (*Wesen*) of the thing. And, as such, he paints it on the canvas. In his 1927 essay "Living Freedom," Guardini writes about the connection between knowledge of art and knowledge of truth, which lies in the honest "looking at" by the beholder (*Betrachter*). The sense of the work of art is that a being, a hidden being, is expressed in form. But not in such a way that one must stop in front of it. The final attitude towards the work of art is not to look at it from a distance. Rather, the work of art is such that one can enter into it. One can be inside it; one is grasped by the formed and forming being and is made right oneself. This entering into the shaped spiritual space of the work of art is also experienced as a free breathing and moving with things and people.[15] It is the process of freedom.

The beholder (*Betrachter*) can become aware of what has happened and is happening in the work of art by encountering it. The true relationship with the work of art is, on the one hand, to become still in order to penetrate, look, and participate in the art and to awaken the senses and open the soul. On the other hand, Guardini states, "To 'see'—perhaps we should say more accurately 'to care', to 'behold'—means first of all and fundamentally to be touched by the 'task' of the object/of the world, which is also a sensory phenomenon in the object and to be called upon not only to understand its content but the 'religiosity,' the being of the work of art." Guardini emphasizes: "It is wrong to say that the eye first perceives mere sensory data in a plant, into which the mind then introduces the concept of life, but rather, it sees this life itself. Yes, this, even before all those individual data; and the position, the spatiality, the firmness, the individual form and color values, relations and movements of a tree, for example, it understands only out of its liveliness."[16]

"The 'eye' is thus much more than the mechanical-biological way of thinking grants it. In this case, 'seeing' is encounter with reality";[17] the eye, however, is simply the human being, insofar as one can be met by reality in its forms assigned to light. In the space of knowledge, light reveals the real. Seeing is the response of the eye and, in the eye of the human being, to

---

15. Guardini, *Vita come opera d'arte*. 104.
16. Guardini, *Wurzeln eines großen Lebenswerks*, 3:187.
17. Translated by the author from Guardini, *Wurzeln eines großen Lebenswerks*, 3:187: "'Das Auge' ist also viel mehr, als die mechanisch-biologische Denkweise ihm zubilligt. 'Sehen' ist Begegnung mit der Wirklichkeit."

the light-related real. To be more precise, it is the *Gestalt* of being (*Wesen*), which is formed in relation to light by the respective real and the eye together, in which being (*Wesen*) takes place. The act of living consists in the manner of expression—not as a simple agglomeration of characteristics, not even as an idea that lies behind it, but in such a way that the thing becomes what it is already but is not yet realized. The thing appears as what it is. This being (*Dasein*) is hidden in our seeing, and all the more so, the higher its rank. But it appears, becomes present, becomes evident in what is directly there.[18]

In a 1924 postscript to Kleist's "About the Puppet Theater," Guardini recalls a conversation five years earlier in Mainz, to restate this connection. He had spoken "about the enigmatic twoness (*Zweiheit*) that lies within [the work of art]. This is the dichotomy between what is initially tangible, perceptible—the real stone, the colors, the sounds, which is nevertheless all only a means and an indication—and what is actually meant, the inner figure (*Gestalt*)."[19] But the twoness is in opposition to its religious being, which means to be lively-concrete; and, at the same time, it is a promise, which will emerge in the moment of the encounter.

The promise is not real but rises in the spirit of the beholder (*Betrachter*) when he encounters what the artist has done artistically in his sensually tangible signs. The beholder (*Betrachter*) needs the courage to re-configure (*erschaffen*) them anew, inwardly.

Guardini described a performance (*Schauspiel*) where he saw how the duality can become particularly strong:

> For here, as in every work of art, not only does the outwardly visible lag behind what is actually meant, but it even interposes itself in an inhibiting way between the latter and the contemplator, who is called upon to work creatively himself. He always tends to attract our attention; that we see him in his real or claimed personal merits, in the bravura of his performance and forget about the real. We then have our pleasure in the next given, external; we indulge in expert judgments about the artist's conception and performance, and shirk the actual, great task of the beholder: to build up that piece of the human world which we are supposed to build up, in other words we want to stand in the "community of beingness"

---

18. Guardini, *Wurzeln eines großen Lebenswerks*, 3:190.
19. Guardini, *Wurzeln eines großen Lebenswerks*, 2:196.

(*wesenhaften Gemeinschaft*) of the artist and the beholder and so we want to be real beholders and not only entertained people.[20]

In this postscript, Guardini apparently speaks of the "artist" as the "creative person"; but the question is, who is the artist in the puppet show? Is he the author of the play, or the actor, or the director? However, if one reads carefully, one sees that Guardini speaks here of our mission, our "should," which we have received from our creator (i.e., God), to participate in the "becoming world" (*Weltwerdung*) of the second world, the human world—culture.

When considering the threefold seeing, Guardini's thoughts often return to the origin of things. In his reflections on seeing, Guardini speaks of knowledge in the "look of Christ" and not explicitly of *Gestaltung/Schaffen*.

Guardini writes in his text about "the beginnings of all things (1956/57) that there is a beginning from which I can know myself, and the human brothers and sisters, and the world in its being and "becoming." God's will that I be, his creative sense directed towards me: that is my beginning. To the extent that I know—let us rather say, to the extent that I become at home in the mystery of this manifestation—is the extent to which my life finds its sense.[21] And that, for Guardini, is real knowledge.

Guardini also seeks and describes this announcement and realization of himself as the outcome of my being (*Wesen*) in all actions: in creating art, in praying, right down to the simplest gestures, as his early reflections on the "Sacred Signs" (1922–1925) testify.[22] In the original preface, which today is accessible only in the first to third editions themselves, Guardini not coincidentally also opens with the image of the tree.

Guardini says, "We no longer think of things but of words."[23] When one talks about a thing, it is often no longer really in front one's eyes, in its greatness and inner being (*Wesen*). It becomes only a word with an certain quantitative value.

> Saying a word, one may have a glimpse or a past memory of earlier experiences in one's mind. This thinking in only words has no relevance for reality. These words no longer have any visual power; they don't go to the heart. Although one speaks words, makes forms, lives in a world of signs, the connection to the reality

---

20. Guardini, *Wurzeln eines großen Lebenswerks*, 2:196.
21. Guardini, *Anfang aller Dinge*, 16.
22. Guardini, *Von heiligen Zeichen*, 14.
23. Guardini, *Von heiligen Zeichen*, 7.

> that they mean has been lost. Only when we stand in front of the real, in front of the things themselves and their being (*Wesen*), in front of the soul, and when we feel their push, something new can grow, a rejuvenated culture and a renewed life. Words must again become images of things, full of sense, and bodies of events, full of sound in the soul; and actions must be filled with inner reality, so that reality is actually grasped in word and deed. Guardini is convinced that we have to pause, marvel, and ask the being (*das Seiende*), to feel its push; and this push has to flow back effectually in our word and work. Only then will there arise a power for renewal. But Guardini is not concerned with getting rid of the obsolete and inventing the new, but, rather, to "give back their sense" to words and forms, seeing the reality that lies behind them. When we reexperience what is expressed in them, they are filled with inner fullness.[24]

Guardini then goes on to describe kneeling, standing, and folding the hands as responses to this "push of the being."

Therefore, if, as Guardini writes, the power of the beginning also lies within us, it means that we, too, can work creatively, in the freedom into which God has placed us. Guardini describes this relationship of creating in freedom towards this beginning in the creative work of the artist and analogously in the encounter of the beholder (*Betrachter*) with the work of art.

According to Guardini, in the space of the work of art, one encounters a promise, which, because the artist as a creature of God and in the comprehension of the whole and true being of the painted "things," the artist has more or less comprehended and has, therefore, consciously or unconsciously, incorporated it into the work of art.

What is done as a creative work (*Schaffen*) in the second world (culture), we can encounter in a work of art, independent of a direct, mostly impossible "encounter" with the artist. The artist's being, but also his "genius," goes into the work of art and becomes figures (*Gestalt*). But this is not meant as the "promise" inherent in the work of art, which God alone conveys as the creator of the human being. God incarnates it in the work of art itself.

The work of art's real sense, however, consists in the fact that it forms a world in which the being of things and, at the same time, interwoven with it, the creative human being himself is revealed more sincerely and

24. Guardini, *Von heiligen Zeichen*, 7–14.

fully than in reality—just as the represented, at first fragmentary, section of this reality is formed into a whole, which forms a symbol of the whole of the being (*Dasein*). The beholder (*Betrachter*) enters this small world, which is clear in its being (*Wesen*), and senses the whole, which can never be grasped directly. He becomes more intimately aware of his own being and experiences a shaping that comes from a deeper essentiality. In this, too, lies freedom: a widening of seeing.[25] Therefore, in the work of art, God *provokes* or calls out the human to seek an encounter with himself, to accept himself and the struggle with his beginning and origin, and to walk the path towards it.

The secret of Guardini's comprehension of art and knowledge of art lies in the connection between becoming human and seeing an artistic creative process that has taken on the *Gestalt* of the being (*Dasein*) in the work of art, with the idea that a "new human being" is incarnated.

Art often speaks unconsciously of a new being (*Dasein*). In it everything is open, the things are in the "heart space of the human being" and the human being lets his own being (*Wesen*) flow into the things.[26]

Where things stand in the heart space of the human being and the human being lets his being flow into things, there is the new being (*Dasein*), where everything is open. Art often does not know that it is talking about this newness.

Guardini understood perfectly what Van Gogh wrote about Delacroix, when Van Gogh said: "Je suis la peinture" (The painting is me).[27] Thus, when Delacroix speaks of color, the color itself becomes the "task." Van Gogh embraced this existential dimension of art. Guardini, through his love and study of Van Gogh's art, also grasped the true dimension of modern contemporary art.[28]

Therefore, in the work of art lies the beginning and the possibility to start new; in its structure and being lie the vocation of the beholder (*Betrachter*) and of the artist who encounters the vocation of the thing/world. In the process of the creative act, the artist can see the vocation of the thing/world, created by God, the God who wants to see his creation strong and constantly alive. The freedom of man is, as Anselm of Canterbury says, that the moment of originality, of the productive, has reached a maximum here.

---

25. Guardini, *Freiheit, Gnade, Schicksal*, 41.
26. Guardini, *Über das Wesen* (1959), 30.
27. Delacroix, "Fragments du journal," 928; Nizon, *Van Gogh*, 214, 224.
28. Dohna Schlobitten, "Romano Guardini and Van Gogh."

Freedom is the human creative act par excellence. Anselm of Canterbury calls it *sub Deo omnipotentia* (omnipotence under God). Only that form of comprehension that is borne by reverence, in the true sense of the word, the attitude that is demanded towards freedom and its sovereignty, does justice to it.[29]

In the heart, there is the amazing ability to turn to good or evil, to decide against righteousness and, at the same time, for or against one's own origin. Freedom is the open side of the human being and includes the freedom to fail.

Guardini understood the dimension of the numinous in the work of art. For this reason, he formulated a comprehension of art and knowledge of art that takes seriously the human as well as the theological dimension in the work of art. Thus, he anticipates the contemporary discourse on the nature of art-making, as also found in the writings of other philosophers on contemporary art such as Jean-Luc Nancy, Didi-Huberman, and Merleau-Ponty.

Didi-Huberman speaks of a kind of ritual from which the subject is constituted, when contemporary art wants to make us feel like a blind man reaching out his hand.[30] This experience does not extinguish transcendence and does not take refuge in a dull materiality.

Through this encounter, humans can approach an openness that is for us the true sense of conversion, and which Guardini calls a catholic comprehension of the world (*katholische Weltanschauung*)—that is, a way of seeing things and participating in them as an inescapable task of humans not to superimpose an imagined sense on the world, not to limit the world to a particular sense, and not to attribute the phenomenon to the appearance of a background world from which it does not originate. World-comprehension, rather, means restoring the fullness of ties to the world. It concerns the authentic experience of specifically human beings.

Contemporary art therefore gives great importance to the notion of experience originally associated with ritual acts, which is experience as an approach "in motion"—as Merleau-Ponty would say, to accept things actively and passively at the same time and to be accepted by them.[31] This experience is an experience of otherness, which is about not only taking but accepting, in a gesture of playful acceptance, as a response of the person

---

29. Guardini, "Freiheit und Unabänderlichkeit," in *Aus dem Bereich*, 117–37.
30. Dohna Schlobitten, "Imparare ad abbandonarsi."
31. See especially Merleau-Ponty, *Auge und Geist*, 275–317.

who has experienced an authentic conversion. In this sense, contemporary theological and philosophical discourses on art appreciation as knowledge have a great affinity with Guardini's art appreciation, with its theoretical and conceptual categories.

The quality of the work is no longer seen from a purely formal point of view. Its authenticity depends essentially on its spiritual, living, and founding power. Only a work that succeeds in imposing itself on the world and thus opening its own world and its own comprehension of being reaches the highest level of quality. In this sense, Kandinsky speaks of the prophetic character of the work of art, of it becoming world and of it being able to be inhabited by people.[32]

Guardini is not only in the wake of this tradition but has gone beyond it and thus was able to formulate an independent comprehension of and theology of "promise," of the religious-eschatological character of a work of art.[33]

CONCLUSION

From these considerations, it is plausible to derive a triadic structure that can order the three forms of knowing: theoretical, experiential, and contemplative (*Weltanschauung*), which is also able to look in between the first two. We can also talk about a *religious epistemology of the knowing of art*, which defines *Weltanschauung* as a kind of encounter of the world, of the self, and of God at the same time. Guardini avoids the danger related to understanding the process of creative knowing as an encounter with an ideal of perfect self-reflection, which means being and knowing are juxtaposed in the sense of a subject-object relationship and a trialogical encounter. Instead, Guardini speaks of a "triadic/trinitarian structure of seeing" (*Blick Christi*) between the author, the work, and the beholder (*Betrachter*), as a paradigm of the comprehension of the world. The true ethos of this contemplative seeing of the world consists of the sincerity of the look (*Lauterkeit des Blicks*).[34] The *Weltanschauung* is a kind of world-comprehension in contemplation. It is a look that is embedded in life near me, closer than

---

32. Kandinsky, *Über das Geistige*, 24.

33. Guardini, *Vita come opera d'arte*, 115.

34. Guardini: "Das eigenste Ethos des Weltanschauens besteht gerade in der Lauterkeit dieses Blickes." Quoted in Gerl-Falkovitz, *Romano Guardini*, 274.

all sciences. *Weltanschauung* speaks of duties and demands that the world addresses the subject.

The person is more than subject and will, and the world becomes more than totaling a sum of objects. Both are phenomenally deeply related and dependent on each other. Only in opening oneself to others, finding oneself in the opposite, and appearing in the receiving space and the receiving time can we encounter each other in the light.

In a Christian formulation, the encounter of eye and light creates an "incarnation," namely, the "incarnation of the world."[35] This expanse holds its center in the vitality of the creator or, more precisely, in the vitality of the Logos, which creatively radiates through the world, offering itself into the encounter.

YVONNE DOHNA SCHLOBITTEN

---

35. Gerl-Falkovitz, "Auge und Licht," 34–35.

Acknowledgments

I start by stating, perhaps presumptuously, that the Holy Spirit has guided this work. However, if the author of Second Peter is correct, and I pray so, then the Holy Spirit's wisdom must have been present in my efforts. As the author writes, "First of all you must understand this, that no prophecy of scripture is a matter of one's own interpretation, because no prophecy ever came by human will, but men and women moved by the Holy Spirit spoke from God" (1:20–21). Therefore, I thank the Spirit's guidance and take responsibility for any interpretative errors. I pray this work is "a lamp shining in a dark place" (1:19), guiding its readers to a fuller understanding of Peter and his mystical theology.

    Life is a stew of plans, goals, and hopes that simmer in a cast-iron pot and is seasoned by trials and ordeals. The finished meal can be surprisingly different from the original recipe and often result in a sumptuous delight or flat disappointment. What makes life a delight is the partners with whom we share it, the living stones that God places next to us as he creates a spiritual house. I am blessed to be placed next to Lanie and mortared together in a delightful marriage. We are two stones that strengthen each other, forever holding hands.

    I have been equally blessed by my academic colleagues who have encouraged me to craft this work. President and Dean of the Virginia Theological Seminary Ian Markham spurred me to move this project from a future fancy to an urgent endeavor. I am indebted to him for offering me the Dean's Scholar position at the Seminary, by which I had the space and time to pray, think, and research during the spring semester of 2021. Equally, the head librarian Mitzi Budde has given me invaluable guidance and accommodated my requests during the Bishop Payne Library's major renovation. Her assistance and the hospitality of the library staff saved me countless hours and eased my research tasks. I am also grateful to Stephen Cook and his students.

Yvonne Dohna Schlobitten, who is associate professor of history and cultural heritage of the church at the Pontifical University Gregorian, invited me to join her in the development of Romano Guardini's threefold seeing. Since late 2019, we have frequently met online to deepen our understanding of the look of Christ and how it applies to our areas of study. Her passion for Guardini's work and her commitment to bringing it to the greater church is a benefit to Christianity as a whole that will enlighten generations to come. As you will see, my reliance on the threefold seeing is crucial to this book's insights into Petrine mystical theology. Thank you, Yvonne.

I must thank Rowan Williams as well. Our conversation in his book-filled study helped me discern vital aspects of this book. He patiently and carefully evaluated my thinking and guided me toward best academic practices. His encouragement gave me the wherewithal to forge ahead. I am equally grateful to Charles Mayer. He is a trusted friend, whose advice has never steered me wrong. This book would not have been completed without his encouragement.

I am also grateful to my prayer group. Peter states, "For the eyes of the Lord are on the righteous, and his ears are open to their prayer" (3:12). My work has been empowered by the prayers of a righteous group for whose prayers I deeply appreciate. Its members are Martha Barnett, Carolyn Castelli, Melina Dezhbod, Mark Fitzhugh, Kate Haslett, Lauren Kuratko, Lloyd Lewis, Mary McCarthy, Donyelle McCray, Jennifer Owen, James Pahl, K. Jeanne Person, Degen Sayer, Elijah Soko, and Cynthia Byers Walter.

Finally, an editor and the publisher's editorial team are the unsung heroes of any book. Each editor with whom I have worked has taken my writing to the next level. This work is no different. I am especially thankful for George and Emily Callihan and the rest of the team at Wipf and Stock. From beginning to end, this book has been improved by their tireless work. Thank you!

Scripture Abbreviations

Old Testament	OT
Genesis	Gen
Exodus	Exod
Leviticus	Lev
Deuteronomy	Deut
1 Samuel	1 Sam
1 Kings	1 Kgs
Esther	Esth
Psalm	Ps
Isaiah	Isa
Ezekiel	Ezek
Jonah	Jonah
Malachi	Mal

New Testament	NT
Matthew	Matt
Mark	Mark
Luke	Luke
John	John
Acts	Acts
1 Corinthians	1 Cor
2 Corinthians	2 Cor
Ephesians	Eph
Philippians	Phil
1 Thessalonians	1 Thess
1 Timothy	1 Tim
1 Peter	1 Pet
2 Peter	2 Pet

1

Mystic and Mysticism

Introduction

For many, *mystic* and *mysticism* are odd words. What do they mean and attempt to explain? Is a mystic a mysterious guru, spiritual leader, holy person, or just close to God? Yes, these might all be true. Mysticism also is a term not often understood and at times mischaracterized. Is it the study of strange encounters had by mystics who try to place these encounters in the greater experience of other religious people? Or does mysticism explain the nature of unseen realities that point to heaven and God? Both may be true. Moreover, would you say that the apostle Peter was a mystic? Most people do not think of him that way. This book will show you how Peter was a mystic and had mystical experiences, which shaped his life and writings and who we are today. You will also be excited to discover that his two letters overflow with a beautiful mysticism that is still relevant to the church and its members today.

Mysticism, as used in this book, is the study of individuals who have connected to God through an encounter that leads to a changed life demonstrated by faith and action. While mystics are often considered unusual people who claim to have a special relationship with God, I will show that mysticism is not so strange or exceptional. Peter's divine encounter in Acts 10 and the letters of Peter show that Peter had a mystical experience that changed his heart, attitude, and life. The divine interaction set him on a course by which God led others to Jesus in ways Peter could not have imagined prior to his encounter.

In his chapter on "Mysticism," David Perrin writes, "A definition of mysticism . . . is not an easy task to accomplish, if possible, at all."[1] As William James and others have described, one reason for the difficulty is such occurrences are a challenge to put into words. Another is the nature of the experiences themselves. Readers must rely on the personal statements of those experiences, which may be unreliable, since they cannot be well put into words. Additionally, the author of the accounts can often be people outside the religious elite, which adds another measure of questionability. The challenge then is one of characterizing the mystic and critically evaluating the writings produced by the mystic. Once the definition of a mystic is set, the term *mystical theology* must then be carefully crafted to meet the high standard expected of any theological study.

Mysticism and mystic are not medieval relics and should not be relegated to the back closet of Christianity nor be hushed words whispered in select company. They do not have to be strange or foreign concepts. By the time you finish reading this book, you will see that mysticism is a rather common occurrence in our world today and that you, too, can acknowledge your experiences of God and the holy or desire such an encounter that transforms you. You may become an ambassador for God.

PETER

When we read the Gospels, we find that few people had a closer relationship with Jesus than Peter. Peter was often in the group of three who went alone with Jesus—at the Transfiguration, in the garden of Gethsemane, and elsewhere. Some Christian traditions teach that when Jesus announced that Peter was the rock, Christ would physically and spiritually build his church on him. Jesus was also speaking to Peter when he said, "I will give you the keys of the kingdom of heaven" (Matt 16:19). Other Christian traditions see Peter as the best student or the leader of the disciples but not having an exclusive role. They avow Jesus as the foundation (1 Cor 3:11) and chief cornerstone, and *all* the apostles and prophets as the foundation (Eph 2:19–22). None claim that Peter was a mystic, and this is where I make a paradigm shift in the tradition.

These images of Peter as the rock, the keeper of the keys to heaven, the top student, or the leader of the disciples seem fitting for a man who ran a commercial fishing enterprise. They are not the images usually identified

---

1. Perrin, "Mysticism," 442.

with a mystic. Peter, however, was a person who had rich mystical experiences. One of his encounters put him on a path that shaped and changed the world forever. Moreover, his letters illustrate a robust, empowered, and beautiful mystical theology. His writing also provides twenty-first century Christians a way by which they can embrace the mysterious presence of God in their lives.

Resolving the tension between (1) Peter as the bedrock of the Christian faith and the co-leader with Paul of the evangelistic movement to the gentiles and (2) his characterization as a mystic who penned one biblical letter and strongly influenced another is not simple. It involves first determining the definition of words that have been hard to explain over two millennia of Christian history. The challenge starts with the concept of mysticism. For my purposes, mysticism studies mystics, evaluating their transformative experiences through their writings and actions. I must, however, acknowledge that my simple definition may be, for some, insufficient.

The Mystic

First, who is a mystic? A general definition of a mystic could be *a person who has had an experience resulting in a moment of sudden religious insight or awakening*. However, that definition is too broad. A 2009 Pew Research Center study reported that about half the U.S. public has had such an experience.[2] A mystic must be more special than half the people in the grocery store's checkout line (although that would be cool, right?). A narrower definition is needed, but writers have not yet agreed on one. In *The Naked Now: Learning to See as the Mystics See*, Richard Rohr writes, "The word mystic . . . simply means *one who has moved from mere belief systems or belonging systems to actual inner experience*."[3] Rohr's definition is still too broad but highlights the transformative nature of the mystical experience necessary to be called a mystic. In *Christian Spirituality: Themes from the Tradition*, Lawrence S. Cunningham and Keith J. Egan state, "The mystic is one whose single-minded love of God and love of neighbor leads to an awareness of the presence of God."[4] This definition describes several mystic characteristics: religious commitment, love in action, and awareness of the divine. While these definitions provide a framework by which a mystic can

---

2. Heimlich, "Mystical Experiences," para. 1.
3. Rohr, *Naked Now*, 29–30 (italics in original).
4. Cunningham and Egan, *Christian Spirituality*, 128.

be identified, they do not sufficiently clarify the special nature of certain people who are commonly referred to as mystics.

Instead, some writers have sought to categorize mystical experiences, creating a distinction between the many people who have had such moments of awakening and the few who are deemed true mystics. In *Mysticism and Philosophy*, Walter Terence Stace divides mystical experiences into two classifications: extrovertive and introvertive. In *extrovertive mysticism*, the mystic "looks outward through the senses. [Extroverted mystics] using their physical senses, perceive the multiplicity of external material objects . . . mystically transfigured so that the One, or the Unity, shines through them."[5] *Introvertive mysticism* "looks inward into the mind" and "by deliberately shutting off the senses and obliterating from consciousness the entire multiplicity of sensations, images, and thoughts, to plunge into the depths of his own ego."[6] Stace begins to delineate the types of mystical experiences. The Christian tradition, however, holds more specific distinctions between those who have a kind of mystical experience and those who are mystics.

Mystics predate Christianity. Bernard McGinn notes that historically great Jewish figures such as Abraham, Jacob, and Moses were mystics.[7] He also echoes A. J. Festugière's claim that Plato was a mystic.[8] Early Christian writings influenced the awareness of mystics in Christianity. For instance, gnosticism, which was influenced by the language of the Gospel of John, has mystical elements. In the third century, the Christian philosopher Origen developed a theory regarding mystics that influenced Christian spirituality.[9] He used the metaphor of ascent to describe a mystic's development, thus creating a progression of mystical categories based on his interpretation of several biblical books.[10] He tied his progression to Proverbs, Ecclesiastes, and the Song of Songs, creating a structure to the mystical experience and the way one became a mystic. Thus, he created a distinction between true mystics and people who have had a mystical experience.

By the early sixth century, Pseudo-Dionysius the Areopagite outlined a threefold pattern to mystical experience, which narrowed the definition

---

5. Stace, *Mysticism and Philosophy*, 61.
6. Stace, *Mysticism and Philosophy*, 61–62.
7. McGinn, *Foundations of Mysticism*, 4.
8. McGinn, *Foundations of Mysticism*, 5.
9. McGinn, *Foundations of Mysticism*, 110.
10. McGinn, *Foundations of Mysticism*, 116–17.

of a mystic. It included (1) the purgative, in which a person experiences a severe absence of God's presence; (2) the illuminative, which occurs when someone has an initial spiritual awakening; and (3) the unitive, which happens for only a few people and during which a person loses all sense of being and reality, uniting completely with the divine spirit or God. Perrin explains, "Based on the threefold ascending itinerary of the purgative, illuminative, and unitive way to God mentioned in the writings of Pseudo-Dionysius, there developed a preoccupation with degrees of perfection, and what 'must be done' to climb the mystical pathway."[11] The Pseudo-Dionysius view took hold in Christianity and created a way to discern who were mystics. Only the people who reached the unitive experience—an encounter that unites one with God or a sensation that all else fades until only God is left—could be considered mystics. As a result, the number of Christian mystics was limited to an elite few.

Several difficulties arise with this threefold approach to identify a mystic. First, not all who have been called mystics follow this progression. For example, several great mystics do not fit the pattern. The Beguine Mechthild of Magdeburg (c. 1207–c. 1282) received her first mystical experience when she was twelve:

> Unworthy sinner that I am, in my twelfth year I was greeted, while alone, by such an outflowing from the Holy Spirit that after that I could never find it in myself to commit any grave venial sin. This very precious greeting came every day and lovingly turned all the sweetness of the world to sorrow for me and the strength of this greeting is still growing day for day. This happened for thirty-one years . . . God Himself is my witness that I never, either through will or desire, asked Him to give me these things which are written in this book.[12]

Mechthild's experience did not start with a negation or absence of God in her life followed by divine illumination. She began in the unitive phase and remained there for many years. She also did not try to ascend to a union with God. It happened to her over and over without her willing it.

Augustine of Hippo (354–430), the early church theologian from North Africa, has also been identified as a mystic. As the nineteenth-century Anglican writer Evelyn Underhill admits, "The wealth of his intellectual

---

11. Perrin, "Mysticism," 446.
12. Andersen, *Mechthild of Magdeburg*, 70.

and practical life" obscured his mysticism.[13] Like Mechthild, Augustine's intense first spiritual experience also demonstrates a break from Origen's threefold progression. His encounter facilitated his conversion, and surprisingly, he and his mother shared the same experience. In *Confessions*, he describes what happened:

> My mother and I were alone, leaning from a window which overlooked the garden in the courtyard . . . . We were talking alone together and our conversation was serene and joyful . . . . Thinking and speaking all the while in wonder at all that you have made. At length we came to our souls and passed beyond them to that place of everlasting plenty . . . . And while we spoke of the eternal Wisdom, longing for it and straining for it with all the strength of our hearts, for one fleeting instant we reached out and touched it. Then with a sigh, leaving our spiritual harvest bound to it, we returned to the sound of our own speech.[14]

Augustine and his mother reached the unitive state in a moment of ecstasy. They did not work through the progressive states of negation or illumination. They reached a rapturous state that did not merely lead to Augustine's acceptance of Christianity and his conversion but also moved him to pursue a life wholly devoted to Jesus. Underhill notes, "The immense intellectual activities by which he is best remembered were fed by the solitary adventures of his soul."[15] She also states that later mystical writers of the medieval period looked to Augustine and saw a theologian and a mystic.[16] Our highly rationalistic culture has, unfortunately, focused too much on Augustine's theology at the expense of his deep mysticism.

The Italian mystic Catherine of Siena (1347–1380) is as much a mystic as Mechthild and Augustine. She was the twenty-fourth child of Lapa Piacenti and Giacomo Benincasa. Catherine was an intelligent, stubbornly independent, devout Third Order Dominican, who declared her virginity to God at age seven.[17] About Catherine's initial mystical experience, Shawn Madigan writes, "In 1368, while at prayer in her room, she experienced the mystical communion with Jesus Christ that would grow throughout her

---

13. Underhill, *Mysticism*, 338.
14. Augustine, *Confessions*, 197.
15. Underhill, *Mysticism*, 338.
16. Underhill, *Mysticism*, 338.
17. Madigan, *Mystics, Visionaries, and Prophets*, 209.

life."[18] While her experience occurred during an intense period of prayer and fasting, as Underhill described, it happened at the unitive level.[19] Catherine's encounter does not indicate a threefold spiritual development pattern, and yet she must be considered one of Christianity's great mystics. Her interaction with the divine led her to "rejuvenate religion" in Italy and beyond, write hundreds of letters full of spiritual advice, compose the *Divine Dialogue*, and actively seek the pope's return from Avignon to Rome.[20] As with the mysticism of Mechthild and Augustine, Catherine's mysticism occurred outside of the normative understanding of mysticism.

While the threefold ascent to union with God has been central to defining a Christian mystic, it is not the only way to evaluate who is one. Just as often, the divine initiates the mystical interaction, and it happens in whatever way God chooses. We should not try to contain the triune workings and agency within a convenient conveyance. If we include the free and unanticipated divine agency and the progression of the mystical state used by many Christians, a cohesive definition of *mystic* seems beyond reach. Must we be forced into a clouded definition? Perhaps not.

Christian Mystic Definition

If we can reshape the qualities of a mystic, we can define what a mystic is. First, *a mystic is a person who has had an encounter with God or the Holy*. The person must also have been moved to action because of the experience. Underhill states, "To go up alone into the mountain and come back as an ambassador to the world, has ever been the method of humanity's best friends. This systole-and-diastole motion of retreat as the preliminary to a return remains the true ideal of Christian Mysticism in its highest development."[21] Echoing what Underhill espouses, Thomas Merton agrees: "Go into the desert not to escape other men but in order to find them in God."[22] The mystic is one who treasures the experience but also acts on it by connecting with other humans. A mystic is not a hermit. For a hermit is too self-oriented and isolated to merit the distinction.

---

18. Madigan, *Mystics, Visionaries, and Prophets*, 209.
19. Underhill, *Mysticism*, 347.
20. Underhill, *Mysticism*, 347.
21. Underhill, *Mysticism*, 133.
22. Merton, *New Seeds of Contemplation*, 53.

The compulsion to write is another quality of a mystic. The mystic, however, is not a reporter. In *The Cambridge Companion to Christian Mysticism*, Charles Stang observes, "It is not fair to the historical record to suggest that mystical writing is only a kind of vehicle (form) for the transfer of a certain experiential cargo (content)."[23] As more than just describing a mystical experience, Stang argues, "Mystical writing can serve as a spiritual exercise in the service of soliciting an encounter with the mystery of God."[24]

Some mystics, however, never directly address their encounter with the Holy in their writings. Regardless, those who write of their experiences, either directly or indirectly, both describe and expound on the wisdom gained through the incident. *A mystic is one who receives wisdom and shares it.* Stang adds that some mystics "write in order to become mystics."[25] The purpose of the act of writing is twofold. The mystic writes to relive, reaffirm, and clarify what happened, and to expand and deepen the received wisdom. The mystic also writes to tell others. As Sara Poor writes, "Transmission, the communication of God's truth in his own words as spoken to or through the mystic is thus embedded in mystical experience and text."[26] In the highest and fullest sense, one is not a mystic without putting pen to paper. Poor's statement certainly applies to many mystics in both Western and Eastern traditions.

Finally, *the mystic's writings must be deemed valuable and edifying to the greater Christian community*. The work of a high-order mystic must also be passed down from generation to generation. Thus, one's life and worth as a mystic is dependent upon the writings having an accepted degree of authority. The influence of the writing is qualified by each generation of the Christian community's ability to see the work's wisdom. As Mary Frohlich observes:

> In Christian theology, the ultimate source of [authority's] power resides in God, and it is mediated through Jesus, the Holy Spirit, the scriptures, and the church. Yet the meaning given to each of these terms, and the way they are played out in social structures and relationships, changes radically in different eras and cultures.[27]

---

23. Stang, "Writing," in Hollywood and Beckman, *Cambridge Companion*, 252.
24. Stang, "Writing," in Hollywood and Beckman, *Cambridge Companion*, 252.
25. Stang, "Writing," in Hollywood and Beckman, *Cambridge Companion*, 253.
26. Poor, "Transmission," in Hollywood and Beckman, *Cambridge Companion*, 241.
27. Frohlich, "Authority," in Hollywood and Beckman, *Cambridge Companion*, 305.

A mystic's writings may be forgotten or considered heretical, but then, the faithful of a new generation could immediately affirm its importance.

The four qualities mentioned above help define who is a mystic. Without relying on a process or system, the qualities focus on the mystics' actions and their writings' wisdom. Importantly, the Christian community has the final say regarding who is a mystic. If Christians see relevance and learning in what the mystic shared, then the mystic can rightly be called a mystic. By looking at the qualities rather than trying to determine if one has progressed far enough, we realize that God's interactions with people are free, flexible, and unexpected. God selects the mystic, and the community can affirm only what God has determined. A mystic does not graduate to mysticism, nor can one proclaim oneself a mystic.

Mystical Theology

Just as the term *mystic* can be broadly defined, so, too, can the term *mystical theology*. A basic understanding of the term is the interpretation of mystics and their experiences and writings. Mystical theology also seeks to assess the wisdom of the theology found in a mystic's writings; but how did mystical theology first develop? The Platonic tradition and other early writings underlie Christian mystical theology. The sixth-century writer Pseudo-Dionysius, however, was the first to use the term when he titled his short work *The Mystical Theology*. In *Pseudo-Dionysius: A Commentary on the Texts and an Introduction to Their Influence*, Paul Rorem explains that Pseudo-Dionysius likely understood the term *mystical theology* to mean God's Word "which is hidden to others but revealed to those initiated into the mysteries" or "the secret God-word."[28] Pseudo-Dionysius's work had a great influence on medieval mysticism, which greatly expanded on his work. The mystical writers of the Middle Ages found insight in the heart of the message of *The Mystical Theology*, which they referred to as "the spiritual ascent to union with God through knowing and more particularly through unknowing."[29] The focus on the union, also described as betrothal and espousal, has been a central expression of Christian mysticism and its theological interpretation for more than ten centuries. The way or process of obtaining union has also been a key aspect of mystical theological writing.

---

28. Rorem, *Pseudo-Dionysius*, 184.
29. Rorem, *Pseudo-Dionysius*, 214.

Not all theologians, however, saw the focus on the process of ascent to God or union itself as productive or relevant. In the nineteenth century, many German Protestant theologians criticized and dismissed mystical theology. For example, as McGinn notes, Albrecht Ritschl stated, "Mysticism therefore is the practice of Neoplatonic metaphysics and this is the theoretical norm of the pretended mystical delight in God."[30] McGinn also notes that twentieth-century neoorthodox theologians Karl Barth and Emil Brunner gave little value to mysticism. McGinn sums up the German Protestant scholars' criticism by stating that they viewed "mysticism, at least the God-mysticism or the mysticism of union with God, as essentially world-negating and solipsistic."[31] Their critical views against mysticism have continued to be argued by some Protestant scholars.

Those German Protestant scholars, however, were not the only voices of the time. In *The Mysticism of Paul the Apostle*, the polymath Albert Schweitzer explained his version of intellectual mysticism as being concerned with "Being in its ultimate reality," focusing on the Pauline phrase, "being in Christ."[32] The nineteenth-century Anglicans William Ralph Inge, Evelyn Underhill, and Kenneth Escott Kirk also supported in-depth consideration of mysticism and theology. McGinn summarizes their view, writing, "These Anglicans insisted that true mysticism (which they understood in somewhat different ways) involved an affirmation of the goodness of the world and the continuity between nature and spirit, as well as the recognition that the mystic life finds its true expression in active love of neighbor."[33]

The development of the theology of mysticism continued in the twentieth century. Karl Rahner argues, "There is the mysticism of everyday life, the discovery of God in all things, that is, the unthematized experience of transcendence at the basis of all human activity."[34] He also objects to the idea of elitist mysticism but still recognizes a distinct category of special mystical experiences, to which he refers as "a paradigmatic intensification of the experience of God that is open to all."[35] Rahner saw the breaking of God into people's lives as a regular and common occurrence. He also recognized that some people, by practice or divine will, were to have more

---

30. Ritschl, quoted in McGinn, *Foundations of Mysticism*, 267.
31. McGinn, *Foundations of Mysticism*, 275.
32. Schweitzer, *Mysticism of Paul*, 3.
33. McGinn, *Foundations of Mysticism*, 275.
34. McGinn, *Foundations of Mysticism*, 287.
35. McGinn, *Foundations of Mysticism*, 287.

intense and moving experiences than typical encounters with God and the Holy.

Defining mystical theology cannot be concluded without the contribution of the Orthodox Church. In *The Mystical Theology of the Eastern Church*, Vladimir Lossky states, "The eastern tradition has never made a sharp distinction between mysticism and theology; between personal experience of the divine mysteries and the dogma affirmed by the Church."[36] He adds, "If the mystical experience is a personal working out of the content of the common faith, theology is an expression, for the profit of all, of that which can be experienced by everyone. Mysticism is . . . the perfecting and crown of all theology: as theology *par excellence*."[37] In the Orthodox tradition, as described by Lossky, the church plays a central role in mysticism not in terms of regulating the personal experience of the mysterious divine but, rather, in framing its interpretation within the Church's teachings. Central to its teaching, though, is the way of union with God. In the Eastern Church, Lossky notes that personal union with God is mysterious:

> The way of mystical union is nearly always a secret between God and the soul concerned, which is never confided to others unless, it may be, to a confessor or to a few disciples. What is published abroad is the fruit of this union: wisdom, understanding of the divine mysteries, expressing itself in theological or moral teaching or in advice for the edification of one's brethren.[38]

The Orthodox mystic is a theologian, sharing the knowledge and insight gained through the close connection with God. The experience itself matters little, when compared to the result of the encounter.

Two Branches of Mystical Theology

The theological study of mysticism highlighted here illustrates two important branches. *The first branch of mystical theology is the close study of the process of the ascent to God or union with God.* The idea of spiritual ascent predates Christianity, finding a home in, among other traditions, the Hebrew Scriptures. McGinn notes, "The highest spiritual experience [in the

---

36. Lossky, *Mystical Theology*, 8.
37. Lossky, *Mystical Theology*, 9.
38. Lossky, *Mystical Theology*, 20.

Jewish tradition], the essence of a visit to the Temple, was 'to see the face of Yahweh'" (Deut 16:16; Ps 11:4–7).[39]

Encountering God on the mountaintop was a familiar path for both Jews and Christians, who looked to Abraham, Moses, and Elijah's spiritual experience. The concept of ascent continued in the Christian tradition. In the seventh century, John Climacus expanded the concept in his treatise on the spiritual life, titled *The Ladder of Divine Ascent*. The process also became known as a quest or pilgrimage. *The Pilgrim's Progress*, the great allegorical work by seventeenth-century English Puritan John Bunyan, is a good example. As defined in *The Oxford Dictionary of the Christian Church*, the theological study of this spiritual quest process takes on an almost scientific approach.[40]

Within the tradition of spiritual process or pilgrimage are the three stages of the mystical life. As previously stated, the process begins with the purgative step, but that is not always the case. Some start it with the illuminative step, followed by a purgative period, and conclude with the unitive state. The goal and proper identification of a mystic in this regard is the attainment of the unitive state. Not surprisingly, the study of the unity has been carefully analyzed, almost scientifically. For example, Underhill states, "The mystic in the unitive state is living in and of his native land; no exploring alien, but a returned exile, now wholly identified with it, part of it, yet retaining his personality intact."[41] Underhill explains the characteristics of the mystic in the unitive state, and she comments on its effect on the mystic: "Awe and rapture, theological profundity, keen psychological insight, are here tempered by a touching simplicity."[42] To determine the qualities and impact of the unitive state, Underhill analyzed the readings of dozens of Christian mystics covering many centuries.

Theologians are not the only ones to study the unitive experience, of course. In recent years, medical researchers have examined the unitive state, creating a new field of study called neurotheology. In *How God Changes Your Brain: Breakthrough Findings from a Leading Neuroscientist*, Andrew Newberg and Mark Robert Waldman observe, "Such experiences involve a degree of self-transcendence and a suspension of personal egotism . . . . In

---

39. McGinn, *Foundations of Mysticism*, 16.
40. Cross and Livingstone, *Oxford Dictionary*, 1127–28.
41. Underhill, *Mysticism*, 313.
42. Underhill, *Mysticism*, 314.

such a state, some believe they are in the presence of God."[43] The study of the unitive state reveals qualities that indicate who is a mystic, but it says little about such experiences' theological characteristics.

The second branch of mystical theology focuses on the fruit of the experience that is produced for others and the church and provides a richer theological understanding. This branch deemphasizes the process and states of experiences, instead focusing on the results: what the mystic does after the experience. Central to this branch is the premise that the mystical experience leads to new wisdom, which is followed by Christian service and action. Newberg and Waldman state, "Nearly every spiritual experience, in some small way, changes our sense of reality and the relationship we have with the world."[44] What separates the mystic from the ordinary person's experience is the degree of wisdom obtained and its impact on others' lives.

The wisdom received must be conveyed in order to distinguish the mystic and to share the theology gained. In the Western tradition, this is done through the written word. Stang notes two reasons for such writing: (1) the mystic writes to inspire others to have similar experiences, or (2) the mystic writes as a part of "a spiritual exercise in the service of soliciting an encounter with the mystery of God."[45]

In addition to the two reasons from Stang, my research reveals a third reason, namely, *the telling of the encounter*, either in written or spoken word, allows the mystic to relive the event. To share the experience, the person accesses the memory; in remembering it, the encounter is relived. As with many dynamic memories, each reliving evokes the emotions that occurred the first time and can create new feelings. The spirit is also reengaged. The neural pathways used to access the neuron storing the memory become more robust, and in turn, the memory and its accessibility increase. Brain chemistry helps make the event more significant and real. Regardless of the reason for writing about a mystical experience, each reason is valid and is an appropriate motivation for the mystic to write about it.

The mystic may also write theologically in order to try to comprehend the experience. My research indicates that expressing the spiritual event, especially one that a person has not previously mentioned, is vital for that person's spiritual growth. Both Teresa of Avila and Mechthild of Magdeburg waited years before they spoke about their mystical experiences. Their

---

43. Newberg and Waldman, *How God Changes Your Brain*, 81.
44. Newberg and Waldman, *How God Changes Your Brain*, 81.
45. Stang, "Writing," in Hollywood and Beckman, *Cambridge Companion*, 252.

confessors had to encourage them to reveal their experiences, help them understand their encounters, and organize their writings, so others could read and reflect on them. The creation of their mystical theologies needed to be coaxed from them, but the process of writing helped clarify the wisdom they gained.

Regardless of the motivation or reason to write, the mystic's writing allows others to access the events and the accompanying wisdom. What happens, however, when the mystic cannot write? Because of illiteracy or cultural emphasis, the mystic might not always write about what occurred. In those situations, the expression of the mystical wisdom takes on different forms. For example, the Orthodox practice of writing icons is a method by which mystical experiences can be encouraged, expressed, and shared with others. The Mexican religious tradition of community feasts, such as the Day of Our Lady of Guadalupe, is an additional way of expressing encounters with God through saints.

Other cultures might use embodied expressions such as dancing to pass along the experiences of the Holy and of one's encounters with God. In the book of Exodus, Miriam and "all the women went out after her with tambourines and with dancing" to express their gratitude to God for saving them from the pursuing Egyptian army (Exod 15:20).

The written word is a critical component of the Western Christian tradition, but it does not represent the only way of expressing mystical occurrences nor the mystical theology that emerges from them. The reader and scholar must not disregard other methods that fall beyond their cultural context. While this book will not engage non-written mystical theologies, our wisdom will be limited without their inclusion.

Paradigm Shift

I intend to create a paradigm shift in this book regarding the discussion of Peter's contribution to the church, as well as to identify the mystical theology in the Petrine letters. Claiming Peter's position as an unexpected high-order mystic, yet a mystic nonetheless (even though he did not ascend to a mystical union using the three-step process), the text will argue that his received authoritative written wisdom validates him as such. This book's theological focus will thus not be process-oriented.

God thrust himself into Peter's life and did so when Peter least expected it. Peter's theology reflects those encounters. His mystical theology does not emerge within an ordered structure of rules or guidance but develops as fruit produced in the two letters that bear his name. Acknowledging the question about whose hand actually penned the letters and setting aside any argument about Peter's lack of intelligence to develop such thinking, I argue that the letters provide a robust, empowered, and beautiful mystical theology that is certainly worth the church's attention and devotion.

I am not the first to identify a mystical theology in Peter's writings. Arthur McGiffert identifies a mystical nature in First Peter. He sees a mysticism not as "controlling" as Paul's but one that includes "the mystical conception of redemption and the Christian life, and also the principle of Christian freedom."[46] McGiffert does not expand on his observation, which leaves off important aspects of Petrine mysticism. He also ties it too closely to Pauline mysticism. Peter's theology is normative for its time but is distinctive and characteristically Petrine.

One of the main challenges of a mystical exploration of the Petrine texts is the state of New Testament studies. In his chapter on "Hermeneutics and Exegesis," Dennis Edwards writes, "Postmodern biblical interpretation consists of virtually unlimited approaches that employ the terms *criticism*, *hermeneutics*, and *biblical interpretation* interchangeably."[47] The "heyday of historical-critical study of the Bible" is gone, replaced by a variety of methods, including the "theological interpretation of Scripture."[48] Such an interpretive approach is not a "precise method of interpretation" but, rather, is "more like the exercise of a type of wisdom."[49] Yet in the current iteration, a theological interpretation of Scripture can tend toward "methodological ambiguity."[50] The aversion to critical methods has also led some to affirm precritical methods, which is unwarranted and unhelpful. Edwards concludes, "Many postmodern interpreters agree that we will always need to employ elements of historical-critical methodology."[51]

---

46. McGiffert, "Mysticism in Early Church," 408.
47. Edwards, "Hermeneutics and Exegesis," 64.
48. Edwards, "Hermeneutics and Exegesis," 67.
49. Edwards, "Hermeneutics and Exegesis," 67.
50. Edwards, "Hermeneutics and Exegesis," 69.
51. Edwards, "Hermeneutics and Exegesis," 81.

Methodology

The variety and diversity of the types of approaches to biblical study during the first two decades of the twenty-first century have shifted the interpretive landscape. Is it, therefore, possible to approach the New Testament accounts of Peter and his writings and of Petrine mysticism, specifically, with a sense of academic firmness? I believe so. In *Seeing the Word: Refocusing New Testament Study*, Markus Bockmuehl establishes several markers by which an interpreter can navigate the tricky twenty-first-century harbor of scriptural analysis.

While Bockmuehl notes that scholars are "unlikely to recover a coherent subject definition," he states that "an understanding of the New Testament as the church's Scripture is indispensable."[52] He argues that studying the Christian religious texts from "any approach that aims to do justice to the texts themselves" must acknowledge that the biblical text forms the basis of sacred revelation for the world's largest religion and that the New Testament has had an influence on human history.[53] Therefore, the interpreter must approach the text from one of two methods. I would add that a combination of both methods would also aid the interpreter's study to appropriately address the text.

Bockmuehl's first method is to "adopt the history of the influence of the New Testament as an integral and indeed inescapable part" of the study of the text.[54] The change of orientation would shift the analysis from behind the text to the text's "foreground." Bockmuehl writes, "The whole battery of historical-critical and synchronic tools could usefully be applied to approaching the New Testament from its meaning and function 'in front of the text.'" The text becomes "not just a historical but also a historic document."[55] This first method allows for the additional examination of "how the New Testament texts have in fact been read and lived."[56] The inclusion of the way that believing communities across the millennia have embodied the text opens interpretation to differing voices within a common faith tradition.

Bockmuehl's second method permits a broader range of appropriate interpretations. He argues for the inclusion of the "implied or model

---

52. Bockmuehl, *Seeing the Word*, 63–64.
53. Bockmuehl, *Seeing the Word*, 64.
54. Bockmuehl, *Seeing the Word*, 64–65.
55. Bockmuehl, *Seeing the Word*, 65.
56. Bockmuehl, *Seeing the Word*, 67.

reader."⁵⁷ While he admits that a "precise identification" of such a reader may be "elusive," he argues that a "core of basic characteristics" can be discovered.⁵⁸ The purpose of these identifiers is "to impose constraints upon readerly whimsy (*intentio lectoris*)"⁵⁹ and not allow a superfluous reading of the text to stand without rigorous qualifiers. Brockmuehl ascribes "five simple theses" to define the implied reader. The reader must (1) have a personal stake in the truthful reference of what [the text] asserts; (2) have undergone a religious, moral, and intellectual conversion to the gospel; (3) view the texts as authoritative; (4) be situated ecclesiastically; and (5) be "inspired," in the sense of Spirit-filled.⁶⁰

Bockmuehl's two methods clear away some of the challenges of the current state of New Testament studies to allow for a manageable way forward. The New Testament texts must be explored by employing critical tools to a historical text that is also read and interpreted by religious believers and nonbelievers. In *The Revelatory Text: Interpreting the New Testament as Sacred Scripture*, Sandra Schneiders writes, "The goal of criticism is not only to sift the text for error, deceit, and distortion (i.e., to protect the reader from the text), but also to protect the text from a premature appropriation by the reader."⁶¹ She does not, however, view critical analysis as an endpoint. Schneiders states, "Unless the text, once criticized, can again be brought close, can again become transparent, the transformative encounter between reader and subject matter cannot take place."⁶² In reading sacred texts, the endpoint is "transformative interpretation," in which "the critical interpreter enters into a genuine dialogue with the text that, like all dialogue, not only permits but demands development of both the interpreter and the text."⁶³

In a time of such diversity within New Testament studies, I have sought an approach to the interpretation of First and Second Peter that brings together Bockmuehl's two methods and Schneider's transformative interpretation. The purpose is to allow the Petrine texts to illuminate the mystical theology present within a rigorous framework. Without a useful

---

57. Bockmuehl, *Seeing the Word*, 68.
58. Bockmuehl, *Seeing the Word*, 69.
59. Bockmuehl, *Seeing the Word*, 68.
60. Bockmuehl, *Seeing the Word*, 66–67.
61. Schneiders, *Revelatory Text*, 171.
62. Schneiders, *Revelatory Text*, 171–72.
63. Schneiders, *Revelatory Text*, 174.

approach that would meet these qualifications, I sought an alternative. The study of aesthetics within Romano Guardini's theology, spearheaded by Yvonne Dohna Schlobitten of the Pontificia Universita Gregoriana, provides a sufficiently rigorous method that affirms the transformative potential of interpretation. In chapter 2, I will outline methodology of the look of Christ and the way it illuminates the Petrine mystical theology, and in chapter 3, I will lay out a way to deeply know the text and its theology.

The Book's Structure

This text will examine Peter's mystical theology in three phases. After laying out the approach to Scripture, (1) I will examine Peter's rooftop encounter in Joppa as seen in Acts 10. Peter's interaction with God sets the stones upon which the mystical theology rests.

After examining Peter's mystical theology, (2) I will outline the mystical sayings in First Peter, using the way of seeing that is outlined in the methodology chapter. In examining Second Peter, I will assess its mystical words, phrases, and verses that further explain Peter's mystical theology and its practice. I will also look at the author's concept of knowledge and knowing, which is integral to Christian spiritual maturity.

Evaluating Peter's experience and the specific Petrine documents leads to (3) the broader question of trajectory. I will also answer several questions that arise from Peter's mystical theology and relate them to the twenty-first century: What does this theology say about Peter, the person? What does it say about God? What does it say about divine communication? How does it inform human self-knowledge and metanoia?

As an Episcopal priest and a lifelong Christian, I acknowledge that my viewpoint comes from within the ecclesial Christian tradition. I affirm the core statements of the baptismal covenant as detailed in the *Book of Common Prayer*, as well as affirming the Nicene and Apostles' creeds. I also profess a liberal education's critical thinking, which was instilled in me during my education at Trinity College (Hartford, Connecticut). My seminary education confirmed those tenets, which are best described in the words of William Sparrow of the Virginia Theological Seminary (1801–1874): "Seek the truth, come whence it may, cost what it will."[64]

I am also someone who has had several mystical experiences, and so I can affirm the potentiality of such occurrences to transform people's souls

---

64. These words are inscribed in stone at the seminary library's entrance.

and lives. My self-implications allow me to balance the tools of modern criticism and an aversion to saccharine devotion with a belief in an immanent and mysterious divine agency. Despite and because of my personal ethos, I hope that this work will paradigmatically shift the Petrine conversation to allow the robust, empowered, and beautiful mystical theology to emerge.

2

THREEFOLD SEEING

ONE EARLY SPRING AFTERNOON during my junior undergraduate year, I sat in a large lecture hall in the science building at Trinity College, listening to Old Testament professor Theodor Mauch describe the account of Moses and the Israelites crossing the Red Sea. He read from the book of Exodus, and then he proceeded to deconstruct the event. After speaking about the wind that blew all night piling up the waters, he implied that it wasn't a miracle but a natural occurrence. The chariots carried armored soldiers, so, of course, the chariots' wheels would have sunk into the soft bottom of the sea, while the thousands and thousands of footfalls of the Israelites would not have, even though they were laden with Egyptian gold.

Professor Mauch's description was the first of many scriptural critical analyses that I struggled to accept. He did not explain his methodology but instead his interpretation seemed like fact. Instead of listening to him coldly pick away at the text, I started skipping his lectures, happily accepting a solid B minus for my final grade.

My decision to pass on his lectures was my loss. Father Mauch, as students called him, was passionate about bringing to life the accounts of the Hebrew Scriptures. While he was a typically trained mid-twentieth-century biblical scholar, he had a deep love for his students and for the prophet Isaiah, and I would receive my divine admonishment one day. During my seminary admissions interview at Virginia Theological Seminary, three people met me, including the Old Testament professor, Stephen Cook, who had been a year ahead of me at Trinity. As the four of us talked, Cook pulled out my undergraduate transcript and said, "I see you got a B minus in Old Testament. That's good." Cook, a top religious studies student at Trinity, an exemplary graduate student at Yale University, and a distinguished scholar, was coolly admonishing me. God's divine hand of retribution poked my soul, filling me with shame.[1] I sheepishly explained my decision to skip the Old Testament lectures.

While Cook held a deep respect for Professor Mauch, he was from a new generation of scholars. In Cook's lectures (for the record, I never miss one of them), I discovered a different approach that included the traditional critical tools and also honored the text's wholeness. I was relieved and delighted, but some seminary students, who had longed for a pure deconstructionist approach, were less enthusiastic. Cook and other scholars of his ilk highlight the critical tools' weaknesses without discarding them, as previously noted. The challenge they face is to balance the necessity of those tried and tested analytical methods with letting the text be and speak as divine revelation and a locus for divine encounters.

The Threefold Seeing

This challenge lies at the heart of the threefold seeing (gaze), which is spiritual, textual, and polyhedral. The descriptors have specific meanings. While the term *spiritual* can be understood broadly, here it refers to the actions of God and the Holy Spirit in the world and presumes that God can personally interact with a group or individual. Peter affirms this viewpoint, writing, "The Holy Spirit [was] sent from heaven" (1 Pet 1:12), and Christians "are blessed for the Spirit of glory and of God rests on you" (1 Pet 4:14). Peter espouses a spirituality centered on a divine presence that was sent from heaven to closely interact with people, even rest on them. Eugene Peterson echoes Peter, ascribing that "God [is] alive and active and present."[2]

The word *textual* specifically refers to the biblical text in a robust sense as a communication between God, the writer, and the reader. Werner Jeanrond states that the text "invites recipients to become engaged in its communicative potential through an act of reading or hearing."[3] The text

---

1. The matter was all the worse because Stephen is also a fraternity brother of mine.
2. Eugene Peterson, "Spiritual Formation," in Vanhoozer, *Dictionary for Theological Interpretation*, 768–69.
3. Werner Jeanrond, "Text/Textuality," in Vanhoozer, *Dictionary for Theological Interpretation*, 782.

can be a specific verse, chapter, book, or a larger portion of the Bible, even the entire Bible. As much as textual refers to the words, it also is the act of engaging with the text.

The third word is *polyhedral* and is the adjectival form of polyhedron. A solid object with many faces is a polyhedron. I use polyhedral to describe the multiple viewpoints of a text that come to light when a reader reads the text with different people in mind. For instance, a reader typically reads Peter's rooftop experience in Acts 10 from Peter's point of view. However, his is not the only view. The reader can also consider the author's, the first-century reader's, and most importantly, God's vantage point. In any biblical reading, several viewpoints exist. A polyhedral approach considers each one.

Within each polyhedral perspective, a specific action occurs. When reading Acts 10, the reader considers Luke's viewpoint; they read the text knowing that he was a physician, whose intent was to carefully describe the account. When the reader takes Peter's point of view, his words, actions, and perceived personality traits add to the account. That Peter is a faithful Jew matters when understanding what he said. If we read the passage without recognizing the audience for which Luke was writing, we lose its meaning. First-century Greek readers would want to understand why Jewish dietary laws were important to Peter's actions and questions. We cannot move on from the passage without considering God's actions. The question, why did he want Peter to change his view about what he can or cannot eat, is a central aspect to the interaction between Peter and the voice he hears. As we will discover, the encounter has many layers and multiple intentions. The totality of the reading's meaning cannot gain clarity or be without each polyhedral view.

The threefold seeing or gaze represents the task of looking, reading, or viewing the text. What the historical-critical and modern approaches to biblical reading lack is a focus on the spiritual way of knowing. While critical reading of the text gives us much in the way of historical and literary understanding of Scripture, the Spirit and spiritual learning is limited to a subsidiary role. As a result, the ability to gaze upon the Spirit's work poured out on the biblical text is diminished. Unfortunately, the risk present in any of the "spiritual sense" approaches to reading a text is that they focus on "a Spirit-conferred understanding of the biblical text."[4] The knowledge gained

---

4. Francis Martin, "Spiritual Sense," in Vanhoozer, *Dictionary for Theological Interpretation*, 770.

has a subjective taint, and good critical readers will question the validity. Any such method, therefore, requires a structured format by which careful discernment of the text may occur. The gaze creates the necessary structure for it.

If the threefold seeing is a spiritual-based consideration of biblical texts, why would I not be better served to use spiritual exercises to analyze the Petrine texts? Opposite the critical methods are spiritual exercises and techniques. Many of the exercises have ancient origins, but they fell out of use after the Reformation and the development of modern critical tools. As spiritual tools, their use, however, has returned in recent years. For instance, some spiritual directors have their directees employ them to connect with God more easily. However, spiritual exercises fall short of the rigor necessary to properly interpret the biblical text. One reason is their starting point—namely, to help Christians grow their relationship with God.

The ancient practice of contemplation and, more specifically, *lectio divina* helped Christians obtain union with God.[5] Divine reading of the Scriptures, which is part of *lectio divina* (along with prayer, mediation, and contemplation), allows Christians to approach the Word of God with solemnity and reverence. In chapter 48 of St. Benedict's *Rule*, Benedict urged monks to set aside specific and regular time for manual work and "prayerful reading." In *Christian Spirituality: Themes from the Tradition*, Lawrence S. Cunningham and Keith J. Egan state, "*Lectio* does not mean technical biblical study (which is the task of the professional biblical commentator) or the mere scanning of the text for the sake of information or the 'story.' It means a close, prayerful openness to the text so that one both reads the text and, with patient expectation, is open to the text speaking back to the person."[6]

The prayer might not only lead to insight regarding the biblical text but might also lead to insight about a person's life. Noting the work of the Jesuit biblical scholar Carlo Martini, Cunningham and Egan suggest, "One should also seek from the prayerful readings of scripture a sense of hope and courage (*consolatio*) which leads one to life choices (*discretio*) motivating the will (*diliberatio*) to a course of activity (*actio*) either for a present situation or as a life choice."[7] A person does not use this approach to learn

---

5. Cross and Livingstone, "Contemplation, Contemplative Life," in *Oxford Dictionary*, 409.

6. Cunningham and Egan, *Christian Spirituality*, 38.

7. Cunningham and Egan, *Christian Spirituality*, 39.

about the Bible and its stories but to inform one's life and actions. Thus, the focus is personal and is, therefore, problematic as a means of discerning a mystical theology within the Petrine letters.

Another spiritual approach is the spiritual exercises of Ignatius. In *Spiritual Freedom: From an Experience of the Ignatian Exercises to the Art of Spiritual Guidance*, John J. English states, "The book of the *Exercises* . . . deals with all the basic human responses to the triune God."[8] Considering the analysis of the exercises by scholars, English writes, "The purpose of the Exercises is for the one making the Exercises to arrive at some kind of decision. But others suggest that the Exercises are meant to be a school of prayer or an instrument for bringing one into union with God."[9] About his exercises, Ignatius explains, "The name of spiritual exercises [is] given to any means of preparing and disposing our soul to rid itself of all its disordered affections and then, after their removal, of seeking and finding God's will in the ordering of our life for the salvation of our soul."[10] As such, the Ignatian is too focused on the person's relationship and interaction with God and thus not useful for the task of the gaze. Spiritual exercises tend toward the anthropocentric and, therefore, are not oriented correctly.

Threefold Seeing Description

While many spiritual-based approaches to the biblical text produce fruitful personal encounters with God, the threefold seeing has a broader and richer intent. It is based on Romano Guardini's understanding of the "relationship between spiritual theology, aesthetics and Christian spirituality."[11] Guardini's thinking echoes a verse in the Sermon on the Mount: "Blessed are the pure in heart, for they will see God" (Matt 5:8). Dohna Schlobitten states, "In his literary interpretations, Guardini recognizes a model of artist-poet, whose work revolves around the authenticity of his experience and around the 'sincerity with which the eye relates to the world, to the specific, formative, shaping force of artistic production.'"[12] Whatever the artist's intent, "the true meaning of the work comes first of all from God."[13]

8. English, *Spiritual Freedom*, 1.
9. English, *Spiritual Freedom*, 18.
10. Ignatius, *Spiritual Exercises*, 21.
11. Dohna Schlobitten, "Aesthetics of Metanoia," 1.
12. Dohna Schlobitten, "Aesthetics of Metanoia," 4.
13. Dohna Schlobitten, "Aesthetics of Metanoia," 4.

Threefold Seeing

Therefore, the purpose of gaze is to unearth the true meaning that God wants to be expressed to the reader and beyond. For the biblical writer's work, that discovery is essential.

The threefold seeing provides its users with a structured, dynamic, and powerful way to experience God's revelation in the world and the word. It offers a conduit to reaching in, through, and beyond the text. Dohna Schlobitten draws on Guardini to explain the observer's look (threefold seeing), "You don't want a complete shared knowledge of this or that kind of art or period, but you really want to know what you've chosen, to penetrate it and become a close friend; one who is loved."[14] The close reading or careful exegesis of a text is a step along the way for the text to be *known and known by heart*.

Critical-method tools are a part of the close reading of the text, but they are not an end in themselves. The discovery of how a writer uses rhetoric or unique wording is helpful only if it points to the meanings God intends. God can, of course, enrich a text with multiple meanings or layers of meanings. The gaze allows a text's meanings to speak as gifts from God.

The threefold seeing allows the divine to be present in a triadic relationship. The world or word can be itself, become its intended actuality, and let the viewer or reader be and be transformed through the word. It affects the reader on three levels. On one level, the gaze develops a unique view that is metaphysical, pointing to the nature of a being in existence in space. On a second level, it is phenomenological, relating to the conscious experience of a being and its intentionality. On a third level, the gaze is ontological and explores the essence of a being in terms of its transcendency.

As a practical application, it focuses on the relationship between myself and me, between the object and me, and between the transcendent and me. In this way, the gaze becomes a sacred act, engaging intellectual, sensual, and contemplative aspects of the human experience. Also, the triadic relationship answers these questions:

- What is the word, and what does it intend?
- What is a person's experience of the word (be it the author or the reader)?
- What is God saying through it?

These questions can be asked and answered simultaneously.

---

14. Dohna Schlobitten, "Aesthetics of Metanoia," 5.

THREEFOLD SEEING ANALOGIES

The difference between the threefold seeing and other approaches can be described as follows: one might see critical tools in the way mechanics use tools and evaluative methods to restore an automobile. During disassembly, mechanics carefully separate one piece from another. The mechanics analyze the parts, assessing them for their usefulness, and then place the valuable ones in a specific order for the rebuild. The mechanic then reassembles the car with the original and replacement parts.

The process mirrors the critical tools scholars employ when looking at a biblical text. They carefully investigate a text in various ways, separate the text into its words or phrases, apply historical and contextual frameworks, discard meaningless results, and reassemble the text to its appropriate truth.

However, the analogy of restoring an automobile falls short. Often, when scholars disassemble and reassemble a text or a work of art, a piece is missing.

Instead, looking at Scripture is more like baking a loaf of bread. A baker must use a variety of ingredients to make bread. Once baked, however, the loaf cannot be taken apart. The baker cannot then separate the flour, water, sugar, salt, butter, and yeast. Baked bread also has a different purpose than its separate ingredients. Likewise, Scripture has a different end than the words themselves. Once crafted and acknowledged as holy writing (be it a divinely inspired written work or the irrefutable divine word), rending it into its pieces cannot return it to its origin. Scholars often gain insight into scriptural intent and design using critical tools, but critical tools cannot prove Scripture's sacredness.

Here is a different comparison that draws on poetry. The critical-method process is also like a rose. A person can pluck the petals from the blossom and admire each one. The hand of the divine architect is evident in each part of the flower's beauty and craftsmanship. Once the rose is pulled apart, someone can gather its pieces and call them parts of a rose, but they are not the original rose and cannot be reassembled. The pieces of the flower and the flower itself represent different things.

The poet knows this. In her poem "A Rose," the nineteenth-century American poet Emily Dickinson begins by naming the parts of a rose, "A sepal, petal, and a thorn," and ends by stating "And I'm a rose!"[15] Her focus is on its parts to name the flower. Whereas, in "Nobody Knows This

---

15. Dickinson, *Complete Poems*, 19.

Little Rose,"¹⁶ she employs the flower to express the complicated feelings of death. The unknown rose that she plucked will die without being missed by anything other than a bee or butterfly and, therefore, can end its life easily. Focusing on the whole flower, not just its parts, allows Dickinson to contemplate the finality of death, the death of a life not regarded highly, the loneliness of grief and loss, and the question of life's purpose.

The twentieth-century German poet Rainer Maria Rilke loved roses and wrote a collection of poems titled *Roses*, which was published posthumously. Like Dickinson, he uses his rose poems, written in French, to express many emotions. In the following poem, he uses a rose to express loss. In the first lines, he writes, "A single rose, it's every rose / and this one—the irreplaceable one." The poem describes the rose and the emotions of grief from a loss. In the poem, Rilke adds, "How could we ever speak without her."¹⁷

In their poems about the rose (and not its separate parts), Dickinson and Rilke illustrate a more profound topic. The reader can appreciate death, grief, and loss anew. In effect, a different understanding emerges of the rose and the transcendent topics. The internal feelings and the external issues of life can be explored by looking at the rose. Similarly, the gaze allows the text to be and be known by heart. For in the completeness of the text, a vision emerges that can transform the reader's heart and soul.

The Threefold Seeing Encounter

The threefold seeing allows greater appreciation and a deeper understanding of the writings themselves. By letting the text be—whole and known by the reader in heart and totality—the text can point to more significant and more profound concepts. The gaze distinguishes itself by looking at the world and the word to see what it is, how it is experienced, and how its transcendence can be discovered. In actuality, the observer or reader beholds the text and thus moves beyond a method of seeing the world or reading the biblical text. In beholding, the Holy Spirit catches the observer or reader. As Dohna Schlobitten explains, "God reveals himself and manifests himself in forms that can be perceived within creation."¹⁸ The gaze acknowledges the divine presence through a "process of aesthetic cognition"

---

16. Dickinson, *Complete Poems*, 35.
17. Rilke, *Roses*, 37.
18. Dohna Schlobitten, "Aesthetics of Metanoia," 6.

that incorporates the "metaphysical anschauung with the phenomenological anschauung," leading to the ontological vision of the world and word.[19] *Anschauung* roughly translates from the German as an immediate, intuitive perception or sense of an object that emerges from the object rather than from the viewer. Dohna Schlobitten notes that Guardini defines "anschauung as a relationship to the living concrete."[20] The *Anschauung* of the biblical text is the encounter of the holy word that has an emerging vision to it.

The vision is an encounter that demands and requires a transformation for the gaze to be completed. The phenomena of the experience of the world or the word is not passive but an active revelation. Schneiders states the meaning of revelation well: "If the Bible is literally God's discourse, then revelation means primarily, if not exclusively, propositional communication by God.... Divine revelation is a far richer reality, a far more personal and engaging encounter between God and humanity."[21] The revealing of God's vision includes a truth that must be discerned, for it indicates what God wants the reader to encounter. In "The Faith in the Reflection," Guardini notes:

> Values, norms essences, ideas, complexities of meaning; the same truth and the good of God—all this is really accepted in the act of thinking, evaluating, wanting, doing when it is thought, evaluated, wanted, done not only in an "exact" way, but also with resolution, depth, the power of performing what is vitally corresponding. It is not enough that those contents are "understood" correctly, be designated with references, determined appropriately, judged to be valid in an objective sense. The content of meaning should be realized in the act, in the unfolding of life.[22]

The threefold seeing is more than viewing the world or word, but it also produces an *Anschauung* phenomenon that causes the reader to wrestle with its meaning and truth related to life. The reader must then allow the meaning and truth to transform the heart and soul.

The wrestling that arises from the emerging vision's demand often causes turmoil in the observer or reader. The word becomes the midwife to what is disordered and askew in the reader's soul or spirit. Once alerted to the truth, the reader reels in spiritual disconcertment. The word challenges

---

19. Dohna Schlobitten, "Artistic Contemplation and Prayer," 13.
20. Dohna Schlobitten, "About Trees and Spaces," 23.
21. Schneiders, *Revelatory Text*, 33.
22. Dohna Schlobitten, "Artistic Contemplation and Prayer," 13.

the reader to become what the person is not. For example, Acts 10 records that Peter was praying on a rooftop when he had a vision. A large sheet filled with "four-footed creatures and reptiles, and birds of the air" descended from heaven. A voice said, "Get up, Peter, kill and eat" (Acts 10:12–13). As he wrestled to understand what was happening, Peter challenged the voice. He was not given an interpretation of the vision. He instead had to let what he had seen be.

The vision emerging was an *Anschauung* event on a metaphysical, phenomenological, and ontological level. By the time Peter watched the Spirit's work at Cornelius's home, the vision had transformed his understanding of God and the divine intention to save the gentiles. The act of looking also feeds the spirit or soul, because the person is directed toward God. By this time in Acts, Peter was no longer the head of the Jerusalem church, and he was on the road with an unclear purpose. The vision on the rooftop and the proceeding struggle allowed Peter to reach his greatest potential, which in turn also allowed the gentiles to seek their greatest potential. The gaze intends to bring out the greatest potential of our common human existence. At its core, the threefold seeing is about accepting what God is calling the reader and the world to become.

Threefold Seeing Process

The threefold seeing is an exercise in seeing the biblical text in a multifaceted way. Its polyhedral nature describes the method or process by which the gaze becomes complete. In the Sermon on the Mount, Jesus said, "Blessed are the pure in heart, for they will see God" (Matt 5:8). The polyhedral aspect allows for the reader's heart to be purified. Once the heart is purified, the reader moves from a self-focused orientation to a new orientation. Many spiritual exercises tend to engage the reader at a personal psychological level, permitting the reader to become more aware of one's self. The gaze has a broader scope—namely, to discover God's purposes emerging in and through and beyond the Scriptures. Critical tools play a part in the threefold seeing and can facilitate the reader's ability to encounter the Holy Spirit and open the reader's heart and soul, making transformation real and present.

The threefold seeing has three stages. Within each are segments crucial to the text, to the experience of reading, and to the transcendent interaction.

Behold

In the first stage, the reader or observer starts with a prayer to orient oneself to the text and purpose of the activity. While the Holy Spirit's work is unhampered and not incumbent upon the reader's actions, prayer assists the reader's spiritual engagement and directs the reader's attention appropriately. When I use the threefold seeing in preparation for my Sunday sermon, I say this prayer:

> Almighty and blessed God, from you comes all knowledge and wisdom; direct my thoughts as I read your holy word and look upon your world. Send your Holy Spirit to counsel and guide my experience of gazing on the Scriptures. Help me behold each experience of the word for what it is, letting the text be known and known by heart. Allow the Spirit to catch me where your word matters most this day. Make me aware of your vision's demands emerging before me, and grant me the courage to affirm them. Assist me in making plain what needs to be born anew in my listeners and readers, identifying the greatest potential of our common human existence. May my words inspire people to bring the Holy to others and the world, making them more sacred all the while. Do not let me finish without arousing my inner self to act on your behalf. In Christ's name, I pray. Amen.

The prayer highlights each stage in the process, shifting the reader's intention toward God and from the self. It is the first step by which the reader sets aside personal objectives for divine ones. Since the gaze is a spiritual activity, seeking the Holy Spirit's guidance and God's direction are necessary to ground the observation and experience in faith.

The word *behold* is not often used in the vernacular today. Readers of the Bible's King James Version are likely more comfortable with its usage, but the word was often used in the biblical Greek to prompt someone's attention (e.g., John 4:35). As the first stage of the gaze, however, I use it more than as a tug on a line. In the first volume of *Silence: A User's Guide*, Anglican solitary Maggie Ross explains the word behold through the works of the twelfth- and fourteenth-century mystics: Richard of St. Victor, Julian of Norwich, Meister Eckhart, and the unknown English monk who wrote *The Cloud of Unknowing*. She explains that *to behold* is "without activity; it is a resting, loving, wondering apprehension of the manifestation of the divine."[23] She supports her definition with two verses from the letters to the

---

23. Ross, *Process*, 113.

Corinthians, stating, "Contemplatives behold directly without any shadow or veil" (1 Cor 13:12), and "it is in *beholding* that one sees face to face" (2 Cor 3:18).[24] To behold is more than seeing or observing an object or words; it is to stop, pause, and become deeply aware of the text or object before the viewer. It is to sense the Holy Spirit at work in, through, and beyond what is observed.

After an initial reading of the verses, account, or pericope, the reader undertakes the crucial activity of self-implication. To behold is a personal encounter with the text but without self-interested intent. Instead, it seeks God's vision, demand, and metanoia. In "Writing in Spirituality as a Self-Implicating Act," Belden C. Lane states, "The author's self is always inescapably present."[25] The question, therefore, is how to identify what involves the self and what belongs to the text and God. Lane suggests a threefold pattern: (1) openly identify the authorial self, (2) recognize the instructive potential of the authorial self as a bridge figure between the reader or listener and the Other, and (3) deconstruct the authorial self to avoid self-indulgence.[26] For example, one may ask, what is there about me and my experiences that makes the text a concern or interest? The process, therefore, of identifying the reader's observations regarding what one brings to the gaze is an act of letting the biblical text be what it is, and it begins the process of letting it be known by heart.

Once the reader has noted the aspect of self-implication, the next segment is polyhedral. The beholding involves looking at the text from a variety of viewpoints. Each view follows a different person mentioned or involved in the reading. Through it, the reader discerns how God illuminates the text. Each beholding also shows God in, through, and beyond the text. Take, for instance, the passage in 1 Pet 3:21–22: "And baptism, which this prefigured, now saves you—not as a removal of dirt from the body, but as an appeal to God for a good conscience, through the resurrection of Jesus Christ, who has gone into heaven and is at the right hand of God, with angels, authorities, and powers made subject to him." While it may not be immediately evident, there are several perspectives to this text.

The beholding starts with the viewpoint of the audience. To whom is Peter writing? Historical- and literary-critical tools suggest that Peter is likely writing to Roman and Greek pagan gentiles, although some scholars

---

24. Ross, *Process*, 113.
25. Lane, "Writing in Spirituality," 57.
26. Lane, "Writing in Spirituality," 57–58.

have seen this text's audience as formerly Jewish people living in Asia Minor. The audience's households include pagan gentiles. They also work and live in multireligious communities where they are a small minority group. Their Christian beliefs have notable implications. For instance, they cannot worship the gods of their parents or grandparents, and they cannot participate in local religious festivals that include feasts of meat and food sacrificed to pagan gods. Their decision to worship God began to have implications, giving rise to business losses, criticism from friends and family, and shunning by the community. Their Christian values had changed them, and life was no longer straightforward or easy.

Beholding the text from the audience's point of view begins to separate the reader from self-interest and allows the first-century cultural and contextual situation to inform the reader. At this point, the typical twentieth-century exegesis and the beholding are similar. However, if the exegete decides that their modern-day community and context and the first-century communities of Asia Minor can speak to each other and decides to go no further, the beholding is incomplete. Only one aspect has been finished. The polyhedron needs to be turned, and a new viewpoint needs to be taken.

The next vantage point is that of Peter. In other instances, the author's view would be best undertaken later. For example, when reading Luke's account of Jesus and Zacchaeus, the views would include those of Zacchaeus and Jesus before considering Luke and Theophilus's view. In First Peter, since the author and the primary speaker are the same, Peter's perspective can be viewed first. Peter's offers the Christian communities encouragement to remain faithful and to be confident that their decision to be baptized had been worthwhile. Unlike Paul, Peter emphasizes positive aspect of the baptismal decision, rather than the sinfulness and corruption of the human condition. With difficulties increasing outside of the community, Peter offers hope, rather than guilt or fear. He gives a pep talk, urging his readers not to give up.

While the reader might recognize the speaker's main intent, the view of the author and his purposes is not central to most readers. The question of an author's purposes is often beyond the central focus of the preacher's or reader's interest. A thorough exegetical analysis will uncover it, but the authorial aim is more to add color than it is a central aspect of the study. In a polyhedral approach, however, the author's goal gives equal weight to all other viewpoints, as well as that of the audience for which the text was written.

Threefold Seeing

Concerning the reading from First Peter, we consider God's view next. The reader must consider why God caused or inspired Peter to write the text. What are God's purposes that are being made real in the verses? What is God doing? What message has God spoken? God has affirmed the decisions and baptisms of these Christians. In doing so, God has empowered people to live in a new way that is wholesome and affirms a positive moral life. God wants Christians to recognize the impact of their choices, and although difficulties may arise, those Christians will be rewarded in both the present and the age to come. The creation of a good conscience through baptism suggests a willingness on God's part to see people change and grow. God also wants Christians to understand Jesus and the position and power he holds. Although Jesus has died, he has risen and sits at God's right hand. Jesus now enjoys a full reign of power, which includes spiritual authority. God's resurrection of Jesus not only changed the course of events on earth but also changed the course of events in heaven.

The polyhedral beholding that focuses on God is central to the method. The reader does not serendipitously consider divine intent, but building on multiple viewpoints, the person can identify God's presence and intentions in the biblical text. The reader is now far removed from self-interest and can effectively see such influences, which may be unlike those of God's intent. Notably, the person does not attempt to resolve any opposing viewpoints. The tension between opposing viewpoints does not need to be resolved but, rather, simply needs to be known. God's vantage point may create unexplainable mysteries or may clarify the text. Either way, textual tensions must not be hastily resolved but should be uncomfortably dwelled on.

In other biblical readings, the polyhedral beholding may include more aspects. The crowd, the disciples, the Pharisees, a specific person (e.g., Zacchaeus or Martha), Jesus, the Holy Spirit, and others would need to be included. Each perspective must be valued no differently than another. The point is not to close off any view but to let each be and be known. It is also to examine the verses, account, or pericope thoroughly and then carefully view them to let them be known by heart. The reader does not so much understand the biblical text as to see it for what it is—what God wants it to be.

To behold an object or text is to enter a sacred encounter. In the opening chapter of Matthew's Gospel, when the angel appears to Joseph, the narrator exclaims, "But while he thought on these things, behold, the angel of the Lord appeared to him in a dream" (1:20 NKJV). In the opening of

John's Gospel, when John the Baptist sees Jesus, he announces, "Behold! The Lamb of God, who takes away the sin of the world!" (1:29 NKJV). The verses demand the reader notice not just a change in the narrative action but the encounter taking place. Because the encounter issues from the text, the reader must not casually gallop through, carefully pull apart, or carelessly project self-interest on the text. Instead, the reader must humbly observe the complex and beautiful workings of the Holy Spirit laid bare and made vulnerable for lowly humans to grasp.

3

Dianoia

Ron is an energetic, open-minded, prayerful man who retired a few years ago and, to his delight, has discovered the joy of reading the Bible and participating in group Bible studies. During the height of the COVID-19 pandemic, he joined an online Bible study of Acts, which I co-led with a Roman Catholic priest and friend named Brian. At the opening of one of our classes, Ron leaned toward his computer camera—the warm glow of a morning fire in his stone fireplace shown behind him—and asked, "How do we know?" and he shifted in his seat for emphasis. He had just asked one of the fundamental questions of human existence.

In October of 1226, Francis of Assisi wrote his testament just days before his death. He began by remembering when God led him among the lepers, an encounter that changed him forever:

> Thus did the Lord grant to me, Friar Francis, to begin to do penance: that when I was exceedingly in (my) sins, to see the lepers seemed a bitter thing to me. And the Lord Himself led me among them and I worked mercy with them. And when I was fleeing from them, because that seemed to me a bitter thing, it was changed for me into sweetness of soul and body.[1]

The encounter transformed Francis's way of knowing who the lepers where—not as things to be avoided but as humans in need of kindness. He also become self-aware, and his change in knowing is clear, as well. At first, being with the lepers was a "bitter thing," but God changed his

---

1. Francis, "Testament of St. Francis," 1.

understanding into a "sweetness of soul and body." Like Ron, we may want to ask, "How did he know what happened to him was from God?"

In chapter 22 of Luke's Gospel, the narrator describes Jesus's arrest. As he was brought to the high priest's house, Peter followed the arresting party at a distance. As foretold by Jesus, Peter denied his association with Jesus and his Galilean identity three times. Luke next powerfully and poignantly states, "The Lord turned and looked at Peter. Then Peter remembered the word of the Lord, how he had said to him, 'Before the cock crows today, you will deny me three times.' And he went out and wept bitterly" (vv. 61–62). His tears and angst arose from the knowledge of his betrayal and that Jesus foreknew what was to happen. It seems that certain knowledge can pass between people even through a look.

In the Second Letter of Peter, the author uses no less than six different words related to knowing or thinking. One of them is *dianoia*, which means a type or mode of thinking and can be a noun or verb. As a noun, it refers to the deep thought or mind but is not understood as intellect or a rational principle. Instead, *dianoia* is a disposition of one's mind and heart as intuition, understanding, or even imagination. In the Petrine letters, the verb *dianoia* is understood as a readiness of mind and soul or disposition and the ability to perceive God's will and action in the world (e.g., 1 Pet 1:13 and 2 Pet 3:1).[2] Thus, in the Petrine letters, *dianoia* is a spiritual insight given as a gift from God and facilitated by the Holy Spirit. It is a way of knowing that is less involved with deductive or inductive thinking and more the result of beholding, waiting, and perceiving the text as an encounter with God who wants to impart mystical knowledge.

More broadly, the synoptic Gospels link *dianoia* to how a Christian loves God. Jesus modifies the fourth clause in the Deuteronomic command to love God (Deut 6:5 LXX) with *dianoia*, replacing *dunameōs*, which means "might" (Matt 22:37).[3] When Jesus changed the words, he dramatically shifted how people loved God, from loving God through power to an intuitive or spiritual consciousness. It is a mystical way of loving and being.

However, *dianoia* within Jesus's mystical call to love God is not an abstract concept, and its mystical qualities are evident in both the Hebrew and Christian Scriptures. In the opening verses of Psalm 1, the reader learns

---

2. "Dianoia," in Danker, *Greek-English Lexicon*, 92, and Kittel, "Dianoia in New Testament," 4:967.

3. In both Mark 12:30 and Luke 10:27, the writers add *dianoia* to Jesus' command and do not delete the reference to strength.

that blessed or happy are those whose "delight is in the law of the Lord, and on his law they meditate [groan or murmur] day and night" (Ps 1:2). The psalmist implies that the law is physically internalized, causing a constant sound, as it is read and studied. Near the beginning of his book, a voice commands Ezekiel, "O mortal, eat what is offered to you; eat this scroll" (Ezek 3:1). Upon mystically eating it, he says, "In my mouth it was as sweet as honey" (Ezek 3:3). After consuming the word of God and now full of knowledge, Ezekiel goes to the house of Israel to proclaim God's prophecy. In the Revelation to John, the author looks up "and there in heaven a door stood open!" (4:1). Next, "in the spirit," John mystically enters heaven and receives knowledge of things to come. These examples illustrate the varied way God communicated with his prophets and others, expressing the qualities of *dianoia*. These examples demonstrate receiving prophecies or visions and knowing as a mystical activity generated by an encounter with God.

For the biblical writers, gaining knowledge was not limited to the studying of the law or the word of God. While a way to understand the world, rational learning was not more significant than knowledge gained through mystical encounters. As spiritual consciousness, *dianoia* provided an additional and critical way of knowing. As seen through Jesus's command, it was a centerpiece to the Christian way of being, encountering God, and learning about God's will and actions.

The PostModern Mind

Unlike the early Christian awareness of *dianoia* as a spiritual consciousness or mystical encounter, the mind—a word translators use for *dianoia*—has an elusive definition today, like trying to describe the wind. When I posted on social media the question "What is the mind?," the brave souls who posted answers could not give a simple one, and no two were the same. The *Cambridge English Dictionary*'s entry does not provide clarity either: "The part of a person that makes it possible for him or her to think, feel emotions, and understand things." Just which part? Can you be more specific? Thinking, feeling, and understanding things are decidedly different activities and cause various bodily responses. Daniel Siegel defines the mind as "a process that regulates the flow of energy and information."[4] But what kind of energy and information? Where do they come from? How does one regulate them? The *Merriam-Webster Dictionary* adds that it is

---

4. Siegel, *Mindful Brain*, 5.

"the organized conscious and unconscious adaptive mental activity of an organism." So, just to be clear, that definition includes just about every possible mental activity. Thus, in the mind, hunger and lust can be on par with prayer and contemplation. When a word is too vague or broad, it loses any sense of definition.

Despite the puzzling descriptions, we can deduce a few of the mind's qualities. (1) Our postmodern age values the mind and mindfulness, which is akin to being purposely present in what one is doing. (2) The mind is related to brain activities involving thinking, feeling, and understanding. (3) The mind is not the brain, ego, or emotions, though it can involve them. (4) The mind is a process or mode of engaging the world and oneself, by thinking or feeling and understanding them.

The difficulty with these postmodern definitions is their omission. By their carefully avoiding any association with religion, spirituality, and mysticism, the word lacks its true intent. With its aversion to aspects of faith, postmodern secularism's sense of mind is incomplete. To understand what Jesus meant in the Great Commandment, the mystical aspect of *dianoia* must be included. When one reads Scripture with an intention of encounter and seeing God's will and work, *dianoia* is critical. Thus, *dianoia is the process or mode that is the bridge connecting the rational and spiritual self to the rational and spiritual world. Its energy is mystical and engages emotions and thought, which allows for intellectual and spiritual understanding and growth.*

Spiritual Discernment

When Ron said, "How do we know?," he asked more than a philosophical question. He was asking a crucial spiritual one that seeks to identify with whom or what is a person communicating. Since biblical times, people have wanted to know the answer to that question. The Pharisees debated the question regarding Jesus. In the Gospel of Matthew, the Pharisees said, "'It is only by Beelzebul, the ruler of the demons, that this fellow casts out the demons'" (12:24). Jesus answered, "No city or house divided against itself will stand. If Satan casts out Satan, he is divided against himself; how then will his kingdom stand?" (12:25b–26). The Pharisees wanted to know from whom Jesus received his knowledge. On the surface, it was a perfectly legitimate question of spiritual discernment.

Spiritual discernment is a classification of spiritual thinking with several categories, one of which is *dianoia*. Fundamentally, spiritual discernment seeks to understand spiritual knowledge and identify from where it comes. For instance, when the Pharisees asked about Jesus's relationship to Beelzebul, they wanted to know if Jesus's knowledge and power came from an evil source. When Jesus spoke about a house divided, he was telling the Pharisees in no way was his power coming from evil. Thus, spiritual discernment is not as simple as hearing an incorporeal voice and acting; we must know who the speaker is.

Determining the locus of spiritual authority, power, and voice are the first steps. Morton Kelsey explains, "Discernment is necessary because there is a real spiritual world with elements that are neutral, elements that are destructive, and elements that protect one and lead one to God."[5] Gerald May also states, "Classically, discernment involves distinguishing among inclinations that may be of God, or the evil spirit, or of oneself."[6] On the one hand, we might conclude that there is a one-in-three chance that any spiritual communication is actually from God; on the other hand, we realize that such activity is complicated and serious. As Luke Timothy Johnson confirms, "The process of discernment is risk-filled and never self-validating. The interpretation of the present moment is perilous, prone to error, always in need of renewal and revision."[7] It crucially involves spiritual senses that are not often used in our normal day-to-day worldly experiences. Therefore, without a proper process, spiritual discernment can become warped and destructive.

Many people have falsely claimed and misidentified spiritual authority, power, and voice. For instance, as Gordon Mikoski observes, "The oracle at Delphi turns out to be nothing but a colossal sham. That whole enterprise of discerning the divine will for human life by some women getting high and then having their incoherent babbling 'interpreted' by money-grubbing priests is religious charlatanism."[8] The seventeenth-century tragedy in Salem, Massachusetts, that led to the infamous witch trails is another example. More recently, in the 1990s, the Branch Davidian sect's fateful standoff against the Federal Bureau of Investigation and the Heaven's Gate cult's mass suicide are also calamitous outcomes due to misidentification of

---

5. Kelsey, *Discernment*, 8.
6. May, *Care of Mind*, 41.
7. Johnson, *Scripture and Discernment*, 31.
8. Mikoski, "Discerning Divine Direction," 308.

spiritual discernment. With these fateful examples in mind, we turn to the process of spiritual discernment.

The Process of Spiritual Discernment

The process of spiritual knowledge begins by recognizing its difficulties. Ladislas Orsy writes, "If we knew God's providence in all its intricacies, it would be easier to handle the practice of discernment. But we have no such knowledge. The will of God is a complex expression."[9] In *Discernment and Truth*, Mark McIntosh states, "The 'perspective glass' of spiritual discernment is a gift, a sharing in knowledge greater than one's own, and yet a real sharing, sufficient to lead one toward truth more mysterious and wonderful than one might ever have imagined."[10] While McIntosh correctly states that discernment is a gift and includes mystery, his words do not fully capture the difficulty of the process. Human knowledge and divine knowledge are rightly separated. Divine knowledge is beyond the reach of human cognition. The gap between the two can be bridged only by the divine gift of grace.

Even so, theologians and mystical writers have identified several characteristics that can facilitate spiritual knowledge. The first is *humility*. Orsy writes, "In our religious context, discernment is nothing else than putting ourselves into a state of readiness to surrender to truth—or into a disposition to reach out for the good—natural or supernatural."[11] What are the hallmarks of that disposition? In examining Catherine of Siena's writings, Diana Villegas notes, "Humility is the virtue that emerges from a balanced knowledge of God and self, and humility is necessary for the practice of discernment," and it is "a natural fruit when a person's intended capacity for love becomes ordered by grace."[12] McIntosh observes that John Climacus wrote, "John thus proposes a test for each stage of spiritual discernment. For the basic level, the measure that indicates a true discernment of God's will is 'growth in humility.'"[13] In the second-century text *The Shepherd of Hermas*, the author also gives guidance to the community regarding discernment, stating, "Someone who has the Divine Spirit that comes from

---

9. Orsy, *Discernment*, 4.
10. McIntosh, *Discernment and Truth*, 4.
11. Orsy, *Discernment*, 1.
12. Villegas, "Discernment," 30–31.
13. McIntosh, *Discernment and Truth*, 41.

above is meek, peaceable, humble, and refrains from all the sin and vain desire of this world."[14] Whereas the person who has received an "earthly spirit" is one who "is bold, impudent, talkative, and lives in the midst of many luxuries and many other delusions." Thus, humility recognizes the difficulty of perceiving spiritual knowledge and recognizes it as the divine gift that is to be cherished and appreciated.

The beholding of a text does not guarantee immediate spiritual knowledge. The workings of the Holy Spirit are not predicated on a person's right attitude. The revelation of knowledge is given in God's time, not by human desire. Thus, the second characteristic is *patience*. About its crucial role, McIntosh quotes Catherine of Siena's spiritual advisor, who said, "Do you know where this tree of death [the fallen soul] is rooted? In the height of pride, which is nourished by their sensual selfishness. Its core is impatience, and its offshoot is the lack of any discernment."[15] Thus, the one seeking spiritual knowledge needs patience and is often rewarded for it. McIntosh notes that in discernment "patience, waiting, loving attention is rewarded not only with a glimpse but an embrace of truth."[16] While revelation can flood a person with a vivid encounter with the divine, knowledge or truth unfolds over time. Orsy confirms the need for patience, because it aligns with God's character, writing, "He is the God of patience and forbearance. His pedagogy throughout the time of the Old and New Covenants has been to introduce his people step-by-step into the fullness of truth and love."[17] Humility and patience acknowledge the source of spiritual knowledge lies beyond human perception and control.

Openness follows the first two qualities. First, one must hold off quick determinations about the encounter and its revealed knowledge. Martin Westerholm explains, "The perception required to see the 'scene before our eyes' in anything more than a 'rudimentary sense' is dependent on cultivating a disciplined judgment that is capable of discernment."[18] With respect to openness, a disciplined judgment includes a skeptical attitude, which considers the self's influence upon the encounter. For instance, when Francis encountered the lepers, was it God directing him to reevaluate his attitude, or was it guilt for his wealth or privileged lifestyle that transformed him?

14. Robinson, *Shepherd of Hermas*, 33.
15. McIntosh, *Discernment and Truth*, 118.
16. McIntosh, *Discernment and Truth*, 205.
17. Orsy, *Discernment*, 34.
18. Westerholm, "On Christian Discernment," 459.

Openness to either possibility is essential to discernment. Such openness is also evident in the kind of knowledge and the action of the one receiving the knowledge. Old Testament prophets who spoke on behalf of God called on the Israelites to reform their actions by being more loving to the disadvantaged, not less. Jesus criticized the Pharisees and Sadducees for making life more difficult for the people. One was to be more faithful by being more open and loving, not closed off. R. W. L. Moberly confirms this biblical view, stating, "The true prophet is the one who aptly applies existing religious tradition to the present moment, while the false prophet is the one who appeals to existing religious tradition in a rigid and insensitive way."[19] Being open to the existence of falsity and self-centered desire and keenly aware that divine knowledge promotes such qualities as love are necessary facets of discernment, but in the end, how does one be certain that it has come from God?

As evidenced by the fatal misjudgments at Salem and other places, community affirmation is not always correct. However, the role of the community as an arbiter of spiritual knowledge has merit and is central to the Christian life. Proper Christian discernment includes the *community*. Douglas Koskela states, "It is rarely (if ever) wise for a person to attempt to discern the genuine movement of the Spirit on one's own, even if the sense of the Spirit's guidance addresses one's own life."[20] One can individually discern, but the divine encounter and knowledge are better understood when assessed and affirmed in and by the community—be it a spiritual director, a small group, a denomination, or the entirety of Christendom. In addressing Ignatius of Loyola's understanding of mysticism, Egan notes, "Inner mystical experiences proved their authenticity for Ignatius if they did not hesitate to become visible, that is, by revealing themselves to the light of a living community of faith harmony with "our holy mother the Church, her rulers and teachers."[21] The author of Second Peter also states, "First of all you must understand this, that no prophecy of scripture is a matter of one's own interpretation, because no prophecy ever came by human will, but men and women moved by the Holy Spirit spoke from God" (1:20–21). Even though a divine encounter happens to an individual, moving them in profound ways, the community informs and validates it. The community helps determine the source of the spiritual knowledge and can assist the

---

19. Moberly, *Prophecy and Discernment*, 18.
20. Koskela, "Discernment," 345.
21. Egan, *Ignatius Loyola the Mystic*, 174–75.

person to better understand it. Many people can and do receive spiritual wisdom and attempt spiritual discernment; a central aspect of this way of knowing is its reception by the community of faith.

The final characteristic of the process of spiritual discernment is *Christ*. Despite the awesome display of the divine that may happen in a mystical encounter and a person's excitement at receiving spiritual knowledge, Christians have already received all necessary knowledge of God. Gordon Mikoski rightly states, "The divine will has been made fully known and is completely open to all in the outstretched arms of Jesus Christ on the cross."[22] However, Calvary is not the sole source of spiritual knowledge. Koskela adds, "A first and essential criterion of discernment is Christological. The Holy Spirit points to Jesus and continues to connect us to the work of the incarnate Son."[23] However, even Mikoski's understanding is limited. Spiritual discernment must also include the prefigurement, anticipation, incarnation, life and teaching, death, and resurrection of Jesus, including his continuing relationship with Christians to reveal all necessary knowledge. As Angus Ritchie writes, "The Bible does not present itself as the center of the Christian revelation—which is, of course, the person of Jesus."[24] Why is spiritual discernment so broadly Christological? McIntosh states it well: "In every discerning moment of Christian life, in every act of discerning truth, this welcoming and beckoning to journey's end draws believers onward to that vision of truth which is the very heaven and a new earth's everlasting joy."[25] Revelation and spiritual discernment are not housed in the word but rather in a person, and that implies an ongoing, vibrant, robust relationship, involving mystical encounters available to all Christians.

The process of *dianoia* is not rigid but fluid and includes humility, patience, openness, community, and Christ. The five characteristics create the necessary limits and fencing for spiritual discernment. They fend off erroneous communication and errant conclusions. They support people in the exciting and illuminative process of spiritual discernment, allowing them to grow and spiritually mature through divine interaction. For humans, the relationship with the divine involves limited perception. God provides wisdom in the amount he chooses. The wisdom of revelation will always align with Christ.

---

22. Mikoski, "Discerning Divine Direction," 311.
23. Koskela, "Discernment," 345.
24. Ritchie, "Role of the Church," 254.
25. McIntosh, *Discernment and Truth*, 7.

The next two chapters explore the Petrine letters. Behind the words is the process of beholding and *dianoia*. These concepts inform the analysis of each verse, phrase, and word. The exploration gives evidence of a connection between Acts 10:9–20 and the mystical theology emerging from the letters. The theology also shows how the letters complement each other. The first letter's subject and object are God, and the second instructs readers in proper Christian living and action. The authors are different, but the inspiration is the same, namely, the honor, praise, and glory of the God who acts.

4

The Unexpected Mystic

Some scholars find Peter perplexing. The trouble they have is what everyone has concerning the Galilean fisherman. Markus Brockmuehl observes that while Peter is the only disciple "whom Jesus addressed by name in all four Gospels," we find little information about "his background, childhood, or youth."[1] Despite not knowing much about him, Peter is "referred to in the New Testament 181 times altogether."[2] Those New Testament references paint a well-respected leader of the twelve disciples and yet a man who is "impulsive and enthusiastic."[3] Bart Ehrman states that Peter is "good-hearted and eager to please, but, when it comes to the moment, vacillating, impetuous, unreliable—one who claims to be willing to die for his master but then in fact denies him not just once but three times."[4] Looking at the Gospel of John's Petrine image, Brockmuehl notes, "Peter is a sympathetically fallible man of resolve, eager to demonstrate commitment but slow to grasp the spiritual point at issue."[5] If *we* were to select a leader from the band of twelve, Peter would not have been our first choice. He is not a calm leader who is proactive and underreacts to stressful situations.

---

1. Brockmuehl, *Simon Peter in Scripture*, 21, 25.
2. Hengel, *Saint Peter*, 10–11.
3. Cullman, *Peter, Disciple-Apostle-Martyr*, 31.
4. Ehrman, *Peter, Paul, and Mary*, 21.
5. Brockmuehl, *Simon Peter in Scripture*, 66.

Peter is not the non-anxious, self-differentiated presence so highly valued as a leadership characteristic in our tumultuous society.[6]

His leadership skills and flaws come to the forefront in the Acts of the Apostles. In the book's first half, Peter is the main figure.[7] After the Holy Spirit descends on the disciples on the day of Pentecost, Peter boldly proclaims to the crowd the message of salvation in Christ. Soon after, he heals a crippled beggar and then defends his faith in Christ to the temple leadership. In chapter 5, Peter then accuses Ananias of lying to the Holy Spirit at the behest of Satan and, a few hours later, does the same to Sapphira, Ananias's wife—both of whom immediately fall dead. Peter's shadow also heals the sick and possessed. The Acts narrative then moves to other disciples, except for a brief healing by Peter in chapter 8. When Peter returns in the narrative at the end of chapter 9, he is no longer in Jerusalem but on the road. In chapter 11, he returns to the Holy City to explain and defend his actions in Joppa and Caesarea. By chapter 15, James, the brother of Jesus, is the head of the Jerusalem church, not Peter. Luke does not mention Peter further nor states why he is no longer head of the church. We should not be surprised, of course. The Acts of the Apostles is not about Peter but about the impact of Jesus Christ upon a growing group of people. However, it would have been helpful to have known.

Peter either lost or abdicated his leadership position as head of the Jerusalem church. As Bockmuehl confirms, "As chapters 15 and 21 make very clear, the leading figure of the Jerusalem church is undeniably James the brother of Jesus."[8] Was it due to Peter's forceful accusation, condemnation, and resulting sudden deaths of Ananias and Sapphira, or did the fledgling church grow tired of his impulsive, rough personality? Perhaps, as Hengel suggests, the early church gravitated toward the *monarchial* tendencies of the surrounding cultures and chose James due to his *royal* blood as Jesus's brother.[9] We can speculate about why Peter was no longer head of the Jerusalem church but not about the relationship change between Peter and the Jerusalem followers of Christ.

No longer the celebrated leader, Peter departs Jerusalem. In chapter 9, Peter is on the road with a small group of nameless companions, traveling

---

6. Steinke, *Uproar*, 49–54.

7. Bockmuehl, *Simon Peter in Scripture*, 27.

8. Bockmuehl, *Simon Peter in Scripture*, 28. See also Hengel, *Saint Peter*, 78, and Cullman, *Peter, Disciple-Apostle-Martyr*, 46.

9. Hengel, *Saint Peter*, 51.

"here and there" (9:1) or on a wandering journey. Luke gives us the impression that Peter's activity is aimless. Of course, he is encouraging the growing group of gentile Christians in the area west of Jerusalem. He heals those in need, like the paralytic Aeneas. Similarly to Jesus's healing of the rabbi Jairus's daughter, the widow of Nain's son, and Lazarus, Peter raises Tabitha from the dead. Peter remains in Joppa for a long time, staying at Simon the tanner's home. His mission lacks clarity. Peter seems to be passing time, and unlike Jesus's mission or even Paul's missionary journey's, Luke's narration of Peter lacks force.

His haphazard travels reveal Peter's emotional state. He has lost his job, position, and status and, once again, feels like the failure who denied Jesus three times. Peter has let down God and Jesus. So, he does what first comes to his mind. He moves about healing those in need, encouraging the believers, and inspiring new followers. However, he is a traveler without a home and seems anxious and unable to sit still.

Moreover, he is punishing himself. Joppa is a Jewish town, a place where a fellow Jew like Peter could feel comfortable. Even if he was a follower of a strange new sect, Judaism had numerous sects in the first century. Presumably, he could have met fellow believers in Joppa who would have welcomed him, offering hospitality and a place to stay. Instead, Peter resides in the tanner's home, located outside of the city. Note that the isolated locale of the tannery had more to do with its pungent smells than any religious impurity. Chris Miller observes, "As long as the tanner avoided the carcasses of animals that had died on their own, he would be as clean as any other Israelite. Thus, while the tanner may have been on the lower end of the social scale, he was not a religious outcast."[10] Additionally, while some scholars have highlighted the religious uncleanliness or impurity of the tannery, the cleanliness laws would not have been relevant in this instance. Frances Taylor Gench points out that impurity was not a sin nor prohibited, and unless a person or object was bound for the temple, it could be ignored.[11] Luke provides us no explanation for Peter's choice and makes no mention of the uncleanliness of the tannery. If it was a problem, Luke would have mentioned it. Even though Peter would have had other options in Joppa, he chose the odoriferous one. In his distraught state, he chose isolation; few would be eager to stop by for a visit. Surrounded by such ghastly smells, he might better ignore his anxiety as well.

10. C. Miller, "Did Peter's Vision," 304.
11. Gench, *Back to the Well*, 40–43.

Peter's anxiousness reaches its apex when he goes to the tannery's rooftop to pray. Acts 10:9 notes that about noon Peter went up to pray and became hungry. The unusual nature of Peter's actions reaffirms his mental state. Darrell Bock writes, "This is not a normal prayer time, which would be around either 9 a.m. or 3 p.m." It was also not a normal mealtime for first-century Jews. "Usually, Jews had a midmorning meal and then a late-afternoon main meal."[12] In his despair, Peter finds himself in the wrong city, at the wrong place, with the wrong desire, and at the wrong time. His isolation has, however, placed him in the right place for an encounter with God.

Today, while intermittent fasting has increased in popularity, religious fasting is not fashionable, and most Christians avoid the topic. However, hunger has long been associated with spiritual encounters. Bible readers are familiar with Jesus's forty-day fast when Jesus was sent by the Holy Spirit into the wilderness (Matt 4:1–11, Luke 4:1–13)—during which, while he was famished, the devil came and tempted him. Jesus's hunger did not soften his spiritual awareness or resolve but heightened them. Jesus was not the only biblical figure to fast. While writing the Ten Commandments, Moses fasted for forty days (Exod 34:28). Esther fasted as she considered her choices in the face of Haman's treachery (Esth 4:16–17). The prophet Daniel and the people of Nineveh went without food as well.

Christian mystics have also taught about fasts. Gregory Palamas states, "If we are dominated by passionate emotions, then we certainly stand in need of the physical suffering that comes from fasting, vigils, and in similar things, if we are to apply ourselves to prayer."[13] Catherine of Siena affirms the connection to prayer and fasting: "She should remain fasting and watching, the eye of her intellect fastened on the doctrine of My Truth, and she will become humble because she will know herself in humble and continual prayer and holy and true desire."[14] John of the Cross also adds, "The soul finds its joy, therefore, in spending lengthy periods at prayer, perhaps even entire nights; its penances are pleasures; its fasts, happiness."[15] Therefore, Peter's hunger is not a distraction or an annoyance but a necessary precondition for what is about to happen to him. He must let go of his anxiousness and earthly desires, permitting him to enter the sacred space of encounter with God.

---

12. Bock, *Acts*, 388.
13. Palamas, *Triads*, 49.
14. Catherine of Siena, *Dialogue*, 71.
15. John of the Cross, *Collected Works*, 362.

Peter's *Ekstāsis*

What happens next to Peter changes him forever and marks him as a mystic. On the rooftop, "he became hungry and wanted something to eat; and while it was being prepared, he fell into a trance" (Acts 10:10). The English word *trance* obscures what is happening. First, Peter had clear spiritual intuition and perception—think *dianoia*—caused by his hunger. Then, God displaced Peter from his ordinary state (*egenetō ep auton ekstāsis*). Yes, it was more than a trance; it was a mystical state, not caused by Peter's prayerfulness but God. Remember how Newberg and Waldman described the state: "Such experiences involve a degree of self-transcendence and a suspension of personal egotism . . . . In such a state, some believe they are in the presence of God."[16] What Luke describes as happening to Peter is self-transcendence and a suspension of his ego. Only in Acts does the word *ekstāsis* have this meaning.[17] To understand the word further, Jaroslav Pelikan quotes Chrysostom's *Homilies on Acts 22*: "There was presented to him a kind of spiritual view (theoria): the soul, so to say, was caused to be out of the body." Pelikan also draws on Theophylact's *Exposition of the Acts of the Apostles 10:16*, stating that *ekstāsis* is "that which goes beyond sense-perception."[18] Peter is not in a hunger-induced, vapid stupor; he is in a mystical state caused by God that will change his emotional state and life purpose.

Peter's *ekstāsis* also places him in a sacred but radical space. In biblical times, God did not meet people just anywhere. Yes, Moses met God on a mountaintop. Jesus went off to pray in the middle of the night. However, for everyone else, the temple in Jerusalem was YHWH's home among his people. Where is Peter? He is nowhere near Jerusalem. He is outside on a rooftop in the middle of the day. Like liturgical incense, the stench of acid and animal skins mixes with the smell of food being prepared wafted around him. Moreover, while the first-century temple still conducted animal sacrifices—offerings to God that were holy—a tannery was a place of the earthly use of dead animal parts for commercial, unholy enterprise. Peter is at a place of human work and livelihood, not a sanctuary.

The radicalness of Peter's *ekstāsis* cannot be understated. Marianne Schleicher writes, "When prophecy ceases to be a legitimate activity among

---

16. Newberg and Waldman, *How God Changes Your Brain*, 81.
17. Bock, *Acts*, 388.
18. Pelikan, *Acts*, 125.

the Jews during the 2nd century BCE, direct communication with God is still possible, though limited to the visit of the high priest in the Holiest of Holy in the Jerusalem Temple on Yom Kippur." Even though, by the first century, people started to question the exclusivity of priestly communication with the divine, until its destruction in 72 CE, the temple remained the place to encounter God.[19] Only following the temple's destruction were the Jewish people cut off from customary methods of divine engagement. Peter, however, is cut off by his physical distance from the temple. While he may have hoped God would have heard his prayers on the rooftop, he would not have expected a direct encounter with the divine. Schleicher would agree: "Jewish mysticism emerges as a response to the religious need of still having mediated access to God, God's will and God's perspective in the absence of institutionalized mediators."[20] Peter's isolation creates the situation for a mystical encounter to happen.

Even through Peter had seemingly lost access to the divine, God bridges the divide to meet him. God creates the unexpected meeting place. No matter Peter's or our disgust for the location, the tanner's rooftop becomes the place for a holy encounter, and God forcefully catches Peter's attention. God is fully aware of Peter's personal needs and the next mission for him and the fledgling church.

Peter's *ekstāsis* serves more than just himself. Peter's encounter will help Hellenistic converts accept Jewish religious beliefs. People immersed in the Greco-Roman culture and religions knew about the mystery cults and their ecstatic experiences, in which people communicated with the gods.[21] As Pieter van der Horst states, "Divinely inspired speech was often discussed and described in pagan antiquity," and the gods were "the authors of ecstasy and for the phenomenon of visions as a concomitant of ecstasy."[22] Thus, when Peter describes his *ekstāsis*, the Greeks and Romans will not only believe him but also consider what he claims about Jesus even more credible.

---

19. Schleicher, "Mystical Midrash," 150.
20. Schleicher, "Mystical Midrash," 151.
21. House, "Tongues and Mystery Religions," 137, 139.
22. Van der Horst, "Hellenistic Parallels," 50.

Peter's Vision

What Peter saw challenged his core beliefs and those Jewish Christians who later heard accounts about it as well. Luke describes it in detail:

> And he beheld the sky or heavens opened and coming down was a vessel like a great four-cornered sail or sheet towards the earth. And in it were all kinds of four-footed animals, crawling creatures of the earth, and birds of the air. And a voice came into existence near him: "Arise, Peter, sacrifice and eat." But Peter said, "Absolutely not, Lord, for I have never eaten anything common or impure." And the voice vibrated and oscillated: "What God has purified and made clean is no longer impure or common." This came into being three times, and then the vessel was taken up to the sky or heaven. (Acts 10:11–16) (author's translation)

When Peter begins to pray, the unexpected vision commences. Peter *beholds* the sky or heaven opening. He immediately becomes aware that he has entered a sacred moment of place and time. Note that Peter has entered stage 1 of the threefold seeing. Quoting Ross again, Peter beholds the heaven and the descending vessel, with "wondering apprehension of the manifestation of the divine."[23] He wrestles with his self-implication. When told to kill and eat, Peter challenges the voice. However, God presses upon Peter's conception of religious adherence by forcefully repeating the instructions, now more like an edict. Peter still struggles to overcome his self-interest. If he cannot lay aside his own beliefs, Peter will shake off what he has seen; and if that had happened, he would have completely faded from history. But the encounter's repetition helps him see beyond himself. He will not, however, fully see God's emerging vision until he is at Cornelius's house.

In Peter's *ekstāsis* vision, the next step is not to see the vessel but to see God in, through, and beyond it. The vessel is God's manifestation and conduit that will change Peter, the Jewish Christians, the gentile believers, and the church for ages to come. By beholding it, Peter stops and becomes aware of its potentiality, its promise. Unlike reading a biblical account, Peter's first person encounter limits the polyhedral nature to the triadic relationship—namely, himself, the vessel, and God. However, for him to fully know what the beholding means, Peter must consider the three aspects. We've addressed Peter's own self-interest. Next, the vision's object

---

23. Ross, *Process*, 113.

(i.e., the vessel) and God's manifestation emerge slowly. Being enmeshed in the encounter, Peter cannot immediately know the other aspects. Peter needs some distance, which he can obtain only with time.

However, Peter does not have time. Luke carefully describes the scene:

> Now, while in himself he was utterly at a loss and Peter was perplexed about what the divine sight that had been given through what he had seen might mean. Behold, the men who had been sent out on a mission by Cornelius, having asked for directions to Simon's house, stood at the gateway. And calling out, they were inquiring if Simon who was also called Peter was staying there. While Peter was revolving thoroughly in his mind regarding the sight divinely granted in the *ekstāsis*, the Spirit said to him, "Behold, three men are seeking you." But arise, go down and accompany them without discerning, for I sent them myself. (Acts 10:17–20) (author's translation)

Initially, Peter cannot make sense of what he saw, and while he turns it over in his mind, the three men sent by Cornelius arrive. The Spirit tells him to go with them without hesitation.

Peter's Beholding

The repetition of *behold* is not just a literary transitional device. The word connotes "Take notice! Look what God is doing in the world around you." The repetition of behold also shows Peter's mental state. He remains deep in thought and unaware of his surroundings. As noted by Tage Kurtén, Paul Tillich in *Systematic Theology* explains, "'Ecstasy' (standing outside one's self) points to a state of mind which is extraordinary in the sense that the mind transcends its ordinary situation. Ecstasy is not a negation of reason, it is the state of mind in which reason is beyond itself."[24] Since Peter is in *ekstāsis*, the Spirit has to interject twice for him to return to his surroundings. It must disrupt Peter's beholding to break the trance.

As previously mentioned, the vision emerging before Peter is an *Anschauung* event on a metaphysical, phenomenological, and ontological level. Peter needs to behold the vision before him to perceive its meaning. However, unlike Paul's encounter on the Damascus road, the meaning of Peter's vision unfolds over time. The metaphysical, phenomenological, and ontological will open to him as a hidden landscape in view only after the

---

24. Tillich, quoted in Kurtén, "Ecstasy," 254.

river's bend. He has yet to interact with the wider community, both gentile and Jewish Christian, but in that moment, his *dianoia* commences. As Peter wrestles with what he has seen in the vision, he senses the vision's meaning is more than food purity.

Peter's *Dianoia*

In Peter's rooftop encounter, the beginning and end of the beholding stage for Peter are obvious. The word *behold* demarcates it. The second stage is also evident: as the vessel returned to heaven, "in himself, Peter was utterly at a loss and perplexed." He was not just thinking about what he viewed. Far from it, his emotional state was heightened and in turmoil. Like the psalmist who meditated on God's word in Psalm 1 with groaning and murmuring, Peter's encounter caused a physical reaction in himself.

Just what has upended Peter's thinking? Scholars have debated the meaning of the four-cornered vessel filled with various four-footed animals, crawling creatures, and birds. For example, Clinton Wahlen writes, "Luke presents Peter's vision as a key step toward resolving the dispute over food that arose between Jewish and Gentile Christians."[25] However, most see the vision was about more than food. David Woods states, "Peter's vision had nothing to do with unclean food any more than it did with sheets. The unclean food in the vision was a metaphor."[26] Luke Timothy Johnson adds, "Ultimately Peter comes to see that the vision has still deeper implications: that the basis on which Gentiles are 'saved,' included in the restored people of God, is exactly the same basis on which Jews are saved."[27]

Recently, scholars have examined the interconnectedness of the Petrine narrative and Peter's vision. Tying the two together and linking them to Jewish literature symbolism, Jason Staples states, "Throughout early Jewish visionary literature, to have a vision of animals was to see the nations in symbolic form."[28] Recognizing the missional aspect of Peter's encounter and his subsequent visit to Cornelius's home, Colin Yuckman also observes, "The Peter and Cornelius story (Acts 10:1–48) is the key episode in Acts' construal of universal witness, in part because it marks the crowning recognition of Jesus' universal lordship (10:36), in part because Luke gives this

---

25. Wahlen, "Peter's Vision," 510.
26. Woods, "Interpreting Peter's Vision," 179.
27. Johnson, *Miracles*, 246.
28. Staples, "Rise, Kill, and Eat," 3.

event unparalleled emphasis."[29] Joel Green writes about the ideological differences between the Jerusalem temple as "God's abode" and Cornelius's house as it relates to the "democratization of the Spirit."[30]

Mystical Liturgy

Peter's unexpected encounter has a mystical liturgical ethos. Green's narrative theological interpretation emphasizes "the boundary-crossing mission of God."[31] The liturgical imagery ripples through Peter's vision.[32] When God causes Peter's *ekstāsis*, Peter first beheld the heavens opening. Like other crucial visionary moments in the Bible (see Ezek 1:1, Rev 4:1, and Matt 3:16), the opening of heaven signals that God is about to reveal his intentions. God's action can represent more than revelation. In Mal 3:10b, God exclaims, "See if I will not open the windows of heaven for you and pour down for you an overflowing blessing." The opening of heaven can signal a revelation or a blessing, and it can also indicate God's sovereignty: "Shower, O heavens from above, and let the skies rain down righteousness; let the earth open, that salvation may spring up, and let it cause righteousness to sprout up also; I the Lord have created it" (Isa 45:8). Whether it is revelation, blessing, or sovereignty, the opening of heaven is an action reserved for God. Even though Peter initiates the encounter by prayer, God causes the heavens to open. God is crossing boundaries, doing the unexpected with an unexpected mystic.

Liturgy can be defined as ritualistic actions that pour the foundation for people to encounter God. Peter is the only one to experience the liturgical action, but God does not intend for it to end or remain with him. Like many mystical encounters, it will continue to resonate at Cornelius's home and then in the gathered community in Jerusalem. The encounter begins with Peter, moves to Hellenistic converts, continues to the Jerusalem believers, and extends to the Jewish Christians. As with any efficacious liturgical action, the event obscures time and space, drawing a wider and wider group of people into it.

God's mystical action occurs within ordinary prayer. Peter pauses to worship God. Then God, who has ventured away from the temple and

---

29. Yuckman, "Mission," 108.
30. Green, *Luke as Narrative Theologian*, 174–77.
31. Green, *Luke as Narrative Theologian*, 174.
32. See Barrett, *Acts 1–14*, 507.

beyond all expectations, breaks forth at the tannery rooftop. However, the location should not concern us. As Graham Hughes writes, "Every act of worship assumes or represents some sort of 'virtual frontier' across which the divine-human transaction which is worship is undertaken."[33] Referring to Jesus's teaching about the kingdom of heaven being like yeast (Matt 13:33), Gordon Lathrop agrees, "This dominion of God is not what had been expected; it is not even where it had been expected. It comes with a radical grace to the outsiders and sinners."[34] On top of the tannery, Peter is an outsider, especially to the Jerusalem Jewish Christian community. The opening of heaven signals to Peter and all who hear of his encounter that God is acting, like the Lord's words from Isaiah, "I am about to do a new thing; now it springs forth, do you not perceive it? I will make a way in the wilderness and rivers in the desert" (Isa 43:19). What happens next further supports the mystical liturgy in his encounter.

As heaven opened, a vessel descended. What is this vessel? It is "like a great four-cornered sail or sheet." The Greek word is *skeuos*, which has an uncertain meaning but is often translated as "vessel." The word can also mean a utensil, equipment, or apparatus. The NRSV translation in Acts 10:11 names it as *something*. On the one hand, the word is a toss-away as in *thing*. However, the word is also used in liturgical settings. For example, in Exod 40:10, YHWH instructs Moses: "You shall also anoint the altar of burnt-offering and all its *utensils*, and consecrate the altar, so that the altar shall be most holy." In the LXX, the word for utensil is *skeuos*. The imprecise definition of *skeuos* could lead to conflating what Peter saw into something it is not; but in this instance, given the boundary-crossing action of God, *skeuos* refers to a holy vessel or utensil with a liturgical purpose. God's presence makes it holy.

The mystical liturgical imagery is not just the vessel but what is on it as well. As stated previously, in Jewish literature of the time, the presence of animals in a vision was symbolic of the nations.[35] Also, the animals themselves were both clean and unclean and metaphorically represented both Jews and gentiles.[36] Writing about the vision and Peter's subsequent visit to Cornelius's house, Charles Van Engen emphatically states, "The meaning of the episode is clearly stated and often repeated: The gospel is for both

---

33. Hughes, *Worship as Meaning*, 148.
34. Lathrop, *Holy Things*, 25.
35. Staples, "Rise, Kill, and Eat," 3.
36. Woods, "Interpreting Peter's Vision," 187–88.

Jews and Gentiles."[37] While the living creatures in the vessel could represent the division of the nations, the liturgical aspect cannot be avoided. All the animals in the vessel were sacred. Thus, all people were, too.

The divine voice's instruction affirms the mystical liturgy. A voice spoke, "Arise, Peter, sacrifice and eat." Many scholars translate the word *thyō* as "to kill." Given the mystical, liturgical nature of the vision, its literal translation—"to sacrifice"—is more appropriate. The voice is not merely giving Peter permission to kill clean or unclean animals for his consumption. The divine voice's command is boundary-breaking. Peter must change identities and become a priest who makes spiritual sacrifices, a mediating presence between humans and the divine. In the first century, Jewish priests, as well as pagan religious leaders, performed animal sacrifices. In the Sermon on the Mount, Jesus acknowledges the custom of animal sacrifice (Matt 5:23–24). In the moment, Peter cannot comprehend what God is asking of him, but over time, he will wrestle and struggle with it. We will see the result of his *dianoia* in his first letter.

THEOLOGICAL IMPLICATION

God presses Peter toward an unexpected change. Instead of focusing on the word *sacrifice*, Peter's attention is on eating. He is a hungry fisherman, after all. Various scholars have noted that food was a religious and cultural dividing line between first-century Jews and gentiles. Peter's emphatic objection, "Absolutely not, Lord, for I have never eaten anything common or impure," indicates his Jewish beliefs and the gap God asks Peter to cross. Never mind the distance God has crossed by meeting Peter on a tannery rooftop! Early twenty-first-century scholarship has recognized the change Peter must make.[38] The distance God demands Peter to cross is shocking. Willie James Jennings explains, "It contained animals, clean and unclean, appropriate and inappropriate, appealing and repulsive, desired and despised. The sheet from heaven contained the common."[39] Peter exclaims that he has never eaten such foods and will not do so, because it would be an affront to God, but the divine voice disagrees. As Darrell Brock observes, "The heavenly reply makes clear, however, that God has cleansed the food so that it is not common anymore (Rom 14:14 gives Paul's view, as does 1 Tim 4:3–4; also

---

37. Van Engen, "Peter's Conversion," 135.
38. Green, *Luke as Narrative Theologian*, 175.
39. Jennings, *Acts*, 105.

1 Cor 10:19). That God has the right to declare food clean is the vision's fundamental premise."[40] In a mystical encounter, God sets the ground rules and breaks any barriers deemed appropriate. The greater point at issue is not food but the inclusion of the gentiles as equal recipients of the power, grace, and salvation unleashed by Christ at the resurrection.

The gentiles' incorporation represents a weighty theological move and one aligned with the resurrection of Jesus. Jesus often spoke about the kingdom of heaven, which is a sweeping eschatological theology. The end times are no longer a distant, cold concept but a present reality with daily significance. Peter's *ekstāsis* opens heaven to him, allowing him to see God's intent for the divine kingdom. Paulo Augusto de Souza Nogueira states that such ecstatic visions "can be nothing less than eschatological liberation."[41] Also writing about ecstatic experiences, John B. F. Miller observes, "With the erasure of time, dreamers are able to gain knowledge of past and future, including the eschatological future."[42] Peter would have unequivocally understood that an eschatological nature was tied to the inclusion of the animals. Jason Staples notes, "It is difficult to imagine an apocalyptically minded Jew who believed the messiah had already come interpreting this vision as about anything but the relationship between Jews and Gentiles."[43]

The eschatological theology is the making present and real the kingdom of God in our age in time, pointing to its fulfillment in the age to come. For contemporary Christians, eschatology is brought to light in the celebration of the Eucharist. Geoffrey Wainwright explains, "An eschatology which denies historical progress in the kingdom's establishment is not doing justice, to the present activity of the (re)creative Word and the (re)creative Spirit in the eucharist."[44] The Eucharist is a many-layered theological activity but principally an eschatological one. Wainwright states, "The eucharist both expresses an already existing unity among the Lord's people and also increases and deepens their love for one another until such time as it will have borne its full fruit in the perfect peace and unity of heaven."[45] God uses Peter's *ekstāsis* to change him. Through his *dianoia*, Peter will embrace the actions of the Holy Spirit at Cornelius's house and later convince

---

40. Bock, *Acts*, 388.
41. Nogueira, "Celestial Worship," 181.
42. J. Miller, "Exploring the Function," 448.
43. Staples, "Rise, Kill, and Eat," 11.
44. Wainwright, *Eucharist and Eschatology*, 150.
45. Wainwright, *Eucharist and Eschatology*, 141–42.

others of the broadening eschatological theology and resulting eschatological liberation.

Peter is a high-ordered mystic. While some might say that he had many mystical experiences, mostly with Jesus, those represent a different category of encounter. They are no less important, but Peter's encounter prior to his threefold denial before the rooster call do not represent mysticism by the direct interaction with the present God. Peter's *ekstāsis* falls within the categories I outlined previously. He has an encounter with God and beholds and receives wisdom. While his *dianoia* will take time, Peter will share what he learned with others. He does so, first at Cornelius's house, then twice to the Jerusalem council, and finally to the Asian Minor Christian community. Notably, both the Hellenistic believers and the Jewish Christians will find value in the wisdom that Peter shares. While he speaks about his experience, which will lead him farther and farther into gentile lands, the open question is, does he write about it? The next chapters will address that question, seek to further identify the mystical theology of Peter, and relate it to the twenty-first century Christian.

5

The Mystical Theology of First Peter

In February 2003, I had the honor to study under Katherine Sonderegger while she taught Karl Barth's theology of mission. When I recently reviewed my course notes, I noticed the numerous times I wrote in my reading notes, "I do not agree with Barth." During her lectures, Sonderegger carefully explained Barth's writing on the subject. Even now, I can feel my frustration as I struggled and wrestled with what the German theologian stated about God, divine agency, and Christian mission.

I also fondly remember Sonderegger sitting next to me after she had finished her lecture and the other students had left. As the late afternoon filtered into the classroom, we would spend another hour in deep discussion of Barth's statements. I would often question Barth's premises, and Sonderegger would patiently answer me, noting frequently that Barth answered my point in another section of his approximately ten thousand pages of writing. I had read only about one thousand pages. But, of course!

The discussion and consideration of Christian theology is meant to be a struggle. I recall the story of Jacob wrestling with God (Gen 32:24–32). Jacob's mystical and physical encounter with the divine leaves him physically injured and with a new name and identity. The faith journey often includes such a mental wrestling, especially with theological issues that cause new ways of seeing. Thinking of vital issues, such as divine agency or lack thereof, Christology and pneumatology, Christian mission and evangelism, salvation and reconciliation, righteousness and evil, eschatology, and the

Trinitarian concept, must expend mental energy. Centuries of Christian history and writing provide contemporary readers with a lifetime's work, and still there is more to consider.

Into this struggle comes mystical theology. Rowan Williams states that the mystical "means that our journey into the apprehension and enjoyment of God is not something that comes to an end with a static set of experiences or formulae; it continues to expand into the endless space of God's presence."[1] Adding theology to mysticism, Williams explains, "The mystical here has to do with the way in which divine agency disrupts 'ordinary' self-awareness."[2] He then adds, "The importance of 'mystical theology' is thus profoundly connected with how we are to conceive the recreation or transfiguring of human existence in Christ."[3] Williams also states, "Mystical theology is our attempt to find words for the activation of the finite self by infinite charity and infinite intelligence."[4]

The robust, empowered, and beautiful mystical theology found in the Petrine biblical material includes all of the facets outlined by Williams. It is not static but ecstatic. Peter's theology is meant to disrupt our ordered and tidy theology of divine agency. Peter's writings are God-centered and Christ-centered and are his attempt to set in words the knowledge he received from God. He will attempt to outline a way of faith for Christians to follow into the mystical journey and struggle of faith.

Authorship

When compared to Paul's rabbinical pedigree, many scholars view Peter's "blue-collar" background as a sign of his intellectual limitations. Peter may have been Jesus's aide-de-camp and leader of the disciples and the early church but did not have the ability to speak and write Greek beyond a common level. Bockmuehl states, "The vast majority of leading specialists on both sides of the Atlantic now regard neither of the NT's two Petrine letters as coming from Peter's own pen."[5] A primary factor in support of Peter's lack of education comes from the New Testament. "Peter himself was not schooled, that he was 'illiterate'—the literal translation of the Greek

---

1. R. Williams, "Mystical Theology," 5.
2. R. Williams, "Mystical Theology," 5.
3. R. Williams, "Mystical Theology," 6.
4. R. Williams, "Mystical Theology," 9.
5. Bockmuehl, *Simon Peter in Scripture*, 4.

term used of him and his fisherman companion John in Acts 4:13: 'When they [the Jewish leaders in Jerusalem] saw the boldness of Peter and John and realized that they were unlettered [illiterate] and common, they were amazed.'"[6]

However, some support for Petrine authorship remains. First, while First Peter does not include direct references to Peter's time with Jesus, neither does it fall directly in line with the Pauline letters and other New Testament writings. As Paul J. Achtemeier notes, "The lack of definitive evidence of dependence on Pauline letters or other NT literature weakens the argument against such authorship."[7] Second, the early church did not question the letter's Petrine authority. Bockmuehl states, "It is worth recalling that the apostolicity of 1 Peter was one of the first to be attested in antiquity and one of the last to be widely discounted in the heyday of historical criticism."[8] Third, Bockmuehl additionally notes that Peter's home village of Bethsaida had "little Jewish presence," and his brother Andrew and friend Philip "were known exclusively by their Greek names."[9] Thus Peter grew up in a Greek-speaking area and also would likely been familiar with the LXX, which is referenced extensively throughout the letter.[10] Fourth, after Peter left Jerusalem, he traveled in the Greek-speaking world. Duane Watson and Terrance Callan state, "After working with the Greeks for almost thirty years, Peter likely also developed a familiarity with the LXX."[11] The years spent there would have given him the opportunity to hone his Greek, which he presumably spoke when proclaiming the good news to gentiles. Finally, in Acts, Luke never hesitates to cite the gifts of the Spirit granted to early church leaders. For instance, starting with Pentecost and the gift of languages, Luke observes the special abilities of healing gained by Peter and how "the Spirit of the Lord snatched Philip away" after baptizing the Egyptian eunuch (Acts 8:39). Luke does not observe Peter gaining special ability to interact with Greek-speaking gentiles, especially those at Cornelius's house. While the quality and level of Peter's Greek is questionable, that he was familiar with it is not in question.

---

6. Ehrman, *Peter, Paul, and Mary*, 25.
7. Achtemeier, *Commentary on First Peter*, 42.
8. Bockmuehl, *Simon Peter in Scripture*, 126.
9. Bockmuehl, *Simon Peter in Scripture*, 127.
10. Bockmuehl, *Simon Peter in Scripture*, 127.
11. Watson and Callan, *First and Second Peter*, 4.

However, the authorship issue will remain sticky. With the letter's lack of references to Peter's personal interaction with Jesus, a shadow of doubt exists. Although we can speculate either way regarding the letter's author, Peter's authorship of the first letter bearing his name is plausible even from the distance of nearly two thousand years. Even if it remains a passing academic interest, the authorship bears little importance on 1 Peter's mystical theology.

Beholding and *Dianoia* of 1 Peter

When I beheld the letter, I noticed several verses. Their imagery highlighted their theological statements in ways that drew me closer to the text. I wanted to know more. I had to pause over the text in "wondering apprehension," the description previously described by Ross, at the work of the Holy Spirit. Through metaphors, Peter made crucial theological statements. In those verses, he spoke of divine agency, divine communication, ecclesiology, ethics, mission, and eschatology. While his teachings were and are normative to the church, professing nothing radical or heretical, they are critical and worthy of careful consideration.

Since beholding the verses, I have wrestled with their meaning. Looking at them polyhedrally, I have considered what each says about Peter, God, and the early church as they relate to mystical theology. In describing for my readers each turn of the text, I hope to reveal what each verse mystically captures, allowing for further considerations to emerge, as well as an intended vision for the church today. In my *dianoia* of the verses, I will draw on existing exegesis and criticism but hold them in tension with what my examination reveals. I also plan to draw together the different verses, stating overarching theological themes. In the end, I hope to let the verses be what they are, allowing for readers to enter the process of *dianoia* and see for themselves the mystical theology of First and Second Peter.

The verses I will examine are from various parts of the letter. I was not drawn to the cautionary areas that touch on the negative aspects of the gentile life. Peter is quite clear about what Christians-gentiles should not do. Like a fisherman whose livelihood comes from the travails of open water, he does not mince his words. Peter is not one to exaggerate, telling yarns about the fish that got away.

With respect to my close examination, I will divide it into two sections. In the remainder of this chapter, I will comment on and analyze the verses. In the next, I will investigate 2 Peter. After addressing the third stage of the threefold seeing, I will expound on the mystical theology of Peter that emerges from the verses, phrases, and words I highlight here and in the following chapter. The verses are as follows: 1:3–5, 1:14–16, 1:23, 2:2, 2:5, 2:9, 4:14, and 5:5b. As I develop the Petrine mystical theology in 1 Peter, some may challenge my choices, and others may see additional areas to explore. I welcome both avenues, for by them, the understanding of biblical literature becomes enriched.

1 Pet 1:3–5

> Blessed be the God and Father of our Lord Jesus Christ, according to his great mercy, he rebegat us to a living hope through the standing up again of Jesus Christ from the dead, and to an undecaying, undefiled, and unfading inheritance kept watched in the heavens for you, who by the power of God through his faithfulness are being guarded, into a salvation ready to be unveiled in the last time. (author's translation)

We can hear Peter singing these verses, bringing him to tear-filled joy at the power of God through the resurrection of Christ. His desire to bless God pours forth from his heart as one who was called by Jesus to be a disciple, had bitterly fulfilled his teacher's prediction of denial, was shocked by the empty tomb, was overwhelmed by the Holy Spirit at Pentecost, and was called by God on a tannery rooftop, giving him new purpose when he thought himself out of reach.

Throughout his life, Peter believes in God. Like Paul on the road to Damascus, whose interaction with Jesus was not a conversion to believing in a new god, Peter is not converted on the rooftop. Peter has never been an atheist or a pagan but a devout Jew. Thus, when he speaks of rebegetting (*anagennaō*), using it with "us," he refers to himself and his readers as being rebegotten or regenerated to a living hope through Jesus's resurrection. Rebegetting is spiritual, not physical, intellectual, or emotional. Rebegetting is not even a matter of religion. Peter and the others have been regenerated or invigorated again. They have been filled with a living hope. Think of a log being added to a fire, the energized feeling after exercising, or the refreshment of jumping into a cool river or pool on a hot summer's afternoon. Peter and the others have encountered the Holy Spirit and have been renewed on all levels.

He is still more joyous, and we can feel his voice rising to the heavens. The promise and faithfulness of God fills his soul. He reminds himself and his readers that their worries are over. They have received an inheritance that lifts all burdens of this world. Unlike worldly things, the promise cannot decay, be defiled, or fade. Nothing can harm it, because the promise is stored in heaven.

What is more, it is guarded by the power of God. Therefore, no harm can harm it. Notice that Peter is thinking not only on a physical level. Like many in the growing Christian-gentile community across the Roman empire, his readers face discomforts, prejudice, bias, and even persecution because of their new beliefs. They are not facing systematic emperor-authorized persecutions but the small local fires that will lead to the time of the martyrs. They face more than physical dangers; spiritual ones are close by. As Peter writes later in the letter, "Like a roaring lion your adversary the devil prowls around, looking for someone to devour" (5:8). Therefore, God guards their heavenly inheritance, and the divine promise matters.

Peter assures them that all will be well. Salvation is both present and future. God's power is guarding it in heaven, but its power does not remain there. Because it is being protected, Peter's readers are emboldened to follow the precepts Peter will outline in the letter. Salvation saves them but also permits them to live their lives in a new way.

And what do these verses say about God? Peter blesses God but does not call for physical sacrifices. A post-70 CE date would conveniently explain why. However, God wants blessings, not a legal system of offerings, to be the hallmark of Christian faith. God is to be blessed, because he is too supreme to be pleased otherwise.

God's mercy is an active force in the world, which can instill a "living hope" into his chosen ones. God is more than the creator of the world and has powers that can animate feelings within people. He can change people's outlook and assure them that, even amid rising trouble, he has not and will not forget them. Thus, God is trustworthy. The three adjectives that describe the inheritance also demonstrate God's reliability. People rewrite wills, taking away potential inheritances, but not God. His promise is "undecaying, undefiled, and unfading." When God caused Jesus to stand again, he also assured Jesus's followers that he is not fickle, like the pagan Greek and Roman gods. Notice that God's actions are not reliant on a covenant. The two Hebrew covenants remain intact for the Jewish people, but God has done something new at the resurrection. No longer is his beneficence contractual. Through Jesus Christ, God acted out of mercy.

However, God allows evil to exist. Be it a condition of the finite world or an allowance of his agency, God gives freedom for both good and bad actions and outcomes. Evil is an undisputed fact. Even so, God provides a solution to those in evil's grip, suffering persecution due to their Christian faith. His faithful followers are actively being protected by God. Evil is not eliminated, nor will persecutions be wiped away, but his faithful have a "living hope" that will carry them along to safety. Their hope means that annihilation, the abyss, and complete darkness are not future realities for them.

The early church does not have to act. They cannot turn God's favor toward them. No temple sacrifice will reward them, nor will a particular religious act save them. Salvation has been wrought through Jesus's resurrection. Full stop. What is more, God has filled them with hope that is present with them every day. Their hope is alive. Thus, their position—be it as a slave, woman, child, aged, or even noble—is not their fate. They may not be able to change the system and culture in which they live; however, they can change their attitude and response toward it. In the end, their response is what will change not just themselves but the system and culture in which they live. The inheritance stored in heaven and God's protection of them allow these Christians to take risks, giving them confidence to live a better life. The hope alive in them sets them apart from their neighbors and gives them power to be free.

Commentary Analysis

With its vivid descriptions and compelling imagery and metaphors, 1 Peter 1:3–5 has captured the attention of many scholars. The verses identify, among other concepts, Peter's view of God, rebegetting, hope, inheritance, and salvation. Each of these plays an integral role in the development of Petrine mysticism.

God. The central actor in this passage, which is part of a lengthy sentence in Greek that ends with verse 12, is God. As Joel Green states, "First Peter is about God and the ramifications of orienting life wholly around him."[12] More specifically, in these verses, it is "God's mercy that is on display in his transformation of people by giving them new birth into a living

---

12. Green, *1 Peter*, 3.

hope."¹³ Fred Craddock agrees, "Verses 3–5 celebrate the activity of God that sweeps from our new birth to the final unveiling of God's salvation, activity that is prompted by the great mercy of God."¹⁴ Peter proclaims a blessing to God, by which he thanks God for rebegetting through Christ's resurrection the letter's recipients and himself. That is not all. Peter also praises God for the hope, inheritance, and salvation that God faithfully granted, protects, and sustains. All of these actions were not merited by their recipients but were bestowed by God's mercy.

For Peter, God's mercy is his primary motivation and tool. Unlike other New Testament writers, Peter does not credit God's love (John 3:16) nor his glory (Rom 6:4). However, God's mercy is not haphazardly sown but initiated through and focused on Jesus's resurrection. One may be tempted to highlight the christological action surrounding the resurrection—think of the Agnus Dei, the liturgical prayer that thrice repeats: "Lamb of God, who takes away the sins of the world." However, God the Father in his mercy causes Jesus's resurrection. Seeing the event in historical terms, Duane Watson and Terrance Callan state, "God has raised Jesus from the dead, which results in extending the relationship of parent and child experienced by the Father and Son to include all Christians."¹⁵ The implication of God's action of mercy thus extends beyond the historical first-century event. God's mercy sets in motion a fundamental action, namely, rebegat or regeneration (*anagennaō*), which is a divine blessing.¹⁶

Rebegat or regeneration is a fantastic notion. Peter is the only one to use this word form in the biblical text (*anagennaō*), and only once. The word is a combination of two Greek words, namely, the prefix *ana*, which is used in compound words to signal repetition or intensity, and the stem word *gennaō*, meaning "begat" or "born." In John's Gospel, the Jewish Pharisee Nicodemus asked Jesus how he could perform his signs. Jesus answered him: "Very truly, I tell you, no one can see the kingdom of God without being born from above" (3:3). Is Peter stating the Johannine concept in another way, or does Peter understand rebegat differently, choosing not to follow Jesus's statement? Also, Peter's statement is different from Paul's teaching in Romans, "If you confess with your lips that Jesus is Lord and believe in your heart that God raised him from the dead, you will be saved"

13. Green, *1 Peter*, 23.
14. Craddock, *First and Second Peter*, 24.
15. Watson and Callan, *First and Second Peter*, 14.
16. Achtemeier, *Commentary on First Peter*, 94.

(Rom 10:9). The difference between the Pauline concept of salvation and Peter's is stark. For Paul, the believer's confession causes salvation, but for Peter, God is the actor.

Peter points in a different direction than John and Paul. The facets of rebegat, regeneration, or what some call *new birth* are not baptismal but are no less profound. Green states that this "is a dramatic metaphor for the decisive transformation of life that has come in accordance with God's mercy and by means of the resurrection of Jesus."[17] Achtemeier agrees that *anagennaō* "points to rebegetting rather than a rebirth" and occurs "by God's word rather than through human agency," which weakens any tie to the act of baptism.[18] Green and Achtemeier observe that Peter sees the new state as resulting from God's agency within a mystical act. Donald Senior adds, "First Peter uses the image of 'rebirth' to describe both God's sovereign power (God alone can give life) and the radical change salvation brings (from non-existence to existence)."[19] Like Peter's rooftop encounter, these new Christians seem to have encountered God in a dramatic act that is tied to the mercy that generated Christ's resurrection. Peter wants them to remember that God rebegat them and its benefits result from God's mercy.

Living hope is the first benefit of rebegetting. Senior explains, "The Christian is born to a 'living hope,' no longer condemned to living a life of despair or wanton aimlessness, but alive with the hope that death in all its manifestations can be overcome just as Jesus was triumphant over death."[20] Even though Senior uses the word "born" instead of rebegat or regeneration, he correctly identifies the present nature of the Petrine hope. It ameliorates present suffering. Achtemeier states that it provides the "necessary antidote" and " points the Christian to a future when the present time of suffering will have been overcome."[21] While they were not likely persecuted by official decree or orders, Christians faced discrimination and hostility due to their avoidance of pagan festivals and other socioreligious activities.[22] Therefore, the living hope provided by God's mercy was "motivation for courageous steadfastness in the face of opposition."[23]

---

17 Green, *1 Peter*, 26.
18. Achtemeier, *Commentary on First Peter*, 91.
19. Senior, *1 Peter*, 35.
20. Senior, *1 Peter*, 36.
21. Achtemeier, *Commentary on First Peter*, 65.
22. Achtemeier, *Commentary on First Peter*, 34 and Green, *1 Peter*, 10.
23. Green, "Narrating the Gospel," 275.

Although God's mercy was the primary cause of hope, it was also initiated through and sustained by Christ's resurrection. The living nature of this hope was founded in the historical fact of Jesus of Nazareth's life and resurrection as the Messiah. As Achtemeier writes, the living hope has "its origin in the risen and living Christ."[24] Watson and Callan add, "The purpose of the resurrection is that a Christian's faith and hope might be placed in God instead of pursuing the futile ways inherited from previous generations."[25] Living hope gave the dispersed Christians, to whom Peter wrote, the will and the means to pursue the Christian way of life, knowing God had promised them help now and a future inheritance.

The *inheritance* promised by God is unchanging. Its three adjectives—un-decaying, undefiled, and unfading—describe the difference between the God of Israel, now in relationship with Christians, and the capricious distant pagan gods, whom these Christians had previously followed. Moreover, the three adjectives point to a mystical realm. Earthly things decay, become defiled, and fade, but not the inheritance located and guarded in heaven. Achtemeier explains that the inheritance's "locus ('kept in heaven') indicates that it stands in contrast to any former inheritance, entered into by one's physical birth."[26] The Petrine concepts of hope and inheritance lead to salvation and its culmination "in the last time."

Peter's notion of *salvation* is different from other New Testament writers. Watson and Callan note, "Salvation in 1 Peter is both present and future but expressed as mainly future. It has been made available through the suffering and death of Christ (1:2,10–12, 17–22), can be presently experienced (1:9; 3:21), and needs to be revealed in its fullness (1:5, 9–10; 2:2)."[27] Thus, salvation has not been fully revealed. In Romans, Paul writes, "For I am not ashamed of the gospel; it is the power of God for salvation to everyone who has faith, to the Jew first and also to the Greek" (Rom 1:16). Unlike Paul, for whom salvation is expressed through a believer's faith, Peter claims salvation is not fully revealed and remains in God's complete control. Admittedly, the difference between Paul and Peter here is more nuanced and is not a decidedly different doctrine. Regardless, as Senior notes, "The author

---

24. Achtemeier, *Commentary on First Peter*, 67.
25. Watson and Callan, *First and Second Peter*, 15.
26. Achtemeier, *Commentary on First Peter*, 67.
27. Watson and Callan, *First and Second Peter*, 25.

does not pinpoint the setting or moment in which the Christian first experiences this salvation."[28]

Moreover, salvation is not an act of the individual but is located within the community. Achtemeier explains, "Salvation is to be a constituent element of the community (rather than of the believing individual) in which this future assumes present reality."[29] Here again, the activity is not focused on human agency but on God's mercy as the cause of salvation. One is saved not by praying to accept Jesus as their savior. Rather, salvation is founded on the divine action in the resurrection of Christ. Additionally, the community is involved. However, an open question remains: since the letter is addressed to Christians living in five separate places in the northern Asia Minor region, does communal salvation mean the group as a whole or each separate community? As our examination of 1 Peter continues, the answer to that question will matter.

1 Pet 1:14–16

> As attentively hearkening children, not conforming yourselves to former lusts, which were yours in your anti-knowing. But according to the holy one who called you, also yourselves be holy in all behavior because it is written: Holy you shall be because I am holy.[30] (author's translation)

Here, Peter's voice is that of the kind, compassionate leader of the disciples. It is not of the man who shouted to the crowds on Pentecost, proclaiming the good news of God, nor is it the voice who condemned Ananias and Sapphira. Peter's voice is gentle but firm. He is the wise older brother counseling his siblings. Peter wants his readers to hear his words, which are vital to spiritual growth and also infused with his love for them, God's children, for whom he only wants the best.

Peter calls his readers children and wants them to be those boys and girls who carefully listen to the instructions being given to them. At one church where I was the priest, every week, a four-year-old child named Hannah came to the altar rail to receive Communion. She knelt between her parents, minding each quiet word of instruction they gave her. As I

---

28. Senior, *1 Peter*, 35.
29. Achtemeier, *Commentary on First Peter*, 38.
30. See Lev 11:44–45, 19:2, 20:7.

neared them, she looked expectantly to her mom or dad, who then nodded. She brushed her hair from her forehead and waited. As I drew near, our eyes met. Hannah attentively hearkened to my voice: "May God bless you and keep you now and forever," and then I made the sign of the cross on her forehead. Our eyes met, and I smiled. She returned my smile with a slight one of her own, breathing in deeply as if she could smell the fragrance of the blessing I had just given her. This is the presence and focus Peter desires for his readers when he calls them to be attentively hearkening children.

First-century gentile Christians led a difficult life. They choose to follow Jesus and, for it, gained a new way of interacting in the world. Before converting to Christianity, these gentiles were spiritually ignorant. As if they were breaking laws in a foreign country and did not know the language, they were unintentionally doing wrong. When I was a child, I once touched a hot stove burner. For a moment, I did not know what was happening. Then, a searing pain struck my finger, and I knew. Peter's gentile Christians have learned that their former lusts were wrong but still need reminding of their harm. They are like children who need to touch the burner once more to confirm its hazard.

Therefore, Peter calls them to be holy as God is holy. It is a lofty goal, based on an ambiguous word. Can a person be holy? It is a divine characteristic. Peter knows that and yet maintains it can be a human behavior—even though he is the one who denied Jesus that fateful night by the fire. "Be holy." Peter will initially define it through the negative, naming what not to do. He will then bolster the definition with the positive attributes.

Learning from Jesus and witnessing Christ's life and death did not produce holiness in Peter. The abyss between God and him only widened. Why else did Jesus have to pray for him (Luke 22:32)? It was Peter's encounter with God on the tannery rooftop in Joppa that showed him how to be holy. The same is true for his readers. The shift to a new behavior, in which they act antithetically from their past, is not based on logical, convincing arguments. Its source is a holy encounter that is deeper, stronger, and more compelling than any explanation or teaching. Holiness can be learned only by encounter.

Verses 1:14–16 begin to shift the letter's focus from God to the gentile Christians reading and listening to his letter. Having been begotten again, they are on a new course, but as Peter points out, they are children. They are not spiritually mature.

Commentary Analysis

Peter describes the children as *attentively hearkening*. Many translators use the modern word "obedient" instead. For example, Achtemeier writes, "They are children whose chief characteristic is obedience."[31] Perhaps, many first-century children were obedient, never stepping out of line and dutifully minding their parents, but that is speculative. Even the best children run around, lost in their world of play, vexing their parents. Instead, "attentively hearkening" seems closer to Peter's intent.

Obedient children are those who always do what their parents want and ask, but those who listen attentively retain agency. They hearken to their parents' words, considering and thinking about what is said. They come to understand by wrestling with their thoughts in comparison to their parents' statements. Thus, attentively hearkening children characterizes the gentile Christians, who must integrate Christian precepts with their actions in the world. As children who learn right from wrong and then must choose for themselves, the rebegotten children of God must learn right behaviors and choose those over wrong ones. In light of their new life in Christ, their conduct matters not just to themselves or their neighbors but also God. However, they are no different from children who make mistakes from time to time and need occasional correction.

To *be holy* is the crucial aspect of the rebegotten life and is defined through good behavior. Thomas Scott Caulley states, "Holiness for the readers of 1 Peter is expressed in holy conduct, a practical matter worked out in the rest of the letter."[32] Darian Lockett also observes that Peter is "calling his audience both to understand and to live out their new identity as 'holy ones.'"[33] Being holy is decidedly different from the way their pagan neighbors live.

Holy conduct or behavior is based on a relationship with God. Peter makes this clear by his reference to Lev 19:2. In the case of the Israelites, God defined their relationship through the law in the Torah and gave the Israelites step-by-step instructions to remain in holiness. Achtemeier notes, "The choice of Israel as chosen people makes them holy, which is defined in Leviticus 29–26 as being set apart from all other peoples."[34] By tying

---

31. Achtemeier, *Commentary on First Peter*, 120.
32. Caulley, "Rehabilitating a Theological Stepchild?," 5.
33. Lockett, "Use of Leviticus 19," 467.
34. Achtemeier, *Commentary on First Peter*, 121.

Leviticus to 1 Peter, Lockett states, "The author of 1 Peter is calling his audience to holiness, which includes both a theological relationship, new identity, and ethical behavior."[35] Like the Israelites, the rebegotten are in a relationship with God who is active in the world and thus expects the gentile Christians to behave differently. Being in relationship with God requires a conduct that is holy and means religious and social pagan activities are no longer acceptable.

1 Pet 1:23

> You having been rebegotten not of seed perishable but imperishable, through the living word of God and remaining. (author's translation)

Peter now returns to *rebegotten*, addressing two more characteristics. Using the horticultural term *seed* (*sporas*), he describes rebegetting as a past and completed event. Unlike John's identification of Christians as having the power to become children of God (John 1:12–13) and more akin to Paul's view of Christians receiving adoption (Gal 4:5–7), Peter places the act under God's agency. However, he does not make it conditional, as Paul does. The regeneration and the rebegetting occurred from seed that is unchangeable. The cracking open of the seed has happened. The bell cannot be unrung.

    As a hobby gardener, I am aware of the importance of seed quality. A local farmer once gave me several heirloom lemon cucumbers in the hope I would keep their seeds to grow my own. When I opened them, I carefully plucked the seeds from the pulp. I tucked them away to dry and stored them over the winter. The following season, a goodly harvest emerged. Even though I stored the new seeds carefully, the next season, not one sprouted. Like all seeds, they were perishable. Peter mentions the imperishable seeds to remind his readers and listeners that they are ever reliant on God's power. They must not forget who rebegotten them.

    The imperishable seeds are tied to another of God's actions. The gentile Christians were rebegotten by God's mercy through the hope found in the resurrection of Jesus Christ but learned and experienced rebegottenness through the *living* word of God, who himself remains forever. Through the verse's quote from Isa 40:6–8, Peter illustrates the difference between

---

35. Lockett, "Use of Leviticus 19," 463.

earthly power and God's actions. Humans are grass and its flowers, which briefly live, but the word of God (*rhēma kyrios*) remains. Also, the comparison highlights the seeds' reliance on God's actions. Seeds need the external conditions—soil temperature, moisture, and light—to be conducive to growth. Peter's readers needed external conditions to be rebegotten as well. Those conditions are incumbent on God's mercy and "the living word of God."

Peter changes Isa 40:8 by adding the adjective *living* to modify the phrase *the word of God*. His change is substantial. The seed is imperishable not because of the word of God but due to the living (*zōntos*) word of God. By comparison, in his Gospel, Matthew describes God as living (16:16 and 26:63), but Peter describes the word of God as living. The change makes an important mystical statement about divine communication's ability to sustain Christians.

First, for Peter's readers and listeners, the meaning would have been different than for readers today. We think of the word as the Bible, the complete and fixed canon. As we understand it, the Bible did not exist in the first century. Even though most gentile Christians understood Greek, they were illiterate. They may have thought of the Septuagint as the word of God and were likely familiar with Isaiah's reference to the "word of our God," pointing to that word's permanence. Thus, given that the Hebrew religion was the oldest monotheistic religion, they would likely have agreed with Isaiah's statement, "The word of our God will stand forever" (Isa 40:8b).

The living word of God has a specific reference. Even though Peter quotes Isaiah, he is not copying the Hebrew Scripture. He calls his gentile Christians to become followers of God—the God of the Hebrew Scriptures—but, more so, to become followers of Jesus Christ. In the letter, Peter is moving away from his Jewish heritage and purposely embracing a new religion founded on the Jewish precepts but following Jesus Christ, the Messiah. Immediately after the Isaiah quote, Peter states, "'But the word of the Lord endures for ever.' That word is the good news that was announced to you" (1:25). Unlike Paul, who identifies himself and other early church leaders as heralds of the good news (see Rom 1:9, Phil 1:12, 1 Thess 1:5), by inference, Peter does not refer to himself but to the living word of God.

Like Jeremiah's mystical call (Jer 1:4), in which the "word of the Lord came" to the prophet, for Peter, the living word of God has its own agency. His readers and listeners had encountered the living word of God, and it had changed them.

The method of encounter occurred in either one of two ways. The people gathered to listen to the good news, and the word of God spoke to them as one living person to another; the word became so real and present that it rebegat them. The divine act could then have been confirmed or sealed in baptism. Equally, like Peter's rooftop encounter, God could have spoken to the people individually or in groups. In either case, the word was alive, in the same way that an electrical wire can be live. The living word of God has energy to rebeget people, regardless of whether it is proclaimed by a person or independently. In both cases, the interaction with the living word of God is a mystical encounter.

Commentary Analysis

Some commentators have linked the imperishability and perishability of the *seed* to the verse Peter quoted from Isaiah: "All flesh is like grass and all its glory like the flowers of grass. The grass withers and the flower fails." For instance, Watson and Callan write, "All that is from human procreation is transitory, in contrast to the dynamic and permanent nature of the word of God, which is the power of God, bringing life and salvation into the world through the proclamation of Jesus Christ."[36] While the horticultural reference naturally draws a linkage, the reader must go further.

The seed and its imperishability point to the mystical encounter of rebegetting. The reader must be challenged the same way as Nicodemus, who asked Jesus, "How can anyone be born after having grown old? Can one enter a second time into the mother's womb and be born?" (John 3:4). Green's conclusion illustrates the mystical nature of the living word of God: "In short, the word of God, the good news, is efficacious in generating, cultivating, and sustaining new life."[37] But the word of God's living quality gives it mystical agency.

As previously stated, the *living* word of God is not a reference to existing first-century Scripture. As Green confirms, this is "not the 'word of Scripture' per se, but the word as good news, the gospel concerning Jesus Christ."[38] The living word has its own power, namely, the power to announce or herald the mercy of God through the resurrection of Christ. Achtemeier agrees, stating that rebegetting occurred through "God's word

---

36. Watson and Callan, *First and Second Peter*, 40.
37. Green, *1 Peter*, 54.
38. Green, *1 Peter*, 53.

rather than through human agency."[39] The living word is the vehicle by which God meted out his mercy to each new believer, and current readers must not limit its working to the then-unfinished biblical canon. As Senior emphasizes, "The 'living and abiding word of God' is yet another way of describing the entirety of the Christian message experienced by the readers of the letter."[40] Then, as now, the dynamic power of the living word of God, which, among other things, converts the hearts of sinners, is not fixed to a single set of words but open to its own mystical workings.

1 Pet 2:2

> As newborn babes, greatly desire the spiritual pure milk, in order that by it you may grow to salvation. (author's translation)

In the preceding verse, Peter urges his readers to *cast off* all wrongful behaviors. Now, in contrast, he reminds them to greatly desire the spiritual pure milk. Peter differentiates between the local pagan religions, which are spiritually impure, and Christianity, which is spiritually pure. Peter also views paganism through the immoral behaviors of its followers. Christianity thus has a distinct set of moral behaviors, which is founded in the desire for spiritual pure milk.

To discern what Peter intends by *spiritual pure milk* is not easy. The imagery challenges the concept of a masculine God. His rebegotten readers must desire to suckle the breastmilk of God. Thus, God's gender is not fixed but fluid. What is more, the locus of the spiritual pure milk is God, which highlights two other essential characteristics. First, nursing is not a utilitarian activity. A baby does not drink and go. Nursing is visceral, involving warm milk, bodily warmth, and soft skin. Second, the baby receives both physical and emotional nourishment, which creates a relational bond of comfort, security, and peace. The intimate relationship of mother and baby gives the child the strength and courage to explore the world. The milk Peter urges his readers to long for also creates the intimate relationship of God and the Christian.

Peter also knows the power of the undiluted spiritual milk. Like the nutrients of breastmilk, spiritual milk provides spiritual sustenance to these fledgling Christians. The milk is the knowledge of God's mercy and fortifies

39. Achtemeier, *Commentary on First Peter*, 91.
40. Senior, *1 Peter*, 48.

the followers of Jesus to conduct themselves rightly. The purity of the milk also indicates the power of the intimate relationship. No intermediator stands between God and Peter's readers. They have direct access and experience of God's power. These new Christians must long for the mystical experience, feeding on the spiritual pure milk directly from God.

Commentary Analysis

The *spiritual pure milk* remains a difficult phrase to interpret. Travis Williams observes, "Discerning the precise meaning of this phrase has proven difficult within critical scholarship." He states that some interpreters have looked to the mystery cults of the region and period, and others link it to baptismal liturgy, but he allows the two adjectives to direct the milk's definition.[41] He states, "The milk on which these newborns feast ultimately derives from the procreative seed of God," which is "completely wholesome and uncontaminated."[42]

The scholarship regarding *spiritual* (*logikon*) is not settled either. Williams states that many scholars argue that the adjective *spiritual* (*logikon*) is intended to echo use of *word* (*logou*) in verse 23. Noting the philological argument presented by Dan McCartney, Williams, however, states that *logikon* "is even used, on occasion, to describe verbal communication, which seems to be the case in its present usage."[43] Citing Karen Jobes, Sean Christensen observes, "The adjective logikos would be an unusual relation to the concept of the word of God since the cognate word (in the form of logos) had previously been associated with the metaphor of seed."[44] Thus, the spiritual to which Peter refers can easily refer to a direct mystical communication with God.

An additional point regarding the phrase *greatly desire the spiritual pure milk* helps clarify its mystical association. Watson and Callan rightly note, "This milk has to do with the recipients' experience of the risen Lord." Peter has changed his focus, bringing his attention to the life after being rebegotten. He urges his readers to *cast off* immoral conduct and desire spiritual pure milk. Peter's concern is a life after their mystical encounter. Watson and Callan conclude, "The focus is not on the means by which the

---

41. T. Williams, "Delivering Oracles from God," 347.
42. T. Williams, "Delivering Oracles from God," 349.
43. T. Williams, "Delivering Oracles from God," 350.
44. Christensen, "Reborn Participants in Christ," 351.

Christians have come to rebirth (the word of God) but on the Lord they have found (the Word). Longing for milk is to actively seek a relationship with Christ based on a beneficence and love already experienced."[45] The entire verse calls to mind the intimate relationship with God the gentile Christians now experience.

1 Pet 2:5

> Also, yourselves, as living stones, are being built upon a spiritual house to be a holy priesthood to offer spiritual sacrifices acceptable to God through Jesus Christ. (author's translation)

God laid the house's foundation, about which Peter does not equivocate. God started the building and continues to build it. Thus, as the architect and builder, God directs the plan and anticipates its outcome. Unlike *rebegotten* (1 Pet 1:3, 1:23), which is in the past participle form, *built upon* is in the present continuous form. Thus, having completed the act of rebegetting, God now builds the spiritual house and will continue creating it. Peter does not lose sight of God's agency, even as he continues to write about his readers and the actions they must take.

In describing the gentile Christians, Peter waxes in mystical theology. The people are *living stones* (*lithoi zōntes*) and, as such, have three characteristics. First, since they are alive, they retain agency. They are free to follow the precepts of Christianity, and Peter urges them to do so—the central aspect of which is moral conduct. If they *cast off* their previous bad behavior and embrace the new religion formed within Judaism, to which Peter calls them, then they will be a part of God's great building. Second, they are connected to each other and mortared together, strengthening the house. They are stones, which in ancient times were used to create large buildings that symbolized the power and permanence of Roman civic and religious institutions. Even though the first-century Christians did not have such visible physical symbols, they themselves represented God's power and permanence. Third, Peter is decidedly egalitarian and nonhierarchical. His letter is written to a region that included five distinct Asian Minor Christian communities. By stating that they are *living stones*, Peter emphasizes that each Christian is important, and no one is more valuable than the other. Even the chief cornerstone Jesus is still a stone. Peter is also

---

45. Watson and Callan, *First and Second Peter*, 45.

demonstrating that while he writes to these communities, they are all one *spiritual house*. No one Christian is more or less vital than another, and no one local church is more or less crucial than another. In fact, they are all interwoven together and support each other. Therefore, if one stone weakens, the whole structure could become unsafe or even collapse.

Peter continues with his reader's mystical communal identity by stating that they are a *holy priesthood*. As such, they are set apart from non-Christians. Customarily, priests have specific duties that separate them from others and allow them to perform their duties. Often, they kept themselves in a state of religious purity. For Peter, that state is clearly a moral one.

As previously discussed, holiness derives from an encounter with God. Now, Peter expands on holiness through its ties to priesthood and emphasizes the communal aspect of the Christian communities. Holiness is experienced and worked out individually but is also a uniting factor for the churches. The individuals engage each other as a people united in their worship, glorifying and praising God. They come together for ritual acts that strengthen them to go into the secular world, which can be a dangerous place for them.

As a holy priesthood, they are to make *spiritual sacrifices*. These acts are moral. In the letter, Peter does not highlight specific religious acts or pious duties that the reader might normally associate with sacrifices. He does not vilify the pagan rites or priests, nor does he highlight actions found at pagan religious festivals. In a world where his readers "suffer grief in all kinds of trials" (1 Pet 1:6), interior spiritual work is safer than overt rites. However, spiritual sacrifices had a greater import. Whereas pagan rites would include animal sacrifices followed by celebratory meals, Christian spiritual sacrifices focused on behavior that heightened the relationship between the believer and the object of sacrifice, other believers, and God. Instead of offering an object, such as an unblemished animal, the object of sacrifice was self-oriented. Thus, the cost of the sacrifice was a changed self.

Commentary Analysis

The apposition and contradiction of *living stones* entices the reader to explore the phrase's meaning. As evident by the close textual references to Jesus as the living stone, Peter wants his readers to feel an affinity with Jesus. Achtemeier states, "The phrase is used only here in biblical literature, and surely refers to the fact that Christ, as risen from the dead, lives."[46] Senior adds, "This section binds together the destiny of the Christians with their crucified and risen Master."[47] Christensen also observes, "Peter develops his emphasis on participation in Christ's resurrection through his identification of Christ as the 'living stone' and believers as 'living stones.'"[48] In using the phrase *living stones*, one obvious meaning Peter posits is the relationship between Jesus and the reader; but Peter goes further.

The meaning of the phrase has two more facets. Similar to Christ's rejection, the readers have faced trials and rejection because of their faith in Christ. Achtemeier explains that since Christ was rejected but affirmed by and precious to God, "they too though rejected and alienated in their culture, nevertheless have God on their side and will ultimately be vindicated."[49] However, like previous portions of the letter, the action is God's, and the object is not his readers. In this instance, the living stones are but part of a greater building or group. Senior observes that the sentence's difficult translation makes not the stones but, rather, either the spiritual house or the holy priesthood as the object of God's purpose.[50] The individual reader plays a role in God's broader plan, which is communally focused.

The phrase *holy priesthood* further develops the intent of the verse. Achtemeier explains, "The movement from Christ as elect and precious living stone to his followers who because of their relationship to him are also as elect and precious living stones constituted into a people special to God"[51] shows the relationship between the gentile Christians and God. It also illustrates the solidification of the Asia Minor church to which Peter writes. God has elected Peter's readers to be a priesthood. Achtemeier adds that the group's purpose is "corporate with a function that includes a witness to all humanity."[52]

Holy priesthood separates Peter's readers from those around him and builds them up to a select group. Thus, their affiliation with God requires several tangible changes:

---

46. Achtemeier, *Commentary on First Peter*, 154.
47. Senior, *1 Peter*, 53.
48. Christensen, "Reborn Participants in Christ," 344.
49. Achtemeier, *Commentary on First Peter*, 154.
50. Senior, *1 Peter*, 53.
51. Achtemeier, *Commentary on First Peter*, 152.
52. Achtemeier, *Commentary on First Peter*, 156.

> In a society noted for its hyper-concern with social status, Peter urges that what really matters is one's standing before God. Status is measured according to divine standards. This requires new ways of ordering and evaluating life in the world, but also personal reconstruction within a new web of relationships, resocialization within the new community, and the embodiment of a new life-world evidenced in altered dispositions and attitudes.[53]

The priesthood works together through spiritual sacrifices that produce individuals able and willing to interact with non-Christians and secular institutions without compromising their inner spiritual nature. They also strengthen their social ties to each other, weaving together a social network that invigorates and supports their public actions. By it, they can maintain their new attitudes in the face of growing social tension. As a continually built spiritual house, the churches become a powerful force with the potential not just to face pagan cultural pressures but to overcome them, ultimately changing and overthrowing the pagan world.

1 Pet 2:9

> But you are chosen kin, a royal priesthood, a holy nation, a purchased-possession people so that you may tell out the divine message of the might, acts, and excellencies of him who called you out of the darkness into a marvelous light. (author's translation)

Peter elevates his language again but to a new height. He celebrates God's selection of them and praises his readers for making the grade. Peter starts with the family, moves outward to wider social groups, and ends with the greatest affiliation. Even though Peter's words echo Moses's covenantal declaration of relationship between Israel and God (Exod 19:5–6), he does not view the gentile Christians nor the new religion of Christianity as superseding the relationship of Israel nor the Jewish religion. He is a Jew and innately understands the difference between the two religions. In elevating the relationship of the Christians and echoing the Sinai covenantal relationship, Peter binds the two monotheistic religions together and connects the Christians' trials and suffering to the Exodus ordeal. Through his aspirational language, Peter illustrates the closeness of these new monotheists to the one and holy God who has continued and will continue to value them.

---

53. Green, *1 Peter*, 269.

Peter also declares the vital role that Christians play. They must *tell out* or *herald* (*exaggeilete*) the works of God as if they are his messengers. Peter's instruction is spiritual. The Greek root word is the same as in *angel*. Therefore, they are not mere evangelists speaking the good news. Instead, they bring to their neighbors a spiritual message from God who, unlike the Roman and Greek gods, is intimately involved and deeply concerned for his people.

Peter continues in this spiritual vein. After reminding them whose they are, Peter stresses from where they came and are now. They are now in the light, having dwelled in darkness. Returning to the four descriptors that opened the verse, Peter's elevation of these Christians illustrates what God has done for them. Bringing them from darkness to light was no small accomplishment. Darkness represents ignorance, moral depravity, spiritual emptiness, chaos, and Satan—the things for which humans need God's assistance to surmount. God's gift of light gives their souls a new beginning and a new way of being, one that matters to them and God. The new being is totally transformative. The Christians are rebegotten.

Commentary Analysis

First Peter 2:9 further represents the actions of God. The four titles Peter gives to the Asia Minor gentile Christian community express the identity of these fledgling worshippers and followers of God through Christ, and they name God's power and actions. Senior explains, "The Christians are chosen by God and thereby become God's elect people."[54] He then adds, "Because the church is God's temple, the members of the community are chosen to be in God's presence, to reflect God's holiness, and to be active in worship and service on God's behalf." God's agency creates the community of believers. God creates and sustains the community, the church.

The four descriptors indicate a strong identity as a community of believers of God through the resurrection of Christ. Craddock observes that the titles "are clearly community and not individual designations."[55] Green adds, "These descriptors establish, assert, and uphold a strong semantics of solidarity, belonging, and election within the communities of the letter's destination."[56] Green also states that these Christians are "to relish in their

---

54. Senior, *1 Peter*, 61.
55. Craddock, *First and Second Peter*, 37.
56. Green, *1 Peter*, 33.

corporate status before God."⁵⁷ However, Peter's readers must remember that "this declaration of the honored status of God's people is foremost a celebration of the God who has made them a people."⁵⁸

Notably, by bestowing these laudatory titles upon his readers, Peter does not advocate for a diminished view of the Israelites as God's chosen people—although some commentators leave the door open to a Petrine replacement theory. For instance, Achtemeier writes, "The absence in the letter of any discussion of the relationship between Christian and Jewish communities makes it impossible to determine how the author understood that relationship, whether as continuation or fulfillment or reenactment or replacement."⁵⁹ However, Green avoids any such superseding of the Israelites' preferred relationship by observing, "Peter collapses the historical distinctives between ancient Israel and contemporary Christians in favor of theological unity, but not in order to deny the importance of history. Rather, in a world in which great age is honored, he roots this 'elect clan' in the antiquity of the relationship between God and Israel."⁶⁰ By frequently referring to the Old Testament, Peter makes it clear that his readers were familiar with the Septuagint but does not call into question the relationship Jews have with God nor posits that his readers have a preferred one. Peter honors his Jewish tradition and encourages familial loyalty and respect.

The heraldic role Peter gives to his readers has a singular purpose. Senior explains that *tell out* (*exaggellō*) is used only here in the NT.⁶¹ He adds, "The Christian mission is to proclaim (tell out) publicly to the world the great deeds of God, that is, the acts of salvation that have given life to the Christians and are offered to all who would accept the gospel."⁶² The heralding also has a moral component. Since they are *chosen kin*, the readers' vocation of proclamation is conducted morally. Caulley states, "The believers' proper action is obedience, apparently embodied in the holy conduct that they are to maintain."⁶³ Additionally, Achtemeier correctly notes, "The telling forth of God's acts in 1 Peter is to be done both by act and by word,

57. Green, *1 Peter*, 55.
58. Green, *1 Peter*, 62.
59. Achtemeier, *Commentary on First Peter*, 167.
60. Green, *1 Peter*, 63.
61. Senior, *1 Peter*, 56.
62. Senior, *1 Peter*, 55.
63. Caulley, "Rehabilitating a Theological Stepchild?," 5.

and the latter is surely the intention here."[64] The community of believers has a vocational duty to state God's actions, especially the salvific act that brought them from *darkness to light*.

Commentators have noted the phrase *darkness to light* has several connotations. Achtemeier observes that the "contrast between darkness and light" indicates "God's salvific act in Christ."[65] On the other hand, drawing on Old Testament imagery, Green notes, "The move from darkness to light is a typical metaphor for conversion with roots in representations of exodus and return from exile."[66] Senior echoes Green, adding, "The phrase 'marvelous light' has a special beauty and may suggest the author is speaking of God's own glorious presence, to which the Christians are called and which will be manifest at the end of time."[67] Each of these interpretations points to a mystical framing of the community and its vocation.

1 Pet 4:14

> When you are reproached, chided, or reviled for the name of Christ, blessed are you because the glory and spirit of God rests on you. (author's translation)

Here, Peter reminds his readers of two central aspects of the Christian life. First, they are *blessed* (*makarioi*). However, Peter is not elevating suffering to make it a good or a telos for his readers. He acknowledges that trials and hardship will result because of their belief in Christ and certainly speaks from his own experience. At the close of the Beatitudes, Jesus comforted him and the other disciples: "Blessed are you when people revile you and persecute you and utter all kinds of evil against you falsely on my account" (Matt 5:11). Since Jesus spoke those words, they have grown in importance for Peter. Now, he extends those words of consolation to his readers. Moreover, his words place into perspective the *fiery ordeal* that, like dark clouds gathering in the western skies, looms in the near future. A freshening breeze darting into corners and whipping up dust portends the clap of thunder. So, too, the bitter words of neighbors and friends presage coming

---

64. Achtemeier, *Commentary on First Peter*, 166.
65. Achtemeier, *Commentary on First Peter*, 166.
66. Green, *1 Peter*, 62.
67. Senior, *1 Peter*, 63.

troubles. Peter is preparing his readers for difficulties and gives them words of comfort to withstand what may come.

Second, Peter assures them that the *glory and spirit of God rests* on them. Peter notes that the reason they are and will continue with their *fiery ordeal* is that they have been changed both outwardly and inwardly. In using *glory* (*doxes*), Peter alludes to the time Moses returned from his forty days and nights on Mount Sinai and his face shined with God's glory that had changed him (Exod 34:29). His readers were physically and outwardly altered by God when God elected them. God also rebegat them, transforming their spirits. That God's glory and spirit rests on them is the outgrowth of their rebegetting. Additionally, God's presence in both glory and spirit means God is a present comfort, support, and inspiration that is and will assist them in whatever ordeal occurs. God is with them and knows their pain and suffering. In this short verse, Peter points to the present time and frames it eschatologically. Present trials do not deny but rather make real the future hope of divine protection and reward.

Commentary Analysis

The suffering of Peter's readers in the name of Christ is not a question of if but when.[68] However, as Senior explains, "The 'fiery ordeal' that comes upon the Christians as a 'test' is not formal state persecution or even threat of death at this point, but the steady drumbeat of hostile criticism from the dominant non-Christian majority and the social alienation that results."[69] While their difficulties do not equate to martyrdom,[70] as previously stated, what happens to them has significant costs.

Moreover, Peter does not want his readers to embrace suffering for its own sake. Instead, when they are reviled, God's presence comforts them. Achtemeier observes that Peter does not want them to view the ordeal "as something strange to their way of life, but rather to rejoice in them, because the presence of such suffering means they are blessed by the presence of God's Spirit and have already a share in the eschatological glory yet to be revealed."[71] Callan and Watson also note, "The blessing of the recipients is from the same Spirit of God resting on them and provides a reason why

---

68. Achtemeier, *Commentary on First Peter*, 307.
69. Senior, *1 Peter*, 129.
70. Craddock, *First and Second Peter*, 14–15.
71. Achtemeier, *Commentary on First Peter*, 309.

they can rejoice in suffering: it gives them a foretaste of glory to be fully experienced when Christ returns."[72] With regard to suffering, Achtemeier, Callan, and Watson push up against a troublesome line. They seem to suggest that the readers are blessed because they have suffered. However, that is erroneous. They are blessed, which fortifies them when the suffering comes. The good is not in the suffering but in God's previous blessing, which becomes more evident to the readers when they are reviled.

Interpreters can only speculate about a complete and concise understanding of *glory*. Achtemeier admits the second half of the verse is "complex and difficult."[73] Achtemeier provides several solutions, the last being most helpful: "The thrust would be that both the anticipation of that future glory and the Spirit of God now rest upon the suffering Christians, thus making them truly blessed."[74] Senior, however, separates the two: "Traditionally the Bible associates 'glory' with God's awesome and transcendent presence, a 'glory' that is also inherent in Jesus Christ as God's Risen Son. When that presence is manifest, 'glory' streams out into the world."[75] The glory radiating from Moses's face is a clear example of its manifestation. Having already alluded to the Exodus ordeal by using the blood of the covenant at Mount Sinai in the opening of the letter, Peter now links back to the Sinai covenant with his reference to glory (Exod. 24:5–8). While the reference to Moses's glory could be seen as weak, Peter has associated his readers with the Israelites and their time at Mount Sinai. For him, glory is the physical outward evidence of God's blessing resting on the gentile Christians. Glory is a hallmark of the Christian life.

1 Pet 5:5b

> And to one another gird on yourselves humility, humbleness of mind, because God resists the proud, but to the humble, he gives grace. (author's translation)

Peter now begins his final set of instructions, and at its center is *humility* (*tapeinophrosynē*). As he has done throughout the letter, he uses an antipodal argument, casting pride against humility. As the final focus of his letter,

---

72. Callan and Watson, *First and Second Peter*, 111.
73. Achtemeier, *Commentary on First Peter*, 308.
74. Achtemeier, *Commentary on First Peter*, 309.
75. Senior, *1 Peter*, 134.

humility stands atop of all others, even love. For Peter, love is an action or attitude toward others (1 Pet 1:8, 3:8, 4:8), whereas humility is foundational and aspirational. Humility is also interior and mystical.

Peter knows the value of humility. Being the best of Jesus's disciples both as a student and leader, Peter grew proud. He attempted to walk on water, only to be admonished for his lack of faith (Matt 14:28–31). When he rebuked Jesus for predicting his Lord's death, Jesus admonished him: "Get behind me, Satan!" (Matt 16:21–23). Of course, Peter also thrice denied knowing Jesus before the cock crowed (Matt 26:69–75). Finally, as previously mentioned, Peter lost his leadership role over the Jerusalem church. Peter's humility was hard won, his chevrons earned through chastening experiences.

Peter emphasizes humility for his readers' sake. The rebegetting, holiness, and blessings made real by God come with power. Peter knows this from his experiences of healing the crippled beggar (Acts 3:2–9), healing Aeneas (Acts 9:32–35), and the resurrection of Tabitha (Acts 9:40–43). Such power will change his readers, and Peter wants them to stay grounded. His emphasis on humility will help.

So, too, will Peter's quotation of Prov 3:34. God, who remains the primary actor of the letter, rewards the humble with *grace* (*charis*). God gives the humble good cheer and gratitude. Notice that the action is not self-serving for the gentile Christians. Instead, the reward points them back to God, the central figure of the letter. Moreover, grace provides an additional spiritual benefit, namely, God's actions on the believers' hearts. It also reassures Peter's readers that God does not and will not abandon them. He is not merely present—in the vicinity like a friendly neighbor—but actively shaping and transforming the believers' spirit.

Concluding Thoughts

In addition to glory and the spirit's presence, humility and grace represent several of the spiritual gifts working in the believers and fortifying them for the fiery ordeal to come. Peter's first letter represents the foundation of a spiritual life for his readers. Peter has also demonstrated the crucial value of Christian community. Together, they are God's spiritual house, able to withstand any trials.

I have underscored these eight sets of verses to begin a mystical theology conversation. By no means are they a complete set. Other verses also illustrate the mystical theology present. The highlighted verses are meant to demonstrate its presence and show its robust and dynamic nature.

Moreover, the eight verses spotlight the first two stages of the threefold seeing, namely, beholding and *dianoia*. The ability to behold, letting the text be and allowing God's grace to work on the observer, permits the text to be known by heart. The *dianoia* appears as a struggle to know the intent of the verses. Difficult and complex verses allow for multiple meanings and permit an ever-unfolding interpretive process that delights the mind as much as it causes the reader to labor over intended meanings. The Holy Spirit's work of sculpting the reader's soul and painting new lavish images based on the text in the reader's mind catches the reader. Later, the divine vision will emerge and transform the reader, causing new acts of humility and grace.

6

The Mystical Theology of Second Peter

When I was seven or eight, my mother took me clothes shopping at the local department store. We wended our way through the racks and aisles of boys' clothing, picking a few things for me to try on. As we neared the fitting rooms, I spotted a New York Mets jackets display. I was mesmerized by the bold blue and bright orange piping and lettering alit ever so attractively by several display lights. I had to have one. The "Miracle Mets" had recently won the World Series, only heightening my desire. My mother relented to my pleas, and I proudly wore our purchase home.

As a young boy, I did not know the complexities of being a fan. Unbeknownst to me, my Boston-raised father had been a suffering Red Sox fan—another reason for me, as a teenager and young adult, to be a Mets fan. Remember October 1986? However, when I started wearing the jacket publicly, I discovered that western Connecticut had a diverse baseball fan base, and some of them loathed the Mets. When they spotted me, adorning my allegiance, these haters questioned my loyalty. I recall one man defiantly glared at me, asking if I was a Mets fan. I hesitantly affirmed my loyalty, and he scoffed. From then on, I started wearing my jacket less and less and was relieved when I grew out of it.

The jacket inadvertently taught me a lesson about identity. The jacket was an outward sign of my inward nature. Who I was and what I believed suddenly became visible. Humans like outward social conformity. Wearing plain clothing might be aesthetically dull, but most people will leave you alone. The jacket also represented a new behavior. I had entered the public space of sports fandom and lacked the knowledge, fervor, and fealty for the banter, ribbing, and rejection I would face. By quickly outgrowing the jacket, I was able to return to privately rooting for my team.

In 2 Peter, its author sought to prepare its readers for the criticism, ostracization, and contempt they would endure as Christians. Thus, he set before them a choice. They could follow the false teachers among them and return to the path of self-destruction through immoral behavior or remember the teaching already given to them by the holy prophets and apostles of Jesus. The latter teaching included the precious and very great promises that allowed them to "become sharers of the divine nature" (2 Pet 1:4). Choosing to remember the full knowledge of God and Jesus and embrace the way of Jesus also illustrated for them a dynamic and robust mystical theology that undergirds the very foundation of the Christian way of life. In this chapter, after stating my position regarding authorship and canonical inclusion, I will uncover the letter's mystical theology by examining key words, phrases, and verses.

Authorship and Canonical Inclusion

The question of authorship needs appropriate vetting. If Peter was the author of the first letter, he was not the author of the second letter. The letter's crafting makes it plain but also raises a question about its inclusion in the NT.

The different vocabulary, rare words, literary styles, and tone separate the letters. Citing Jerome, Daniel Harrington observes, "As Jerome noted, if one accepts both 1 and 2 Peter as directly composed by the apostle Peter it is difficult to explain the striking differences in their vocabulary, style, and tone."[1] Lewis R. Donelson agrees: "Readers have long noted the striking differences in language, literary style, and theology between 1 Peter and 2 Peter. It seems unlikely that the same author could have written both letters."[2] Jörg Frey fairly concludes, "Although it is difficult to determine what degree of Greek proficiency can be credited to the Galilean Peter, the elaborate style of 2 Pet does exceed nearly all other texts of the NT and is certainly not that of a Palestinian who originally spoke Aramaic."[3] Even

---

1. Harrington, *Jude and 2 Peter*, 236.
2. Donelson, *I & II Peter*, 207.
3. Frey, *Letter of Jude*, 215.

though the letter credits Peter as its author, the evidence for a different author is not speculative but conclusive. Peter did not write both letters.

The linguistic differences are such that a native second-, third-, or fourth-century reader would recognize the differences. Early scholars such as Jerome and Origen noted the differences and questioned its Petrine attribution. The question then is why include 2 Peter in the Scriptures. The answer can only be speculative. In *The Biblical Canon: Its Origin, Transmission, and Authority*, Lee Martin McDonald states, "No surviving literature identifies the canonical process."[4] McDonald, however, highlights four likely reasons texts were selected for canonical inclusion, writing that (1) "apostles, or those close to them, produced its writing"; (2) the "writings conform to the church's broad core beliefs"; (3) the texts had "widespread use in the life, teaching, and worship of the churches"; and (4) the writings "clarified the church's essential identity and mission as a community of Christ."[5] McDonald's conclusions are fair and reasonably characterize all but a few biblical texts.

However, when examining 2 Peter within McDonald's criteria, the letter's inclusion seems even more extraordinary. First, we cannot know whether someone close to Peter wrote the letter. It could have been the author of Jude or perhaps even Peter's son, Mark. We cannot know, but the letter provides several of the writer's characteristics. Harrington observes, "The actual writer of 2 Peter appears to have been a Hellenized Jewish Christian."[6] He was familiar with the Septuagint and Hellenistic writings. Thus, Harrington's answer is the best presently available. The letter was also rarely referenced by other early church writers. The *Apocalypse of Peter* had wider use in the early church.[7] However, McDonald's two remaining reasons canonically qualify the letter, namely, it holds to the church's core beliefs and features the church's essential identity and mission. As Frey states, "In terms of substance as well, 2 Pet is not a conglomerate of disjointed arguments, but rather a carefully composed and, in form and theme, internally coherent theological letter."[8] That theology avers mysticism.

---

4. McDonald, *Biblical Canon*, 405.
5. McDonald, *Biblical Canon*, 405.
6. Harrington, *Jude and 2 Peter*, 236.
7. Frey, *Letter of Jude*, 202.
8. Frey, *Letter of Jude*, 179.

The Mystical Theology of Second Peter

Key Words, Phrases, and Verses

To determine its mystical theology, particular words, phrases, and verses need examination. We will need to behold key portions of the letter with pure spiritual thinking (*dianoia*), determine their meaning, and then encounter their mystical theology. While First Peter is driven by God and God's actions on behalf of the chosen kin, Second Peter develops the response Christians must take to *become sharers of the divine nature*.

Aretē (2 Pet 1:3, 1:4, 1:5)

Aretē is an unusual word in the NT. Used several times in the Petrine letters and once by Paul in the Letter to the Philippians, the word feels like an odd-fitting borrowed coat. It is a word more comfortable in the Hellenistic world of philosophers and stoics.

In the first chapter of the letter, the author of 2 Peter uses *aretē* twice in close succession. First, in 2 Pet 1:3, he identifies God's calling of the Christian community "by his glory (*doxa*) and goodness (*aretē*)." In 2 Pet 1:4, the pronoun *hos* refers to *aretē* as one of the means by which God gives his "precious and very great promise" that permits them to become sharers of the divine nature. Then, in 2 Pet 1:5, the author places *aretē* immediately following faith (*pistis*) in a progression of descriptors for the Christian life.

In 1:3, the NRSV translation of *aretē* as goodness undervalues the word's meaning. Another definition is moral excellence or excellence of character, and another defines it as the manifestation of divine power or a miracle. When the author first refers to *aretē*, he is associating it with God's power visible to the letter's readers. In 1:4, he then shows how glory (*doxa*) and *aretē* bring forth the promise that, by them, the readers may become sharers of a divine nature. In 1:5, the author changes the word's definition, referring to moral excellence of the reader.

The reader, however, would not forget the concept of God's manifesting power so quickly. The proximity of *aretē* forces the reader to think spiritually, even mystically. The letter is not espousing philosophy but theology. *Aretē* is more than goodness or the manifestation of God's power through excellent moral behavior. The reader is to manifest God's power as an outgrowth of faith. To share in the divine nature is more than being a do-gooder. Once having faith, the Christian suddenly can manifest *aretē*, the power of God, by which knowledge of God increases.

Commentary Analysis

The complexities of the word *aretē* go beyond its rare NT usage. Donelson writes, "The common Greek noun aretē is difficult to translate into English. The usual translation of 'virtue' does not convey the sense of power, capacity, and ability that the Greek word contains."[9] He also observes, "Originally the term apparently had the sense of 'power' or 'prowess.' A virtue is not simply something good; it is also a capacity to do that good."[10] Examining 2 Pet 1:3–4, Frey adds, "Those who are called and who are faithful should then emulate this 'virtue' (aretē) and participate in his nature. The latter is further explicated in v. 4, likewise in the language of Hellenistic religiosity." The author's utilization of a Hellenistic word for Christian purposes causes difficulty for modern translators and commentators. *Aretē* translated as goodness undervalues the original Greek understanding, but virtue misses the mark as well. The saving power of Christ expressed in glory (*doxa*) and *aretē*, promised and given to the Christians by God, is more than a virtuous act. In the list of the spiritual life and growth of the Christian, the author points to the manifestation of divine power more than to the Hellenized virtue of doing good.

Epignōsis (2 Pet 1:2, 1:3, 1:8, 2:20)

The author uses *epignōsis*, defined as full knowledge, four times in the letter (1:2, 1:3, 1:8, 2:20). He also uses several other words with the *gnōsis* root, which is defined as knowledge. Thus, in this letter, the author intentionally differentiates his conception of knowledge.

While *gnōsis* means "knowledge," adding the prefix *epi* signifies a sense of "over" or "full." Some translations define the prefix as "true." When examining its use in 2 Pet 1:2, *epignōsis* becomes a cause, force, or power from God and Jesus that significantly increases grace and peace. It is repeated in 1:3, and there, it is a conduit through which divine power provides the necessity for life and holiness. Thus, the full knowledge of God and Jesus is more than a static rational sense of knowing. *Epignōsis* is active and dynamic.

As an active or dynamic force, *epignōsis* has a spiritual component. Its purpose is more than increasing knowledge and adding to one's

---

9. Donelson, *I & II Peter*, 218.
10. Donelson, *I & II Peter*, 221.

understanding of the physical world. *Epignōsis* also increases the spiritual qualities of grace, peace, holiness, and life with God. In fact, it is a power of realization that allows the readers to see the world's dangerous and destructive forces. As the author notes in 2 Pet 2:20, *epignōsis* is the force by which the readers have escaped the world's defilements.

For Peter, full knowledge comes from his time with Jesus, Jesus's resurrection, and his rooftop encounter. For his readers, full knowledge is more than listening to Peter's encounters; it is when God and Jesus become fully real, the result of a personal mystical encounter. It does not occur through rational deduction or persuasive elocution. In an encounter, the readers experienced the living Jesus and God, which was unlike any interaction with the stone-carved Greek and Roman idols.

Commentary Analysis

The source and object of *epignōsis* is one and the same. It is defined contextually as knowledge of God or of God and Christ.[11] Some commentators narrow its meaning to a "fundamental knowledge of Christ."[12] The context, however, suggests that God is also the object of *epignōsis*. Harrington observes that in Second Peter, "the object of *epignōsis* is in every case God and/or Christ."[13] The object of the verb is God and/or Christ, and its source is God. Green notes that *epignōsis* is "not knowledge of principles and systems but rather the formal aspects of our faith that cannot be segregated from but actually find their meaning within the narrative content and context of God's revelation to us."[14] Green rightly notes the importance of narrative content; but without revelation, the content is just a story. The key component is the mystical encounter, where revelation happens.

In 2 Peter, the author uses *epignōsis* and *gnōsis*. While they both are a form of knowledge, they are not the same. The author uses *epignōsis* to indicate a "foundational knowledge" that comes from "conversion."[15] Since a conversion may take time or occur through a series of events, the author's usage is better understood as knowledge gained through a mystical encounter. *Gnōsis* is knowledge that can be increased or learned over time.

11. Danker, *Greek-English Lexicon*, 369.
12. Kraftchick, *Jude and 2 Peter*, 9.
13. Harrington, *Jude and 2 Peter*, 240.
14. Green, "Narrating the Gospel," 267.
15. Kraftchick, *Jude and 2 Peter*, 177.

Steven Kraftchick calls it "maturing knowledge."[16] The author intends to demarcate the types of knowledge to clarify the difference between the knowledge given via a divine encounter and other types of knowledge, like rational knowledge, which can be taught by the author and church leaders.

The Chain of Christian Living (2 Pet 1:5–7)

Ethical lists, virtue ladders and moral pairings, sorites, or chains were not uncommon to the author's time. In 2 Pet 1:5–7, eight words are grouped together, reminding the readers that the Christian life is a moral one embodied in consequential action. However, the precise meaning of the grouping or order of words is difficult due to the author's writing style. Some translators have added a preposition between the words. For instance, the NRSV inserts *with* between each word (e.g., knowledge with self-control), but the author chose not to include a preposition. Here is a closer translation:

> Also, for this very reason, bringing all diligence, supply in your faith *aretē* and in *aretē gnōsis* and in *gnōsis* self-control and in self-control perseverance and in perseverance piety and in piety brotherly love, and in brotherly love love (author's translation).

The writing style and pace imply a series of steps or a chain leading toward a goal. The eight words feel like a recipe. My wife and I take turns cooking. In her family heritage, cooking is a creative act of generosity, confidence, and love. She will add dashes of herbs and create delightfully tasting dishes. I lack her confidence and prefer a clear recipe with exact measurement. For instance, when I bake bread, I precisely follow the instructions, knowing that if I miss one, the result may not resemble bread.

The author purposely chose the ordering of the pairs. However, one could argue that self-control should be closer to the beginning. Without it, even faith hangs in the balance. Perseverance could also be earlier in the sequence. In the face of difficulties and trials, endurance or steadfastness is faith's mortar. These observations highlight the author's decision. Unlike other NT writers—for instance, Paul in Gal 5:22–23—the chaining of the words implies an additional intent. Pairing the words and repeating all but the first and the last word twice imply a hierarchy or progression that is not typical in other NT virtue lists, especially the Pauline ones (see 2 Cor 6:6–8,

---

16. Kraftchick, *Jude and 2 Peter*, 177.

Col 3:12, 1 Tim 4:12, Eph 4:32). The order, repetition, and placement of the words speak to a progression from faith to love.

The author intended a sequence, the word chain moving from internal qualities of faith, knowledge, self-control, and perseverance to outward expressions of piety, brotherly love, and love. But *aretē* stymies the progression. If it is defined as moral excellence or goodness, as it is often translated, then the internal to external progression weakens. However, due to its repetition in the previous two verses, the author intended *aretē* to mean the manifestation of God's power. Thus, the list is not a progression from internal characteristics to external virtues. Instead, it is the five learning steps of the Christian way, followed by the three expressions of that learning, the three types of Christian love. From faith, Christians can recognize God's presence in their lives and world. From their divine encounter, they become more knowledgeable about the world. From the knowledge they gain, they understand the importance of moral self-control for a life gifted by God. Self-control fortifies readers' perseverance when the temptations of paganistic values and depravity return. These five attributes lead to outward expressions of love of God through piety, brotherly love toward neighbor, and genuine love for Christ's saving action that fills the soul with an overflowing love for existence, others, and creation.

Commentary Analysis

As with other portions of the letter, 2 Pet 1:5–7 has a translation difficulty. Donelson explains that some translators make the sequence of words "unnecessarily complex" by adding an "agency so that each virtue directly empowers the arrival of the next."[17] Harrington adds, "What is not so clear in this list is whether it assumes that there is straight-line progress or movement."[18] The temptation to create a progression or hierarchy exists due to the author's stylistic decision. Thus, readers can see a progression but not one that creates a dogmatic process from the word order. The chaining of the words may best be understood as a bracelet, forever building from one link to the next and ever returning to faith from love.

The eight words are similar to Greco-Roman or Hellenistic groupings of moral qualities. Donelson observes that several words, namely,

---

17. Donelson, *I & II Peter*, 220.
18. Harrington, *Jude and 2 Peter*, 248.

self-control, perseverance, and piety, are common Greco-Roman virtues.[19] Harrington also notes, "The (by no means exhaustive) list of virtues in 2 Pet 1:5–7 contains items that fit well in Hellenistic popular philosophy and Stoicism."[20] Thus, the letter's readers could contextualize the word chain within their greater cultural teachings but also transform the words' understanding to Christian theology and ethics.

The chain of words flows at a point in the letter that has a theological highlight. Sherri Brown states that the "chain of virtues" supports the Christians in sharing the divine nature and has an "effective destiny of theosis," which is a term familiar to the Eastern Church, meaning "becoming like God or participation in the divine life."[21] Kraftchick also agrees that the author "reemphasizes that a moral life is the necessary response to the knowledge God has bestowed."[22] Regarding the theological link to the virtue list, Donelson rightly concludes, "Theology not only leads to ethics; it also requires it. There is an obvious linkage between God's virtue, which empowers the calling of people (1:3), and the virtues enjoined here."[23] The word chain connects the letter's mystical theology of theosis to the real lives of the readers.

The tie to the divine nature and the correct Christian living is inseparable. As Watson and Callan note,

> Second Peter 1:3–7 forms an enthymeme in which the gifts of Jesus listed in verses 3–4 are the basis on which progress in virtue is urged in verses 5–7. The argument can be restated: One who receives everything needed for life and piety should live virtuously. Jesus's divine power has given the addressees everything needed for life and piety. Therefore, the addressees should live virtuously.[24]

The inseparability of the gift and response is a hallmark of Christianity. Kraftchick adds, "In verses 5–7 the author urges a set of virtues that should characterize the recipients of God's promises. Because the readers are destined for eschatological redemption and to become 'partners of the divine

---

19. Donelson, *I & II Peter*, 221.
20. Harrington, *Jude and 2 Peter*, 248.
21. Brown, "Challenge of 2 Peter," 585–86.
22. Kraftchick, *Jude and 2 Peter*, 96.
23. Donelson, *I & II Peter*, 220.
24. Watson and Callan, *First and Second Peter*, 157.

nature,' they must live in a manner consistent with this future state."[25] The precious and very great promise ushered in by Christ engenders a response that is more than thanksgiving. It involves a moral response that moves from faith to love and back to faith again.

And the Morning Star Rises in Your Hearts (2 Pet 1:19)

The author casts a beautiful metaphor of the predawn light, likening it to the presence of Jesus pouring into a believer's heart and soul. In 2 Pet 1:19, he writes, "And the morning star rises in your hearts" (*phōsphoros anateile en tais kardias humōn*). The readers are to wait expectantly for a divine encounter, and until then, the author's prophetic message is a guiding light in a dark world. The author paints a mystical world of overwhelming darkness and the unquenchable light of promises made by the OT prophecies and the return of Christ (2 Pet 1:16–19). The image, metaphor, and promises ripple with eschatological hope. However, the morning star rising in their hearts conveys not just a future reality but a present one as well. The hope is not cast in a final outcome exclusive to the end of the ages.

The feeling of the morning star rising is visceral and palpable. As an early child educator, my wife often has children connect events to feelings. Once, she asked a girl how it felt to hug her mother. The girl said that it made her heart warm. John Wesley had a similar experience. One May evening in 1738, he had a mystical experience. In his journal, he wrote:

> In the evening I went very unwillingly to a society in Aldersgate Street, where one was reading Luther's preface to the Epistle to the Romans. About a quarter before nine, while he was describing the change which God works in the heart through faith in Christ, I felt my heart strangely warmed. I felt I did trust in Christ, Christ alone, for salvation; and an assurance was given me that He had taken away my sins, even mine, and saved me from the law of sin and death.[26]

While grieving the loss of her five-year-old daughter, the nineteenth-century Quaker Hannah Whitall Smith had a similar encounter. In her autobiography, she writes, "I could not endure to think that my darling had gone out alone into a Godless universe; and yet, no matter on which

---

25. Kraftchick, *Jude and 2 Peter*, 98.
26. Wesley, *Journal of John Wesley*, para. 1.

side I turned, there seemed no ray of light."[27] At that time, noonday religious meetings had grown in popularity in urban areas. With little interest, Hannah happened on one and, while there, encountered God. She writes, "Then suddenly something happened to me. What it was or how it came I had no idea, but somehow an inner eye seemed to be opened in my soul, and I seemed to see that after all God was a fact."[28] The sensing of an inner eye and the warm feeling are indicators of mystical encounters. They represent the presence of hope, not as a future promise but a real, felt event.

The metaphorical phrase *the morning star rises in your hearts* also represents spiritual resonance. While the morning star shines, sunlight begins to illume the eastern sky, and nature responds. A soft breeze stirs leaves, and birds begin to sing in anticipation of the dawn. The morning star promises and heralds the greater light that will break the horizon, causing flowers to unfold and turn toward its warm rays. These demonstrate nature's ability to resonate with anticipation of the sunlight. The human soul resonates with God in the same way. The morning star rising in their hearts is Jesus, who can directly affect the readers, creating a mystical encounter that changes them and/or reinvigorates their faith. Their hearts are warmed by the promise of Jesus's return that resonates in all aspects of their lives, leading readers to the light of God.

Commentary Analysis

Morning star (*phōsphoros*) has several connotations. However, in this context, it refers to Venus. Donelson notes, "The compound noun phōsphoros means 'light-bringer.' Though it can refer to any person or thing that brings light (e.g., in Latin phōsphoros becomes 'Lucifer'), in the context of the heavens it normally refers to Venus, the so-called 'morning star.'"[29] Harrington also notes that the morning star is "the first 'star' visible in the morning."[30]

The author uses the image of the morning star visible in the last hour before dawn metaphorically to represent Jesus. As Frey states, "The 'morning star' can be understood here at least implicitly as a metaphor for Christ, whose ascent like the 'break of day' is an image of the complete revelation

---

27. Smith, *My Spiritual Autobiography*, 172.
28. Smith, *My Spiritual Autobiography*, 172–73.
29. Donelson, *I & II Peter*, 229.
30. Harrington, *Jude and 2 Peter*, 257.

that is expected to come with Christ's Parousia."[31] Frey is correct about the tie to Jesus. Harrington agrees, noting the metaphor is also employed in Rev 22:16, "where the risen Jesus is given the title 'the bright morning star.'"[32] However, Frey conflates the dawn image to include the morning star and, by doing so, neglects the anticipatory message of the presence of Christ in believers' hearts before the parousia. The morning star represents not the future eschaton but eschatological hope mystically illuminating the present.

For Whom the Gloom of the Darkness Has Been Kept (2 Pet 2:17)

The letter's second chapter brings to light the letter's opponents. The author does not withhold condemnation nor disgust for these false teachers. Although the author uses crasser language, the image depicted in the verse *for whom the gloom of darkness has been kept* captures the chapter's overall tone.

While the readers who follow the author's advice will have the morning star in their hearts, the false teachers only have darkness. At the end of time, the false teachers will not be annihilated, nor punished in an unquenchable fire, nor continually prodded by the devil's minions; God has reserved for them another fate. They will exist in the gloom (*zophos*) of darkness (*skotos*). Since both words are associated with darkness, the phrase creates a frightening image. God will punish the false teachers with absolute blind isolation. Not even Dante Alighieri's imagination paints such a horrible image of hell.

The author heightens the costs of false teaching to help the readers. By showing them the horrible outcome for opposing the teachings of Jesus Christ, the author hopes to save the readers from error. The readers know well these false teachers, because they had been followers who had turned from the good news, leading some back to their old pagan ways. Thus, in chapter 2, the author chooses extreme images to make his point. Follow the false teachers, and risk dire eschatological consequences.

---

31. Frey, *Letter of Jude*, 305.
32. Harrington, *Jude and 2 Peter*, 257.

Commentary Analysis

The false teachers are the central opponents of the Second Peter author. While the author gives no physical or other characteristics to describe them, several attributes can be inferred. First, the false teachers do not believe in the parousia. Watson and Callan explain that the false teachers "deny the second coming of Christ and the second coming itself,"[33] and Robert Wall adds that they "work against the redemptive purposes of the Creator."[34] Additionally, Donelson connects the false teachers in chapter 2 to the mockers in chapter 3 as having doubts regarding divine judgment and the parousia.[35]

The false teachers make an additional claim. Frey explains that the author's argument is more than an "apologia for emerging Christian eschatology. What 2 Pet articulates in response to the objections of the opponents has shifted significantly from the form of the Parousia expectation in emerging Christianity and is a thoroughly creative development in the dialogue between biblical and emerging Christian tradition and pagan cosmology."[36] Thus, Frey argues, "The appearance of the false teachers corresponds with this prophecy and affirms the eschatological understanding."[37] In contrast to the beliefs of the false teachers, the author wants the readers to anticipate the second coming of Jesus, and maintain "a lifestyle that is appropriate to Jesus' followers who expect to face their Lord and Savior at the Last Judgment."[38]

Your Pure *Dianoia* (2 Pet 3:1)

Having condemned the false teachers, the author returns to his beloved readers. At the beginning of chapter 3, the author notes that he, "Peter," has written to them before and makes both letters' purpose clear. He writes to awaken, stimulate, stir up, or arouse (*diegeirō*) their pure mind (*eilikrinēs dianoia*) to remind them. The adjective *pure* is a compound word, meaning

---

33. Watson and Callan, *First and Second Peter*, 146.
34. Wall, "Canonical Function," 71.
35. Donelson, *I & II Peter*, 210.
36. Frey, *Letter of Jude*, 242.
37. Frey, *The Letter of Jude*, 242. See also Watson and Callan, *First and Second Peter*, 173.
38. Harrington, *Jude and 2 Peter*, 237.

the sun's rays and to judge in sunlight. *Pure mind* can thus be understood as spiritual consciousness judged by rays of sun or in the best light possible.

After harshly condemning the false teachers, the author is unafraid to have his viewpoint examined. He says, "Remember everything you have learned from the OT scriptures and the apostles about the commandments of Jesus Christ and then examine it carefully in the sunlight." The author knows the validity and veracity of what he teaches, so much so he uses Peter's name. His confidence in the validity of his argument is unshakable.

The author then must address the age-old animadversion: "Where is the god who promised a second coming?" To refute their criticism, he uses a theological argument centered on God's word that tames and checks the chaotic waters that otherwise would destroy the world. He also acknowledges that God is not bound by time, and the judgment day's delay is to allow all to repent and come to God.

Therefore, *pure dianoia* is the readers' ability to remember who God is and allows the readers to clearly know God and the world. It exceeds the rational mind's ability to know. The readers understand that God alone gives order to the world, holding back the waters of chaos and the fire of judgment. They have also learned God is beyond human conceptions of time but can still act within time. With an aroused spiritual consciousness, they are now aware that God willingly suffers so that all may be saved from the fires of judgment. Finally, the author reminds them that those with acceptable conduct will dwell in a new earth surrounded by new heavens. *Pure dianoia* allows the readers to recognize spiritual truths not available through rational thought.

Commentary Analysis

Dianoia is a compound word, deriving from the Greek word *nous*. It is a complex word, which has different meanings depending upon its usage. In its non-Christian use, *nous* means mind or disposition and the power of spiritual perception. It also means insight, spirit, reason, and consciousness.[39] Additionally, *nous* can mean understanding or thinking ability or thought as a result of mental activity.[40] Working from Philo's writings, Behm importantly notes that *nous* could lead humans to the knowledge of God. He states that Aristotle considered it as "the finest part of man's

39. Behm, "Nous in Meaning of Term," 4:952.
40. Behm, "Nous in Meaning of Term," 4:953.

spiritual life, the epitome of the divine," and adds that *nous* is a gift from God by which it connects to the cosmic mind or reason.[41] From other Greek philosophical sources, Behm notes that God himself is *nous* in the final and deepest sense. He is the great and perfect cosmic reason creative and at work in all things, the good of the soul and of all things."[42]

Commentators most often think of *dianoia* in its rational and non-mystical meaning. Frey states, "The phrase is concerned with the addressees' capacity for thought and discernment (dianoia), or with its result and thus their comprehension of the teaching. If this is to be 'pure' (eilikrines), this means that the addressees' understanding should not be 'contaminated' with error, but instead correct and in accordance with the truth."[43] Harrington observes that the phrase's "emphasis is more likely on the moral aspect ('sincere, free of dissimulation') rather than on the intellectual aspect, and so 'pure heart' would have been even more appropriate."[44]

When the author of 2 Peter uses the phrase *pure dianoia*, he retains both an ancient Hellenistic philosophical understanding of *nous* and the rational aspect noted by Frey and Harrington's moral one. Greek philosophy reasons the mystical aspect of thinking leads to unexpected and surprising insights and new knowledge. When thought becomes deep and absorptive, it enters into the realm of God. Dempsey Rosales-Acosta describes the process well: "The physical and spiritual senses are interrelated to the point that the latter helps the former to perceive better the reality of the world, serving as a platform for the true mystical perception of the divine reality."[45] The author urges his readers to remember the OT prophets and apostle's teaching through *pure dianoia* to gain spiritual strength and insight to perceive God's presence and work in the world.

2 Pet 3:14, 17–18

> Therefore, beloved, awaiting these things, be diligent to be found by him in peace, spotless and blameless.

---

41. Behm, "Nous in Greek Philosophy and Religion," 4:955-956.
42. Behm, "Nous in Greek Philosophy and Religion," 4:956.
43. Frey, *Letter of Jude*, 370.
44. Harrington, *Jude and 2 Peter*, 281.
45. Rosales-Acosta, "Jesus and the Demons," 309.

> Therefore, beloved, knowing this beforehand, be on guard lest you are led away by the error of the lawless and fall from your own steadfastness. But grow in grace and knowledge of our Lord and Savior Jesus Christ. To him be the glory both now and to the day of eternity. Amen. (author's translation)

As the letter concludes, the author turns to eschatology. Having described the horrors, hope, and promise of the day of judgment (2 Pet 3:10–13), he addresses his readers as beloved (*agapētos*), those who embody *agapē*, the Christian's highest expression of love. The author names them as such to affirm their spiritual maturity and further encourages them to be faithful, pursuing Christian grace and knowledge of Jesus.

The author next identifies both an interior orientation and an outward ethic. Peace (*eirēnē*) expresses the inner orientation. At the parousia, God is to find the readers at peace, which is not an indication of how they are to relate to each other or to their non-Christian neighbors. As spiritually mature Christians, they diligently embody peace. In this way, the author ties back to the mystical post-resurrection encounter between the disciples and Jesus in the upper room. Jesus said, "Peace I leave with you; my peace I give to you" (John 14:27). Thus, as Jesus called the disciples toward inner peace, the author urges the readers to internalize spiritual peace.

His readers outwardly exhibit peace by being spotless (*aspilos*) and blameless (*amōmētos*). The negative particle at the beginning of each word implies not a way of being but a way of acting. The words could literally be translated as "anti-spot" and "anti-blame," which when combined with diligent, implies action against becoming spotted or to be blamed by wrong or sinful action. Both convey a sense of spiritual impurity due to actions, which the reader must work against.

The author knows the dangers the readers face. In addition to the inward work of peace and their outward actions, they must be on guard (*phylassō*), being on the watch for false teachers who arise among them. The author also recognizes that his readers have spiritual stability or steadfastness. However, if they do not beward themselves, they will slip into the judgment day's fiery abyss. Thus, as protection from these dangers, they are to grow in grace (*charis*) as they continue to be influenced by the divine gifts and promises identified in 2 Pet 1:3.

Lastly, the readers must increase their knowledge (*gnōsis*) of Jesus Christ. As a community of believers, they will continually learn about the birth, life, death, and resurrection of Jesus. This is more than gaining factual or historical information about the man from Nazareth. The author makes learning a mystical imperative. The knowledge of Christ causes growth in the readers, which feeds peace, allows them to act blamelessly and be spiritually unblemished, and permits grace to increase in them. The result of growing in knowledge of Jesus Christ shapes them via a mystical encounter through the words taught regarding Jesus; and as mentioned in 2 Pet 3:9, God wants none to perish but all to come to repentance (*metanoia*).

Second Peter's eschatology is dynamic and robust. It is not a future event, stored up in heaven and protected from human influence. Humans' present actions influence its outcome and timing—this is perhaps the most controversial statement the author makes. God is patient (2 Pet 3:8–9), permitting humans to encounter God and discover metanoia. Human agency is preserved. People are not forced into belief and can discover Christ but also fall away. Faith is not a once-and-for-all event but, instead, an interior facet of spiritual growth. Moreover, while God acted through Christ's resurrection and the early Christian community, God continues to work on the hearts of the believers, strengthening them as they continue to discover the meaning and purpose of Christ's dwelling on earth.

Commentary Analysis

The letter begins and ends with admonitions for peace; and as a gift from God, peace protects the readers during the final judgment. Many commentators view peace as an outward action. For instance, Dieudonné Tamfu states, "To be like Christ is to be at peace with him and to strive for peace with others, and those who are at peace with Christ need not fear his judgment."[46] Tamfu identifies peace as an activity toward others and not an interior state of being and notes the quality's protective factor. Kraftchick also sees peace as a part of the "ethical practice of the Christian faith" that represents outward action, but he adds it can, in part, help the readers' "awareness of the danger posed by the false teachers."[47] On the other hand, Frey affirms "in peace" as an interior spiritual quality: "Generally, an existence 'in salvation' could be the intended meaning, in correct faith and the corresponding way of life. Peace (eirene) points to that comprehensive state of being of Christian praxis, which was already mentioned in the prescript

---

46. Tamfu, *2 Peter and Jude*, 75.
47. Kraftchick, *Jude and 2 Peter*, 175.

(1:2)."[48] For the author, peace is the essence of a Christian and has repercussions that extend beyond the present to the "day of eternity."

The author closely ties the inner quality of peace to the outward action represented by anti-spot and anti-blame. Watson and Callan observe that the use of these two words "reverses the description of the false teachers in 2:13 as 'spots and blemishes,' again using these terms as metaphors for ethical behavior."[49] The contrasting descriptors give the readers additional clarity that their right actions must align with God's intentions, which they can do by rejecting the spiritually impure false teachers. Also commenting on two descriptors, Harrington contends, "The ideal of Christian life is to be found without fault or blemish on the Day of the Lord. The consequence of this hope is constant vigilance in the present and confident expectation regarding the Last Judgment."[50] To be anti-spot and anti-blame also includes a mystical connection to Jewish sacrificial temple rites. As Donelson states, "Both terms are used for animals that have been judged to be adequate for sacrifice."[51] The author does not imply that the readers will be sacrificed on the day of judgment but instead metaphorically imagines the readers being worthy to be in the presence of God, much in the same way a spotless and blameless lamb can be in the divine presence at its sacrifice.

The readers live in a potentially dangerous world where they may fall into moral depravity. Watson and Callan explain, "One who knows that incorrect interpretation of Scripture is dangerous will guard against it. The addressees know that the ignorant and unstable twist the meaning of the Scriptures, leading to their own destruction. Therefore, the addressees should be on guard so that they do not fall away from their own firm footing."[52] The author's best protection against an errant unethical fall is to grow in grace and knowledge of Jesus Christ.

Grace and *knowledge* are catchall words used by the author to tie together letter's themes and purpose. As Kraftchick notes, "The nouns 'grace' and 'knowledge' repeat language from the beginning of the letter (1:2)." Thus, they emphasize their importance and ability to shield the readers from false teaching. The readers also grow through their "experience of God's graciousness and knowledge of Christ," which is a "maturing knowledge,"

48. Frey, *Letter of Jude*, 420.
49. Watson and Callan, *First and Second Peter*, 215.
50. Harrington, *Jude and 2 Peter*, 298.
51. Donelson, *I & II Peter*, 280.
52. Watson and Callan, *First and Second Peter*, 217.

not the burst of knowledge coming at conversion.[53] Using these terms at the end of the letter, the author summarizes the readers' interior spiritual nature with the exterior, outward ethical actions. As Donelson states, "The purpose of these terms is to connect in the most general possible way to the larger imagery of the Christian life,"[54] not to frighten the readers into compliance but to encourage them.[55] Petrine mysticism is positive and uplifting.

Concluding Thoughts

The Second Letter of Peter contains a mystical eschatological theology based on divine encounter graciously bestowed by God and growing knowledge of Jesus Christ. The letter's fulcrum anchors in the call to become sharers of the divine nature. To be like God is a radical statement. In the Roman empire, only the emperor himself retained such status and privilege. Yet, the author boldly claims that ordinary humans can be like God. Not surprisingly, some might erroneously teach that divine nature includes unchecked freedom, leading to debauchery. The author instead teaches that sharing the divine nature requires spiritual maturity, ethical action, and learning more about the ways of Jesus. The readers have mystically encountered God and now must live not as privileged religious elite but as people expressing the highest form of love.

---

53. Kraftchick, *Jude and 2 Peter*, 177.
54. Donelson, *I & II Peter*, 285.
55. Harrington, *Jude and 2 Peter*, 299.

7

Metanoia

Victor was about ten years older than I, with a shaved head and a pleasant face. Being a talented musician, he enjoyed the sanctuary's acoustics that enriched the lovely old organ's tones and heightened the organist's skills. Since he always sat in a pew attached to the sanctuary's north wall, with a stone pillar blocking his view of the altar, I figured Victor had found the perfect place to hear the music. I was wrong.

One day, Victor met me in my wood-paneled office and told me about a divine encounter. Early one morning, he had awoken with a start, surrounded by a beautiful light. Thinking it had to be from outside, he had gone to a bedroom window and pulled open the curtain. Victor then had compared the outside light to the light in his bedroom. He was confused because the interior light was different. The two were not coming from the same source.

He chose to worship at this church and in that particular pew for a reason. High above the sanctuary floor were several small windows, situated at ten-foot intervals within the church's stonewalls. Victor discovered that the morning sun's rays pouring through one window was just like the light he had experienced in his bedroom that morning.

Upon seeing the light, he had sensed God was calling him back to church, and after having searched for a sanctuary that held the same light, he attended services regularly. Unfortunately, when he had shared his experience with my predecessor, the priest had had nothing to say. Of course, it could have been worse. The priest could have dismissed Victor's experience.

When Victor spoke with me, I affirmed his experience and helped him identify the divine in it. I regret not encouraging him to speak more about what it could mean, but Victor was satisfied to have me affirm it.

Victor's beholding of the divine light, thinking deeply about its meaning, and positive spiritual transformation is one result of a divine experience, but his is not the only type. John's is an example of different outcome. John was not baptized as a child and went to only a few church funerals and baptisms as an adult. When John met Kathleen, who was a long-time member of the parish, she encouraged him to be baptized. He was. It was a moving, seminal event in his life and was all John could talk about for a long time.

Not long afterwards, John and Kathleen went on a church's pilgrimage to Israel. Kathleen loved visiting all the holy sites, but John became fixated on the group's visit to the Jordan River, where priests and pastors baptize pilgrims from around the world. He insisted that the group's clergy baptize him. Even after the priests reminded him that he had already been baptized, he persisted. The priest capitulated, re-baptizing John in the Jordan River as the others watched. Once again, the experience moved him, and he was delighted.

A year later, Kathleen urged John to meet with me. He desired to return again to the Holy Land for another baptism. After a few minutes into our visit, I put the kibosh on John's idea, explaining that it was not appropriate and that he had misinterpreted the intent of his first baptism. John's error was not in beholding the event nor in his *dianoia* but, instead, in his *metanoia*. As a result, he had mistaken the Holy Spirit's work on his soul. He had confused the experience for its outcome. *Metanoia* is the by-product of beholding a divine encounter and thinking deeply about it. Like the rippling circles extending away from the point where a rock landed in a pond, *metanoia* is the change to someone after a divine encounter's splash, but the change is not the same for everyone.

Earlier I introduced a prayer, *The Prayer for Threefold Seeing*. After asking the Spirit's counsel when reading the Scriptures—to behold the experience of the word and to let the text be known and known by heart—the prayer focuses on the *dianoia* of the divine encounter. The prayer beseeches the Spirit to catch the petitioner where the word matters most and make the person aware of the divine vision's demand and provide the courage to affirm it. The prayer then addresses *metanoia* in two ways. (1) After identifying what needs to be born anew, the person is to inspire others through word and action to bring the holy to others and the world, making both more sacred. (2) The person asks God to inspire the inner self to act on God's behalf. Unlike John's desire for repeated baptisms, the prayer asks that, through an encounter with the word or the world, God will also change the person, not for selfish purposes but for divine ones.

For the encounter to cause the right change in someone, *metanoia* needs *acceptance*. The difficulty John faced was he did not accept the *metanoia* calling him to grow beyond the initial event. In fact, his experience caused angst and hubris. Victor's reaction was different. Even though he desired to see the light again, it inspired him to return to church and become involved with the life of the parish. His *metanoia* brought him peace by leading him to a church community. The difference in their *metanoia* is best described by John of the Cross. In the first commentary section of *The Dark Night*, John explains, "God nurtures and caresses the soul, after it has been resolutely converted to his service, like a loving mother who warms her child with the heat of her bosom, nurses it with good milk and tender food, and carries and caresses it in her arms."[1] Here, John describes conversion, but it can apply to any divine encounter. The intimacy, however, does not remain. Further spiritual development must occur. For the spiritual shift to take hold, the encounter must lead to the right *metanoia*. John writes:

> But as the child grows older, the mother withholds her caresses and hides her tender love; she rubs bitter aloes on her sweet breast and sets the child down from her arms, letting it walk on its own feet so that it may put aside the habits of childhood and grow accustomed to greater and more important things.[2]

After the beholding and *dianoia*, the person reaches *metanoia*. However, it can be misinterpreted or even rejected. If it is, then the encounter is sullied and spoiled. In such cases, the change leads the person away from the good, and growth does not happen.

---

1. John of the Cross, *Collected Works*, 361.
2. John of the Cross, *Collected Works*, 361.

Types of *Metanoia*

The categories of *metanoia* are antipodal. On one side are the *positives*: peace, hope, love, humility, and faith.[3] The *negative* side includes angst, despair, hatred, hubris, and apathy. A person can think deeply about an experience and find a new way of being and meaning that is positive, drawing the person to the light of God. However, the wrong conclusions about the experience can leave someone in a worse state.

When Francis of Assisi encountered God and beheld the lepers, he could have been overwhelmed by the experience, devolving into despair or filled with pride that God had reached out to him while he walked among the lepers, but he did not. Francis instead chose the positive *metanoia*. In his testament, Francis explained:

> The Lord granted me, Brother Francis, to begin to do penance in this way: While I was in sin, it seemed very bitter to me to see lepers. And the Lord Himself led me among them and I had mercy upon them. And when I left them that which seemed bitter to me was changed into sweetness of soul and body.[4]

The sweet change Francis chose was peace and love. Just before his death, he beheld his divine encounter and the metanoia that forever changed him and the world.

John Wesley is another example of a positive *metanoia*. As previously mentioned, he encountered God while in a crowd listening to a talk on Martin Luther's explanation of Paul's Letter to the Romans. Wesley's heart grew strangely warm, indicating the Holy Spirit's work in him—the divine encounter. His *metanoia* was different from Francis's but still positive, and it produced in Wesley faith, peace, and hope. The event at the Aldersgate meeting spurred him to become a leader of a revival movement, which led to the creation of Methodism.

Still another example of positive *metanoia* is Hannah Whitall Smith's experience. As already noted, she was twenty-six years old and suffering from depression. She wrote, "My heart was aching with sorrow. I could not endure to think that my darling had gone out alone into a God-less universe; and yet, no matter on which side I turned, there seemed no ray

---

3. The nine Pauline gifts of the spirit (Gal 5:22–23) may also be seen as positive *metanoia*.

4. Francis, "Testament of St. Francis."

of light."⁵ After her encounter, Smith quickly entered *dianoia*. "God was making himself manifest as an actual existence, and my soul leaped up in an irresistible cry to know him."⁶ She had beheld God, and a passionate desire to know God grew inside her. Her *metanoia* became that of hope, faith, and love. Smith explains, "Since this discovery of the mother-heart of God, I have always been able to answer every doubt that may have arisen in my mind, as to the extent and quality of the love of God, by simply looking at my own feelings as a mother."⁷

Further, Smith expressed her *metanoia* through action. As she states, "The revelation I had had was too glorious for me to withhold it whenever I found an open door,"⁸ and soon she and her husband traveled to England where she became a public speaker, an evangelist for God. As Smith spoke about her direct experience of the holy, controversy followed her. Many could not fathom that God would communicate with her. She became worn down by the criticism, until one night, while on her knees praying, God unlocked a storehouse of patience, which gave her strength.⁹

This additional communication from God, which Smith defined as "the life of faith," was an additional *metanoia* that gave her peace, hope, and faith.¹⁰ Once again, the *metanoia* spurred her to act: "So great was my delight that I felt impelled to speak of it to everybody, and to compel every one to listen."¹¹ After beholding a divine encounter and spending time in *dianoia* to gain *metanoia*, if the change is to be complete, then the Christian's inner self acts on behalf of God, going into the world in service of Christ.

Even though negative *metanoia* is detrimental to spiritual growth, it is not new, having biblical roots. For instance, Jonah's divine experience sent him in flight to Tarshish (Jonah 1:1–3). He was filled with angst and despair, which, while in the belly of the large fish, he finally expressed in prayer: "I called out to the Lord out of my distress" (Jonah 2:2). After traveling to Nineveh and proclaiming God's judgment, after which Nineveh's people lamented and followed, once again, Jonah's *metanoia* was negative:

---

5. Smith, *My Spiritual Autobiography*, 172.
6. Smith, *My Spiritual Autobiography*, 173.
7. Smith, *My Spiritual Autobiography*, 214.
8. Smith, *My Spiritual Autobiography*, 221.
9. Smith, *My Spiritual Autobiography*, 256.
10. Smith, *My Spiritual Autobiography*, 261.
11. Smith, *My Spiritual Autobiography*, 262–63.

"But [God's change of mind about his retribution upon Nineveh] was very displeasing to Jonah, and he became angry" (Jonah 4:1). Jonah's self-centeredness and fear and apathy toward the Ninevites illustrates all five deleterious outcomes (i.e., angst, despair, hatred, hubris, and apathy).

Another example of detrimental *metanoia* is that of Lot's wife. As God destroyed Sodom and Gomorrah with sulfur and fire, Lot, his wife, and daughters fled to Zoar (Gen 19:24). Beholding the act of God and knowing the angels' instructions, Lot's wife looked back and became a pillar of salt (Gen 19:26). Why did she disobey God? We can speculate that she may have been filled with anger at her neighbors who had hurt her and her family. She may have been filled with despair and angst at the power of God. Or she had hubris or apathy toward the angels' directions, thinking it cannot hurt to just peek. Her seemingly minor infraction led to her demise. She did not embrace a positive change in her heart and follow the instructions.

A third example comes from the New Testament. A rich young man approached Jesus and asked, "Teacher, what good deed must I do to have eternal life?" (Matt 19:16). At first, hubris filled the man's heart as he responded to Jesus's inquiry, but then despair or angst poured from him when Jesus said, "If you wish to be perfect, go, sell your possession, and give the money to the poor, and you will have treasure in heaven; then come, follow me" (Matt 19:21). Grieving at Jesus's instructions, the rich young man left.

Angst, despair, hatred, hubris, and apathy are negative metanoia's outcome—when people behold a divine action and, after considering it, follow a path of darkness. Their actions are centered in selfishness. They can stymy spiritual growth and even change for the worse.

Testing of *Metanoia*

The outcome of metanoia can be helped by testing. In fact, it is central to spiritual transformation. In 2 Pet 1:20, the author states, "First of all you must understand this, that no prophecy of scripture is a matter of one's own interpretation, because no prophecy ever came by human will, but men and women moved by the Holy Spirit spoke from God." Thus, as Robert Mounce states, the prophetic word "is not to be interpreted according to the whims of anyone."[12] With respect to his rooftop encounter and what he witnesses at Cornelius's home, Peter closely follows the author's edict. Not even Peter trusts his own interpretive skills. He knew better. Peter did not

---

12. Mounce, *Living Hope*, 120.

immediately test the prophetic word received on the rooftop haphazardly or lackadaisically but patiently waited and involved the wisdom of the believers in Jerusalem.

Metanoia testing must involve others, which may take time. In Acts 11, Peter returned to Jerusalem and was confronted by the "circumcised believers" who questioned him about his visit to and eating with the uncircumcised. Peter spoke about his account, including his experiences on the rooftop and Cornelius's home. He described the Holy Spirit's presence among and effect on Cornelius's entire household. Peter welcomed the opportunity to tell his story. The believers' response demonstrated the power of *metanoia* testing: "When they heard this, they were silenced. And they praised God, saying 'Then God has given even to the Gentiles the repentance (metanoia) that leads to life'" (Acts 11:18). Even though the believers beheld the Holy Spirit's presence among Cornelius's household, affirming the inclusion of gentiles, the matter was not immediately settled. Only later, after Peter criticized the Jerusalem council for its harshness toward the uncircumcised and after Paul and Barnabas spoke about the signs and wonders of God that they had beheld when among the gentiles, did James dismiss the issue of gentile circumcision and permit the gentiles full Christian membership. Thus, while *metanoia* testing involves other believers, the process can take time, perhaps a year or more.

Therefore, testing requires *patience*. We can speculate that Cornelius's household anxiously awaited final word about whether they had to follow the Jewish dietary and circumcision laws. However, they had to wait. In this way, *metanoia* testing is similar to the process of discernment. Luke Timothy Johnson notes, "The process of discernment is slow and messy. But it is neither arbitrary nor authoritarian."[13] *Metanoia* testing can be equally slow and messy and thus requires patience. For example, Peter had great patience after his interaction with the holy, whereas Jonah did not. In the light of Peter's thoughtful reflection and *dianoia*, Jonah's impatience is starkly evident. Jonah ran from God, only to be swallowed by a fish, and later grieved the salvation of Nineveh rather than listening with the ear of his heart.[14] Peter trusted God; Jonah did not. Like the discernment process, *metanoia* testing cannot be rushed and must be accomplished with the assistance of others. Without his openness and trust in the counsel of others,

---

13. Johnson, *Scripture and Discernment*, 111.
14. Benedict, *Rule of St. Benedict*, 15.

Peter may have come to a result that would have led to disunity among the two groups of believers than unity and accommodation.

METANOIA AND DEMAND

Metanoia also creates a *demand*, which, as we have seen, persons either affirm or reject. Whichever one chooses, the demand changes the inner self, albeit with a sweet spirit or a disruptive one. The demand also develops internal or external action or both. For example, when the people murmured against Zacchaeus, Zacchaeus stated, "Look, half of my possessions, Lord, I will give to the poor; and if I have defrauded anyone of anything, I will pay back four times as much" (Luke 19:8). His reaction caused him to self-reflect and submit to God's will. Zacchaeus willingly opened himself to examination and offered restitution to anyone he may have wronged. His encounter with Jesus spiritually transformed him, giving him the courage to face any criticism and the willingness to make amends. Jesus's recognition and acceptance of Zacchaeus demanded that he confront his critics and affirm who he had become, namely, a sinner who was ready for Jesus's salvific work. *Metanoia* always demands an interior change *and* outward action.

The Petrine letters affirm the relationship between *metanoia* and demand. In 1 Pet 1:3, the author states that God rebegat Christians to a living hope through Jesus's resurrection, and to an un-decaying, undefiled, and unfading inheritance, which God watches over in heaven. Since they were emboldened by the living hope, his readers had to respond to the demand emerging from the *metanoia* experience that called them to act differently toward their neighbors and society as a whole.

Second Peter shows that some chose positive *metanoia*, growing to spiritual maturity, and others became false teachers or chose to follow their wrong teaching. Those who chose positive *metanoia* shared in the divine nature. The Spirit rested on them, and they received grace from God as they learned more about Jesus Christ. Filled with a living hope, their positive *metanoia* could and did change the world, eventually transforming them and all of Roman society to Christianity. Then and now, *metanoia*'s demand is primarily this: *In the face of a culture with a separate set of values, Christians must follow God's plan, which has been laid out from the very beginning, and live with steadfast courage fueled by a living hope.*

Threefold Seeing's Goal

Having outlined the individual stages, I will address the three overarching goals of the gaze, specifically with respect to the biblical text. However, we must remain cognizant that the use of the threefold seeing goes beyond the biblical text to include any observable encounter with the divine. Any interaction involving the creator, the created object, and an observer has the potential for beholding, *dianoia*, and *metanoia*. Thus, whether one reads the Bible, poetry, or literature; views a work of art; listens to musicians play; or observes any aspect of creation, the potential for a divine encounter and an ecstatic experience exist. However, while an encounter is latent with divine potentiality, readers or observers play a role in the encounter.

First, readers or observers must remain with the created object. With respect to the Bible, the readers' focus must be the text and remain with the text. What matters most is not the biases, intentions, or even personal interests the readers have as they read the text. The text takes precedence. Thus, if readers disagree or react negatively to the text, they must not quickly smooth over or skip what is said. Instead, they stay with the text, allowing its true meaning for them to emerge. The readers trust that the Holy Spirit will catch them, pointing their attention and interest in the appropriate way. Disagreement, controversy, and confusion regarding the text's meaning is allowed to be, trusting that the text's meaning or vision for them will emerge. In this sense, the object or the text looks directly at the readers.

Therefore, the gaze connotes faith in the text. Bockmuehl notes, "The biblical writers unapologetically presume a readership converted, or converting, to the conviction that their subject makes all the difference in the world—and that their claims for it are true."[15] The threefold seeing presumes a faith in the creator of the text. The readers' faith in the text also permits the potentiality for spiritual influence to work on the reader. Without such, the ability to discern God's emerging vision is irrelevant. It is like hearing a rock splash in the water and not caring about its results. The trust of and faithfulness to the text is a critical component to the gaze.

The second goal is the struggle to engage with God's demand that becomes apparent through the divine encounter. It involves wrestling in body, mind, and spirit. As previously stated, the author of Second Peter observes, "No prophecy of scripture is a matter of one's own interpretation, because no prophecy ever came by human will, but men and women moved by the

---

15. Bockmuehl, *Seeing the Word*, 232.

Holy Spirit spoke from God" (1:20–21). The demand emerges from a text as an expression of a divine encounter, which involves seeing the word and world anew through being rebegotten. Dohna Schlobitten notes that Guardini states, "Seeing proceeds from life and influences life. Seeing means assimilating things, succumbing to their action, and being caught up with them."[16]

The acts of assimilating, succumbing, and being caught by the Spirit are an interplay between the Spirit and the mind, in which a struggle ensues. The body becomes involved as well. The psalmist repeatedly speaks of the bodily effects caused by the spiritual life. For example, in Psalm 22, the psalmist laments God's spiritual distance and its physical effects, writing, "I am poured out like water, and all my bones are out of joint; my heart is like wax." Again, in Psalm 38, David writes, "And your hand has come down on me. There is no soundness in my flesh" (vv. 2b–3a). The physical struggle points to a new vision and its knowledge being begotten. Like an embryo of a seed cracking open the seed coat, the begetting of God's demand is a multiple-level struggle.

The vision and knowledge push the mind to consider new interpretations of the word and world. In turn, the soul wrestles with a new way of being. The vision cannot be diminished, because a reality exists "behind each of [the New Testament's] sentences that transcends what is being said."[17] Caught by the spirit within the gaze, the mind and soul must untangle themselves from an old view of the self and the world and embrace a new reality.

The third goal is *metanoia*. The encounter changes the reader. In truth, the gaze is not about seeing the world anew, but it is about seeing its reality and transcendence. Guardini's threefold seeing reveals God's activity in the world, which is a gift of love. Christians also understand it as grace. Hans Urs von Balthasar summarizes Guardini's understanding of divine grace:

> Indeed, the act of actual divine grace not only illuminates inner-worldly conduct guided by grace, but it also fulfills it internally in such a way "that the water that flows from the eternal spring is provided and, for those who themselves partake of it, there rises from within a spring in its own right"—a spring, however, that

---

16. Dohna Schlobitten, "Art and Transcendence," 7.
17. Balthasar, *Romano Guardini*, 89.

stems from the "original" source and is "never possessed except as a gift."[18]

The reader's inner spirit or soul changes because of the divine gift of grace illuminates and transforms the spirit. Like the flower's stem sprouting through soil, the change demands an outward expression. *The word, read with faith, causes a struggle and moves its readers from interaction to action.*

CONTEXTUAL APPLICATION

The threefold seeing offers a unique way to approach First and Second Peter. The exploration of Petrine mysticism is a paradigm shift. It requires a methodology that honors the critical methods of the recent era and more recent theological interpretation of Scripture approaches. However, God speaks through the biblical text, and careful reading allows the reader to hear God's voice.

While drafting my doctoral thesis, I read Peter's ecstatic experience on Simon's rooftop and noticed his encounter included the hallmarks of a mystical experience. As I read the passage, an unexpected mystic emerged. With Schweitzer's writings on Paul's mysticism in mind, I then studied the Petrine letters. Mystical statements and teachings jumped from the page. Since my thesis examined the intersection of mystical experiences and evangelism, Peter became part of the biblical foundation for my thesis—but I left unanswered the full extent of the Petrine mystical theology that I glimpsed in his writings. Without a tool or method by which I could carefully analyze the text, I left the biblical soil undisturbed.

Upon learning of the writings of Romano Guardini and Dohna Schlobitten's analysis of them, I saw a way to exhume the corpus of the Petrine mysticism in a rigorous and faithful approach. The gaze allowed me to diminish my biases toward the text and the limitations of my analysis by not deconstructing the mystical aspects of the letters and not restricting their potential. While permitting the whole structure of the letters to be analyzed, the gaze also allowed space for tension and seemingly opposite aspects of the letter to exist, without a tidy urge to make them fit within an overall exegetical theory or theological interpretation. In the previous chapters, I have sought to allow the mystical vision of Peter and the resulting mystical theology to flower. In the next chapter, I will gather the constituent attributes of the Petrine mysticism to illustrate its theological whole.

18. Balthasar, *Romano Guardini*, 45.

8

Petrine Mystical Theology

WHEN GOD CALLED ME to the priesthood, I was a member of Christ's Church, Rye, New York. It was a tumultuous time for the parish, and the bishop sent a seasoned priest, George Packard, to help the congregation heal. George helped me discern God's call and guided me through the diocesan discernment process.

While moving through the evaluative steps, I had to write a spiritual autobiography. After George read my first draft, he wondered if I had had any "unusual" experiences, and if so, I should include them. I nodded my head and busily rewrote my work. I included the following unusual encounter.

One warm summer evening, when I was about twelve years old, I stood outside my family's home in Stamford, Connecticut. I faced a large swimming pool, standing right next to the diving board. I spread my arms wide. When I raised them to shoulder height, I closed my eyes. Surrounded by the undisturbed water, a copse of statuesque sable trees, and the soft susurrus of insects, a soft voice said, "Jesus." I snapped open my eyes and turned around. No one was there. I sillily poked the tall grass a few feet behind me at the edge of an embankment. It hid no one.

The encounter and its memory gave me peace and security in a home filled with abuse and kept me grounded with a divine reassurance fortified by regular church worship. It also pulses with mystical theological questions: What does my encounter—or any similar encounter—say about

God? How does it explain to divine communication? What does it say about human self-understanding?

Mysticism's fungible meaning undermines any attempt at a complete theological structure or system. However, mystical theology remains the anchor for all theological questions. As McIntosh states, "In the more ancient and expansive notion, we might say that mystical theology is the heart of Christian theology, theology gazing into the mystery at the heart of the universe, the mystery of union with God."[1] It is not then a subset of another tenet, nor is it a secondary or tertiary subject. McGinn confirms, "Mystical theology is not some form of epiphenomenon, a shell or covering that can be peeled off to reveal the 'real' thing."[2] While the theological spotlight has been elsewhere for much of Christian history, as McGinn claims, "from the start Christianity contained a mystical element."[3] Therefore, that the Petrine letters contain a mystical theology is no surprise and, in fact, should be expected.

The Three Theological Questions

While mystical theology is not limited to the three previously mentioned questions, the Petrine letters elucidate them with particular clarity. Others may desire to explore the christological, soteriological, phenomenological, or ecclesiological mysticisms that are present as well. I will focus on these three questions, because they are foundational to mystical theology and elucidate all other forms of theology as well.

First, *what does the divine encounter say about God?* The question is filled with multitudinous difficulty and a lustrous elixir that entices the human desire for knowledge. The fourteenth-century English mystic Walter Hilton writes in *The Scale of Perfection*, "Contemplative life has three parts. The first consist of knowing God."[4] In *The Fiery Soliloquy with God*, Gerlac Petersen, another fourteenth-century mystic, acknowledges the insatiable desire for knowledge of God. "It is not enough to know by estimation merely, but we must know by experience that the soul looks upon Him Who looks at all things past, present and to come at one glance."[5]

---

1. McIntosh, "Mystical Theology," 27.
2. McGinn, *Foundations of Mysticism*, xiv.
3. McGinn, *Foundations of Mysticism*, xvi.
4. Hilton, *Scale (or Ladder)*, 14.
5. Petersen, *Fiery Soliloquy with God*, 26.

However, God's characteristics or nature are immediately impenetrable. The anonymous author of *The Cloud of Unknowing* states, "No one can fully comprehend the uncreated God with his knowledge."[6] The anchorite Julian of Norwich agrees, "We can have a little knowledge of that of which we shall have the fulness in heaven."[7] Gregory Palamas, the Byzantine theologian, rightly observes, "For God is not only beyond knowledge, but also beyond unknowing."[8] As much as humans desire to know God, the Holy One cannot be truly known by the created ones.

The mystics and other writers have provided several solutions to the conflicting desire for the knowledge of the God and God's unknowability. In *On Learned Ignorance*, the fifteenth-century German priest Nicholas of Cusa states, "The quiddity of things, which is the truth of beings, is unattainable in its purity . . . . The more profoundly we are in this ignorance, the more closely draw near to the truth."[9] Cusa argues that the truth has no limit in both its absolute maximumness and its absolute minimalness, and at its core, both are God.[10] Cusa looked to mathematics to learn about God, recognizing that mathematics and science do not permit full knowledge of God; but instead, learned ignorance, the idea of nothing, is the best way to understand God.[11]

While Cusa's nothingness is one method to know God, others have looked to prayer or contemplation to gain knowledge of God. About prayer, Guardini states, "On this holy ground the reality of God becomes manifest."[12] The Franciscan monastic Ilia Delio writes, "Prayer leads us to know ourselves in God and God in ourselves."[13] Thomas Merton notes, "Contemplation is, above all, awareness of the reality of that Source. It *knows* the Source, obscurely, inexplicably, but with a certitude that goes both beyond reason and beyond simple faith."[14] Prayer and contemplation allow a person to gain knowledge of God by the relationship they create.

---

6. Johnston, *Cloud of Unknowing*, 50.
7. Julian of Norwich, *Showings*, 335.
8. Palamas, *Triads*, 32.
9. Nicholas of Cusa, *On Learned Ignorance*, 90.
10. Nicholas of Cusa, *On Learned Ignorance*, 92.
11. Nicholas of Cusa, *On Learned Ignorance*, 110.
12. Guardini, *Art of Praying*, 19.
13. Delio, *Franciscan Prayer*, 23.
14. Merton, *New Seeds of Contemplation*, 1.

Petrine Mystical Theology

One enters into a holy room where God draws near, and the divine perfume remains upon one's clothing, hair, and skin after returning to the world.

God's gift of revelation through the Bible is an additional way to learn about the God who reveals himself. Eugene Peterson states, "We call this book 'revelation,' God revealing himself and his ways to us, not so much telling us something, but showing himself."[15] The Bible invites Christians into a space where they can learn about God. As Sandra Schneiders states, "Scripture is a medium of the divine self-gift for all who approach it in faith."[16] For most Christians, the Bible remains the locus of divine knowledge and the way to know who God is.

When looking to the word, one must not ignore that its focus is Jesus Christ and God's revelation expressed through him. Thomas Keating observes, "Christianity is not so much a series of propositions about God as it is the communication of the intimate *knowledge* that Jesus had of *Who God Is*."[17] For Christians, Jesus is the ultimate source of revelation and the standard by which all knowledge of God must be evaluated. In *The Lord*, Guardini states, "Jesus did not 'experience' God; he was God. He never at any given moment 'became' God; he was God from the start."[18] Thus, to know God, one must know Jesus; and to know Jesus, one must know God.

Second, *how do divine encounters explain divine communication*? For Christians, God freely interacts with people and the world. Although Jesus avers in the Gospel of John, "I am the way, and the truth, and the life. No one comes to the Father except through me" (14:6), God merrily strews breadcrumbs and delightful clues of divine knowledge. God's agency is never limited. Schneiders explains that the meaning of sacred Scripture as "the word of God is not to literal divine speech" but refers to "the immensely more significant reality of divine revelation, which is certainly not restricted to the confines of human language."[19] Therefore, God can be a burning bush that never burns up, as well as a voice and image of a vessel filled with living creatures descending. The wondrous conundrum is, God is the same person who causes and oversees the ever-expanding universe and the quiet voice who speaks to a boy standing poolside on a summer's night.

---

15. Peterson, *Eat This Book*, 24.
16. Schneiders, *Revelatory Text*, 46.
17. Keating, *Manifesting God*, 6.
18. Guardini, *Lord*, 20.
19. Schneiders, *Revelatory Text*, 32.

Third, *what does divine revelation say about human self-understanding*? Rowan Williams clearly states, "Christian self-understanding is shaped by the 'mystical'—this means that our journey into the apprehension and enjoyment of God is not something that comes to an end with a static set of experiences or formulae; it continues to expand into the endless space of God's presence."[20] Self-understanding is defined by the relationship with the revealing God. The mystical carries humans beyond themselves and their self-interest to a place of divine relationship.

The psalmist illustrates the self-understanding gained through divine encounter. In Psalm 8, after acknowledging the grandeur of God, the author asks, "When I look at your heavens, the work of your fingers, the moon and the stars that you have established; what are human beings that you are mindful of them, mortals that you care for them?" (vv. 3–4). In explaining how self-understanding grows in a divine encounter, John of the Cross observes, "God will give illumination by bestowing on the soul not only knowledge of its own misery and lowliness but also knowledge of his grandeur and majesty."[21] He adds, "We conclude that self-knowledge flows first from this dry night, and that from this knowledge as from its source proceeds the other knowledge of God. Hence St. Augustine said to God: Let me know myself, Lord, and I will know you."[22] Teresa of Avila agrees, "Self-knowledge and the thought of one's sins is the bread with which all palates must be fed no matter how delicate they may be; they cannot be sustained without this bread."[23] Williams explains that the mystical encounter is meant to "disrupt 'ordinary' self-awareness" to allow true self-knowledge to grow.[24] The desire for self-knowledge is not solipsistic but a by-product of relationship with God.

One of the central purposes of the divine encounter is to create or reinvigorate a human self-understanding aligned with true reality. Williams notes that humanity's current context is one "where knowledge is habitually reduced to the acquisition of facts and solutions to determinate problems."[25] Christian self-understanding is expansive and includes an eschatological

---

20. R. Williams, "Mystical Theology," 12.
21. John of the Cross, *Collected Works*, 387.
22. John of the Cross, *Collected Works*, 387.
23. Teresa of Avila, *Collected Works*, 1:130.
24. R. Williams, "Mystical Theology," 14.
25. R. Williams, "Mystical Theology," 17.

hope that is essential "for our survival" and "our well-being."[26] Williams states, "The contemplative who is radically open to the act of God is in this sense an eschatological reality," which becomes a reality that includes others within the Christian community and the world and in the midst of all creation.[27]

Petrine Mysticism

The mysticism encountered in the letters of Peter answers these three questions as well. The words and phrases previously examined highlight the knowledge of God, divine communication, and human self-understanding. They elucidate the Petrine approach to the Christian life that is unique but well within Christian dogmas.

Knowledge of God

God is the one who acts. The Petrine authors make clear that God is not static or passive. God is the primary actor in the letter and causes Christianity to become and be. God is an active force in the world as well. The world came to be and continues to exist because God chooses to make it so.

In *The Doctrine of God*, Karl Barth elegantly states, "God is."[28] He claims that God can be known only by his actions: "God is who He is in His works." Barth is correct, but his precise thinking limits a robust understanding of God. Petrine mysticism avers God is the one who acts. God is more than the qualities of his actions. Barth agrees with that and understands that God is not bound by them.[29] However, God is more than his actions. God's essence is active, alive, concerned, and involved. That is God's personhood.

The Petrine letters, especially First Peter, provide a clear sense of God. The Petrine verses and phrases point to a mystical understanding of God that demonstrates that God is active, alive, concerned, and involved in a way beyond both transcendence and immanence. The Holy One is not

---

26. R. Williams, "Mystical Theology," 17.
27. R. Williams, "Mystical Theology," 19.
28. Barth, *Doctrine of God*, 257.
29. Barth, *Doctrine of God*, 260.

limited in his acts, and his action opens the door to an endlessly deep and broad pursuit of who God is.

1 Pet 1:3–5

Returning to the first letter's opening chapter, verses 3–5 illustrate several central qualities of God. Foundationally, mercy is an action of God, and God is mercy. Peter states that God acted "according to his great mercy." God rebegat Christians into a living hope because of and through mercy. This mercy also caused Christ to be resurrected. Additionally, Christ's resurrection gives hope for an inheritance that is guarded by God. It will never change or diminish. In fact, the inheritance is salvation, and the divine guardian protects it. The motivation and cause for each of these actions is mercy.

God's great mercy has been explained by Christian theologians and mystics. Perhaps best is Karl Barth, who writes, "God's very being is mercy. The mercy of God lies in his readiness to share in sympathy the distress of another, a readiness which springs from His inmost nature and stamps all his being and doing."[30] John of the Cross also identifies mercy as an attribute of God, writing, "He is almighty, wise, and good; and he is merciful, just, powerful, loving, and so on."[31] Teresa of Avila writes, "He never tires of giving, nor can he exhaust his mercies,"[32] and she adds, "God's mercy makes me feel safe."[33] Petrine mysticism differs from others by making mercy the central aspect of God's actions. The most central aspects of God's actions in the world and for humanity—rebegetting, resurrection, hope, and salvation—rest on mercy.

God's mercy implies that human agency exists as well as evil. The letter addresses both. The letter shows God's willingness for readers' freedom to make good or bad choices and that evil, which affects Christians in various ways, is an outgrowth of God's mercy. An unmerciful, ruthless, and cruel god would not permit human agency. Lacking any agency, humans would have no choice regarding their circumstances. God would have no desire for relationship. Such a god would maintain all aspects of evil in himself; a separate evil would be unnecessary. The divine power's actions would

---

30. Karl Barth, *Doctrine of God*, 369.
31. John of the Cross, *Collected Works*, 673.
32. Teresa of Avila, *Collected Works*, 1:172.
33. Teresa of Avila, *Collected Works*, 1:333.

encompass both good and evil, but in truth, the demarcation between the two would be irrelevant. Even though evil is a conundrum and presents a persistent obstacle to faith, evil exists, because God mercifully lets it be so, just as he permits human agency.

In response to evil and its troubles is hope. God gives hope, bathing Christians in its cleansing and life-giving waters. Unlike the dispassionate pagan gods, God's action of mercy creates a living hope, which points to who God is. Once again, God is not cruel, leaving the world and humanity to exist without any sense of divine attention and goodness. Moreover, hope is living, because it's more than a promise or a distant eschatological telos. Hope exists in the present world as a gift to the followers of Christ, and it affirms that God acts in the world and is concerned about Peter's readers.

1 Pet 1:23

The mercy of God exemplifies the activity of God, and so does the *living word of God*. As previously stated, first- and second-century readers would not have heard the phrase and associated it with canonical Scripture. The living word of God signified God's presence through the spoken messages of the apostles and teachers and the word communicated directly to the readers by God during divine encounters. Thus, the living word of God represents the God who acts—active, alive, concerned, and involved.

Furthermore, Peter credits the living word with rebegetting the readers. The image of the imperishable seed increases the power of the living word even more. The living word has agency and immense power. It transforms Christians. Thus, it represents more than Scripture but rather the action of God—the point where God meets Christians in a mystical encounter.

1 Pet 2:5

Peter yet again explains God as the one who acts. God is both an architect and builder of a spiritual house. Soon after the death of Jesus, the first-century Christians were excluded from worship at the temple in Jerusalem. They were also not welcome at regional synagogues, and pagan worship offered no solution. Rising local discrimination left few options for communal gathering for worship. They were not forced underground yet, but

Christians did not have public support, let alone official governmental acceptance. In the face of rising opposition, God answered their need.

Only God can create a spiritual house, using both the body and spirit of Christians. The creation of a spiritual house and the holy priesthood affirms a God who acts. God is aware of the readers' needs and so expands their understanding of spirituality beyond a physical place, such as a temple. He also enlarges their sense of religious community. God aims to create Christianity, not based on the Roman or Greek religious system of gods nor limited to a tribe or people. Instead, God's action and concern know no limit. God builds a spiritual house from all classes, types, and kinds of people.

1 Pet 2:9

As much as he favors Jews, God favors Christians. Peter reminds his readers that God chose them. God made them kin, and they are a royal priesthood because of God. God purchased and possesses them, because God resurrected Jesus. Not one of them chose to be such. God called them into being. Thus, God's actions supersede any decision of faith, altar call response, or choice to be baptized. The one who acts brought them together, and they became the five churches to which Peter writes.

God also instills in the readers a purpose. God makes them into witnesses of God's actions. Having called them out of the darkness, God brings them into the light. Thus, God is one who is concerned for their wellbeing, involved in their lives by giving them a purpose, and active not just in the community but with each individual as well. God takes initiative to save people by creating kinship and purpose. Finally, God gives them the gift of physical and spiritual light, which once again shows God's mercy by allowing them to dwell in a marvelous light.

1 Pet 4:14

God does more than give the readers a purpose and allow them to dwell in light. They are blessed by God, and God's glory and Spirit rests on them. The power bestowed on them cannot be understated. When they face fiery trials, they do so armed with and fortified by divine gifts. To be blessed in such a way allows them to withstand and stand firm against ostracization, prejudice, and hatred. Critically, the emphasis is not on suffering but on the blessing and divine gifts. God's action when they face difficulties is more vital to Peter than what the readers face. The Christians have no need to worry, because God is active, concerned, and involved in their lives.

1 Pet 5:5b

What God values is far different from what humans value. People have always sought power, strength, and success, but God rewards the followers of Jesus who are humble. The Holy One bestows grace on the humble. Christians are no different from anyone else. When using power, even if it comes from God, pride and hubris can follow. Mindful of such a mistake, God rewards the right use of divine power. Gratitude is God's gift for those who act well.

2 Pet 2:17

God guards the readers' inheritance of salvation and also keeps the gloom of darkness for those who lead others astray. God is judgment. God gives humans freedom to make good or bad choices but retains the power to punish people, especially those who work against God's actions, aliveness, concern, and involvement. God creates limits to human agency. God seeks order, not chaos. The author knows this and thus warns those who undermine divine purposes. God's punishment will be severe for false teachers, and while readers may want God to act immediately, God retains autonomy over how and when to punish such people.

2 Pet 3:1

At almost the same level as mercy is God's willingness to be known. Pure *dianoia* is a generous gift from the creator. The ability to unknow the things of this world and to awaken the soul to the actions of God is an unfathomable privilege. While the act of prayer itself is a great benefaction, of greater import is pure *dianoia*, the ability to wrestle with and conceive of divine actions in the world and oneself. Returning to the psalmist's words: "When I look at your heavens, the work of your fingers, the moon and the stars that you have established; what are human beings that you are mindful of them, mortals that you care for them?" (Ps 8:3–4). The ability to interact with the divine is not a condition of the created order but a result of God's actions, aliveness, concern, and involvement with humanity. The ability to pray, learn, and know are generous gifts.

Petrine Divine Attributes

Petrine mysticism illustrates four of God's attributes, namely, active, alive, concerned, and involved. God acts for the benefit of humanity as a divine choice that is completely in God's control. Fortunately for humans, God chose to resurrect Jesus and rebeget Christians, giving them a living hope and salvation ever protected by God. Although perplexing for humans to grasp, evil remains, because God chooses it so. God's action continues through the creation of a spiritual house, shaped and molded from followers of Jesus. These followers have received a divine purpose to be witnesses of God's four attributes, and God has given them power to be messengers, even when they find it difficult. From these divine actions, a Petrine mysticism emerges that shows God is mercy and judgment, which can be understood by humanity and individuals if they so choose to learn them.

Divine Communication

Mysticism presumes divine communication. God, Jesus, or the Holy Spirit can directly communicate with a person. For Peter and the Petrine author, such divine encounters are not rare or unusual. The writers presume God communicates with the gathered community and individuals and thus make no special mention of God initiating interactions.

In Petrine mysticism, divine communication is fluid and intimate, driven by an active and alive God who is concerned and involved in the lives of Jesus's followers. Such communication does not, however, imply that God is a smothering mother-in-law, a tiger mom, or a micromanaging father. Divine communication does not obfuscate or diminish human agency but supports and encourages it.

1 Pet 1:3–5

Rebegetting is the most obvious evidence of divine communication. Since Peter does not explain the characteristics of or the process for being rebegotten, God's method was either obvious to the readers or so varied and fluid that it could not be simply described. Regardless, the instances of rebegetting appear to have happened broadly within the community. What is communicated to everyone is a living hope that resulted from Jesus's resurrection. God gave both the five communities and individual members the awareness of what occurred through Christ.

1 Pet 1:14–16

To attentively hearken also presumes divine communication. If God does not communicate, then nothing can be heard, and hearkening is folly. Attentiveness also implies that divine communication can be missed. To hear what God says requires a willingness and ability to discern, from all other noises and voices, God's words. The readers can hear God speaking when they prayerfully and mindfully seek it.

God's voice can be heard, but God values the sounds of creation and the agency of humans. In the Gospel of Mark, Jesus proved the divine ability to silence the wind by rebuking it (4:39). At Horeb, God speaks to Elijah in a voice from the silence (1 Kgs 19:13). Both examples illustrate the divine ability to control the sounds of creation but also the divine respect for agency among the created order. The wind and fire have their time, and then God speaks.

1 Pet 1:23

The living word of God is the clearest form of divine communication. It comes in two forms. (1) People gathered to hear the living word of God spoken by the apostles and teachers or heard their letters read. As previously stated, the living word is not what contemporary readers know as the Bible but is the good news shared by one to another. (2) God communicated with groups or individuals via direct encounter. Petrine mysticism does not prefer either. Both are valued. However, false teaching is always deleterious and ruinous.

The living word of God is fluid and dynamic. It causes rebegetting, sustains Christians, and brings life and salvation. The living word converts the hearts of sinners and does so through various means. It is not fixed or set but still growing and alive. Thus, the living word of God is mystical, flowing from God's mercy.

1 Pet 2:2

Peter also describes divine communication as spiritual pure milk. Coming directly from God, it provides physical, emotional, and spiritual nourishment. It creates an intimate and nurturing relationship between God and believers. As previously mentioned, John of the Cross writes, "God nurtures and caresses the soul after it has been resolutely converted to his service, like a loving mother who warms her child with the heat of her bosom, nurses it with good milk and tender food, and carries and caresses it in her arms."[34] Feeding the soul comes about through communication directly from the breast of God. The soul grows through tender divine interaction.

Spiritual pure milk also informs the way divine communication occurs. Unlike pagan religions, which often required the services of priests or other types of intermediaries, Christians have direct access to God and can experience God's power directly. Empowering Christians to have direct access instills in them hope, value, and appreciation. God meets their longings, desires, and persistence.

1 Pet 5:5b

God chooses with whom to be in relationship and in what way. God does not interact with the false teachers and mockers. Peter makes no reference to others excluded from divine blessings, such as the sinners and evildoers whom Paul chastises. Regardless, Petrine mysticism understands that God is free to communicate in whatever ways God desires. When in relationship, God can communicate via gifts. In particular, God gives grace, by which God transforms hearts.

Epignōsis (2 Pet 1:2, 1:3, 1:8, 2:20)

Knowing is a form of divine communication. *Epignōsis* is a power from God, a force from God and Jesus that increases grace and peace, and a conduit that provides the necessity for life and holiness. By it, God permits himself to be known by the followers of Jesus. In this sense, *epignōsis* is a means by which revelation occurs. It is a gift from God.

---

34. John of the Cross, *Collected Works*, 361.

2 Pet 1:19

Another gift is the morning star (*phōsphoros*). That it can rise in the readers' hearts illustrates another type of divine communication. God can communicate nonverbally to affect the readers, giving them a present hope. The image represents Jesus who is the light bringer and, of course, is a present reality who communicates God's message of good news. The morning star changes Christians, bringing them out of the murky places into the light of God.

Pure Dianoia (2 Pet 3:1)

Like *epignōsis*, pure *dianoia* is also a divine gift. Through its spiritual wrestling, God permits Christians to gain mystical insight, consciousness, and perception. It is the ability to reason about the divine and to communicate with God through deep, absorptive thinking. In that state of consciousness or depth of thinking, God allows humans into the divine realm. Pure *dianoia* is the foundation of spiritual strength and perception.

2 Pet 3:14, 17–18

Divine communication also implies God's desire for human growth. God enables Christians to develop full spiritual maturity. Growth comes in the increasing knowledge of God and Jesus and also in grace. While knowledge is focused on the act of learning, grace is a spiritual trait. As such, its source is from God, who works on the readers' hearts and helps them perceive God in the world, each other, and themselves. The outgrowth of the gift of grace is an abiding gratitude toward God, who permits the divine to be known and appreciated.

Petrine Divine Communication

In all its forms, divine communication is a gift from God. Be it through the simplest prayer or the innermost contemplation, divine communication is unattainable without God. Thus, as previously noted, God is the source of communication and its subject and object. The resurrection of Christ is also a form of communication, which can rebeget Christians and empower them to learn more about the nature of God. The living word of God, spiritual pure milk, and the morning star bring life, nourishment, and hope to the Petrine readers. They also indicate that God reaches out in various and intimate ways to support Jesus's followers. The sense of learning and spiritual growth pervades the readers, by which God allows them to discover and reach spiritual maturity.

Human Self-Understanding

As previously mentioned, the psalmist writes, "What are human beings that you are mindful of them, mortals that you care for them?" (Ps 8:4). The question strikes at what it means to be human. Even though the question is directed toward God, it is one of self-knowledge. Awareness of the mortality of humans in an enormous universe is itself self-knowledge. Self-knowledge also asks another question, namely, "Whose are we?" In addition to the questions of God and divine communication, the Petrine letters, especially the second one, answer these questions regarding human self-knowledge.

The mystics see knowledge of God and self as intertwined. Knowledge of God cannot occur without true knowledge of self. The author of *The Cloud of Unknowing* writes, "And therefore, do not shrink from the sweat and toil involved in gaining real self-knowledge, for I am sure that when you have acquired it you will very soon come to an experiential knowledge of God's goodness and love."[35] John of the Cross adds, "God will give illumination by bestowing on the soul not only knowledge of its own misery and lowliness but also knowledge of his grandeur and majesty."[36] Thus, the two questions, who are human beings and whose are they, are integral to discovering who God is and a complete view of Petrine mystical theology.

1 Pet 1:3–5 and 1 Pet 1:14–16

These verses begin to explain who Christians are in light of God's particular concern and preference. First, they are recipients of an inheritance and promise of salvation. Second, they are worthy of God's attention and special favor and thus have particular merit as recipients of hope through God's mercy. Third, humans, but specifically Christians, can become holy. They

---

35. Johnson, *Cloud of Unknowing*, 66.
36. John of the Cross, *Collected Works*, 387.

can understand and live out holiness. Thus, Christians are those who have received God's blessings of salvation, hope, and holiness. These three gifts inform a self-understanding that goes beyond the more prevalent Christian views of human depravity and sinfulness. They expand human self-knowledge to include what humans can become. Petrine mystical theology affirms that people have the potential to spiritually transform, grow, and realize spiritual maturity.

1 Pet 1:23 and 1 Pet 2:2

Self-knowledge also defines the relationship between God and Christians. The rebegottenness of Christians has established them as children of God. When God rebegat them, he acted on their behalf, affirming their potential as followers of Jesus. They thus gained access to spiritual pure milk, which nourishes and sustains them. The ability to long for the spiritual pure milk implies they can have an intimate and beneficial relationship with God. Christians can feed directly from God without the need for mediation. Petrine mystical theology affirms the reality of community as egalitarian and unified. Since everyone has access to God, all are valued by God.

1 Pet 2:5

Living stones continues the self-understanding of community. Humans can be built into a spiritual community by the hands of God but also retain agency. They are not to forced to be a spiritual house. The agency means that some Christian communities can deteriorate and crumble. When members choose not to be formed into a spiritual house, the community suffers. However, the potentiality also means that people are not beholden to cultural, communal, or familial constructs. All people are vital, have worth, and have a place in the spiritual house.

The royal priest description extends the idea of community to spiritual action. As a royal priesthood, holiness becomes central to humanity for individuals and communities. The sacrifices the priesthood offers are spiritual, not physical. As opposed to pagan or even first-century Torah-based sacrifices, Christian churches disavow animal offerings. Thus, they elevate a respect for the world and its creatures. As spiritual sacrifices, they place a high value on moral actions. The way Christians conduct themselves with each other, in their secular communities, and toward the world at large matters. Moral actions are spiritual sacrifices.

The images of living stones and royal priesthood embrace a self-understanding that includes the individual and one's family, community, tribe, state, nation, and empire. As a united group of Christian communities, they can influence society on every level. Spiritual sacrifices are conducted by an individual, a church, and a group of churches. Such moral actions redefine acceptable moral and ethical behavior. To remain a living stone in a spiritual house and a member of the royal priesthood, a person must adhere to the appropriate actions that maintain relationship with God through Jesus Christ.

1 Pet 2:9

In 1 Pet 2:9, Peter lists four identifiers of self-understanding. The readers are "chosen kin, a royal priesthood, a holy nation, and a purchased-possession people." Each connotes a sense of group, by which Peter elevates community over individuality. One Christian may be strong and faithful, but an assemblage of Christians is powerful, receiving and giving strength to each member.

The verse also reminds the readers of whose they are. They previously dwelled in darkness and were brought by God to the light. The letter's undercurrent of human living presumes that the readers can backslide into darkness. They retain the choice to be chosen kin, and in fact, the false teachers rejected their divine kinship. The readers are also a people with purpose. The human life can be one of import, with an objective of sharing the good news with other people. Self-understanding includes being a witness of God's actions in them, others, and the world.

1 Pet 4:14 and 1 Pet 5:5b

Christians are also those who can endure being reviled while remaining humble. They are blessed by God, which presumes the power to withstand what others cannot. Unlike many gentiles who believe in distant, uncaring gods, Peter's addressees can be resolute, because God actively blesses them. Moreover, the spirit of God rests on them, providing them with unique powers. The divine spirit makes them exceptional, which could lead to hubris and pride. Since such powers can lead to inappropriate spiritual behavior, Peter's advice regarding humility counteracts spiritual arrogance. As informed by Peter, the human spiritual character is sophisticated and complex. Without divine guidance, it can become unruly, wild, and rebellious.

Aretē (2 Pet 1:3, 1:4, 1:5)

The focal point of the Second Letter of Peter is the self-understanding that the readers can share in the divine nature. As defined previously, *aretē* is the external manifestation of God's power. It encompasses more than belief or the ability to be morally good actors. *Aretē* is the present vitality of God within the believers, which allows them to act differently, be humble, and have hope. Since *aretē* is not static, the believers can grow. Thus, *aretē* represents a key aspect by which the readers express the divine nature God shared with them.

2 Pet 1:5–7

The chain of Christian living represents the process by which the addressees can share in the divine nature. Each of the eight words embodies theosis. Faith, *aretē*, *gnōsis*, self-control, and perseverance are outward qualities that define who are the addressees. The latter three—piety, brotherly love, and *agapē*—that emanate from Christians are spiritual qualities. In themselves, they signify who Christians are compared to others and the apex of all human identity, namely theosis. They are the means by which all people can represent and know themselves as people of God. Thus, divine nature and Christian living are inseparable. If Christians cannot be people of good moral actions, then the divine nature is unknowable.

2 Pet 3:1 and 3:14, 17–18

People can be spiritually awake and can arouse their pure *dianoia*. These verses imply that humans have more than one type or aspect of their minds. The human mind is complex and dynamic. One aspect of it enables spiritual thoughts. To be human is to conceive of God, divine communication, and the spiritual features of the human mind. For full actualization, humans can and must think of ideas and concepts beyond base economic activities.

To be fully human is to know God, increase spiritual strength, and perceive God's presence in the world. Reaching spiritual maturity means people must grow their souls in order to achieve participation in the divine nature.

Additionally, while many people are afraid and live in fear, the addressees can embody peace. With right conduct, they can eschew sin-stained spots and avoid blameworthy behavior. They can also grow in grace, expressing goodness in its highest expression, while increasing their knowledge of Jesus Christ. Thus, humans are mystical learners. They can experience God's graciousness and learn about Christ.

The potential for spiritual growth is latent to the human condition. Newberg and Waldman state that the human brain "is built in such a way that humans can have occasional mystical experiences."[37] Newberg has also determined that human mystical experiences, which "last just seconds to minutes, seem to rewire the brain completely in this very short period of time. It is remarkable that all the different ways a person thinks about the world can radically shift from a singular moment of mystical enlightenment."[38] As Jesus taught, "For nothing is hidden that will not be disclosed, nor is anything secret that will not become known and come to light" (Luke 8:17). Mystical encounters initiate spiritual growth, bringing knowledge of Jesus and the grace of God.

Petrine Human Self-Understanding

Peter and the Petrine author are distinctly aware that to know God, one must know oneself. Christians are recipients of divine blessings that allow them to become sharers of the divine nature. The ability to be holy and sustained by the living word of God are essential aspects of Christian self-awareness. Christians can be directly fed by God as well as molded and shaped into a spiritual community, which symbolizes God's presence in the world.

The communal nature of Christianity eliminates human understanding within classifications. All people can pray to God, dwell in the light, and be messengers of God's holiness and love for humanity. In particular, the Christian community can endure ordeals, because God's Spirit rests with them. They know themselves to never be alone and thus can be moral agents fortified by their belief.

---

37. Newberg and Waldman, *How God Changes Your Brain*, 114.
38. Newberg, *Neurotheology*, 275.

As sharers of the divine nature, the Petrine readers can manifest God's power and allow theosis to take hold in them, living their faith from within themselves. Their awakened spirituality enables them to think deeply about God and their spiritual nature and understand that they are more than their base needs. Being spiritual creatures, the readers can embody peace and can act in ways that expand their expression of grace. Mysticism can be fully realized as a telos of human self-understanding.

9

PETRINE MYSTICISM AND THE TWENTY-FIRST CENTURY

AFTER THE GREAT FLOOD account in Gen 7, what Everett Fox's translation calls the *Deluge*, the nations of the world "migrated to a valley in the land of Shinar and settled there."[1] The people said, "Come-now! Let us build ourselves a city and a tower, its top in the heavens, and let us make ourselves a name (That is, make sure that we and our works will endure)."[2] YHWH's response was contumelious: "Here, (they are) one people with one language for them all, and this is merely the first of their doings—now there will be no barrier for them in all that they scheme to do!"[3] After changing their languages, YHWH then scattered the peoples across the face of the earth. The Tower of Babel was left to decay.

The post-flood mythological account can be interpreted in various ways. In his commentary on Genesis, Walter Brueggemann considers three primary ones. (1) The people feared YHWH's desire to scatter the people and thus drew together. (2) The people sought unity to disestablish themselves from divine mandates. (3) The people resisted the unity God desires and God's purposes, which included scattering.[4] In whatever way one interprets the account, the flood narrative demonstrates a growing

---

1. Fox, *Five Books of Moses*, 48.
2. Fox, *Five Books of Moses*, 49.
3. Fox, *Five Books of Moses*, 49.
4. Brueggemann, *Genesis*, 99–101.

disenchantment with God by humans who sought to replace YHWH with themselves as the pinnacle of existence.

Not since the prehistoric period has human society been as secular and nonreligious, even antireligious, as it is in the twenty-first century. While religion has not disappeared, and God is not dead, postmodern thinking excludes the necessity of either. On the whole, people have not rejected religion as much as drifted away from it. In the coming years, as the younger nonreligious generations become influential adults, they will ferret out moral tenets and cultural values for themselves, without the millennia-old, time-tested values of the major religions. In place of religious teachings will be an amalgam of new-age culturalism, corporate-sponsored adages, and academic philosophical relativisms. These three will create a salad of morals from which the new generations will pick, as if they are in a college cafeteria with food bars from every major culture's cuisine.

Western cultures will be similar to the first-century society, in which the Roman empire's decrees, Hellenistic philosophy, and Stoic wisdom created a moral foundation. The major difference, however, is first-century religions seeped into every aspect of life. Twentieth-century democratic societies that privatize religion and the authoritarian governments that ban public religion have created an ever-changing secularist faith with capricious morals that whiplash people's understanding of the good. Twenty-first century culture can be described as morally relativistic, non-foundational, and highly secular.

Moreover, the fight between free-market democracies and socialistic authoritarianism will contribute to the social and spiritual disruptions many feel now and in the coming years. On the one hand, democracies are messy. They allow for many voices to be heard but grind out change slowly. On the other hand, authoritarian systems are simple. With power consolidated in an elite class of powerful leaders, decisions come more quickly. Few voices are heard, and the masses must accede to edicts from their leaders. In today's complex world, their simplicity is alluring. It is unclear which system will win. Unfortunately, the twenty-first century's wars and economic power-struggles will likely decide whether democracy or authoritarianism will rule over the rest of the century.

In light of the cultural turmoil and power struggles, many people will seek alternative places to live. Some will travel to outer space and establish colonies on other planets. They will do so for various reasons. Some will argue that humanity threatens Earth's environment and will choose to terraform and populate inhospitable planets to create utopian enclaves with no discernable carbon footprint. Others will seek planetary exploration as a natural progression of humanity. Having conquered the known world, they will explore new ones. Still others will extract solar and extra-solar resources, as they pursue other avenues to create power and wealth. These and other motivations illustrate the ever-present human desire to "make ourselves a name."

Religion will continue but will face more frequent and widespread "fiery ordeals" and local pressures. The post-World War II popularity and acceptance of religion in Western societies will be replaced by open rejection and harassment. Further erosion of religious liberty will likely occur as well. Christmas and Easter will become increasingly secular holidays with their own mythological narratives (i.e., Santa Claus and the Easter Bunny). In democracies, religious institutions will be less relevant to society's functioning and will serve it at society's margins, caring for the maligned poor and a growing underclass of noncitizen residents. The separation of church and state will be complete.

Peter

In 1971, Karl Rahner wrote, "The devout Christian of the future will either be a 'mystic,' one who has experienced 'something,' or he will cease to be anything at all."[5] Future, mystical Christians will need to properly frame and conceptualize the divine encounter or else they will not comprehend the "something" of which Rahner refers. Thus, they will require sound teachings grounded in Christian mystical theology to perceive the wisdom attached to their experiences. With its robustness, empowerment, and beauty, Petrine mystical theology must now garner its appropriate place, and Peter, the unexpected mystic, can lead new generations to the Christian way of living. By learning Petrine mysticism, future Christians will spiritually mature. Petrine mysticism can nurture and sustain the increasingly isolated Christian communities.

In the twenty-first century secular society, Petrine mystical theology can flourish. This book has outlined the reasons. First is the man himself. The First Letter of Peter ripples with mystical theology written by a man who had followed Jesus himself and had an intense, rebegetting encounter with God. Peter may have been impetuous and gruff but was also a student

---

5. Rahner, "Christian Living," 13.

who learned from his mistakes. He is the prime example of divine forgiveness, redemption, and rebegetting. Peter's commitment to God can be a light shining in the gloom of secularism.

What does Peter's rooftop encounter and the first letter disclose about the entrepreneurial fisherman from a small village on the Sea of Galilee, a remote body of water on the desert's edge? Five traits best elucidate his character.

Peter is *faithful*. Although he has lost his leadership position, Peter remains in relationship with God. His role is now subordinate to others, as he is obligated to report to the Jerusalem believers regarding his actions. Because of such an abdication, demotion, or rejection, Peter could have become angry with God and even Jesus, but he does not. Instead, he prays in an odd place and time; he seeks comfort and guidance from God.

Moreover, when his experience takes him beyond himself in a strange vision that challenges his faith practices, Peter remains faithful. He could have shaken away the encounter, denying its validity. He exclaims that he had never broken the dietary laws but does not reject the voice's demand. His faith in God carried him through the bewildering, radical request. Peter questions but does not deny the Spirit.

Rebegetting expresses Peter's faith. During the rooftop encounter, God rebegat Peter. In 1 Pet 1:3, Peter states, "He rebegat us." It is the only time in the letter he uses the first-person plural *us* and thus includes himself in God's act of rebegetting. Like his readers, God initiated a change in Peter, giving him a new mission and purpose.

Peter is also *patient*. When the Spirit confronts him with a new understanding of the dietary rules, he does not rush to solve the confusion in his heart and mind. Peter remains open to the possibility of a new way of eating and following God. When he sees the Holy Spirit descend on the people at Cornelius's home, he does not reject what he witnesses. When the Jerusalem believers question the account, Peter responds with patience. Of course, his patience is an outgrowth of his faith. The two synchronously work. Peter's faith and patience allow the Spirit time and space to influence and change him.

First Peter shows him *hopeful*. Peter passionately speaks about hope in his letter and does so because, like his readers, God rebegat him. When he was regenerated, his self transformed. God gave him a new hope. His soul burned with living hope, which is why the words of 1 Pet 1:3–5 are powerful, clear, and bold.

Notably, the letter is not about his time with Jesus, the empty tomb, or the resurrection. His readers had previously heard about them—likely from Peter himself. They had already been baptized as well. Instead, Peter explained the effect of rebegetting and the power of living hope that they also embodied. Living hope allowed Peter and the readers to remain firm in faith and live the precepts of a Christian life.

Peter is also *humble*, having been humbled several times. In the Gospel accounts, Peter was the disciples' best student, repeatedly answering first and asking Jesus questions, but his impertinence tripped him up. Peter names Jesus the Messiah, but soon after, Jesus calls him "Satan" (Matt 16:13–23). At the transfiguration, God chided Peter for not listening. Peter's denial of Jesus is his greatest humbling instance. However, Peter learns from these experiences and become humble. His patient witness of the Holy Spirit at Cornelius's home demonstrates his growing humility. Peter learns from his failures and becomes a humble person.

Finally, Peter is *peaceful*. His interactions at Cornelius's home and later at the Jerusalem council show a person at peace with himself and God. Peter is not frightened by what he encounters, worrying what the gentile inclusion would mean. He is no longer the impertinent disciple nor an anxious leader. He was not defensive when he made his report to the Jerusalem believers. He calmly described his actions "step by step" (Acts 11:4). Later at the Council at Jerusalem, Peter once again calmly recounted God's actions (Acts 15:7–11).

In the First Letter of Peter, he yet again exudes peace. He describes the "exiles of the Dispersion" as chosen, destined, sanctified ones (1:1–2). He also calls them to be "like obedient children" (1:14) and "like newborn infants" (2:2) and names them "beloved" (2:11, 4:12). He ends the letter with a blessing of peace. In contrast, in several of his letters, Paul is cantankerous and brusque. For example, to the Galatians, he writes, "I am astonished that you are so quickly deserting" God (1:6). Even when he calls the Corinthian church "beloved children," an admonishment prefaces it (1 Cor 4:14). At the end of the letter, his closing statement includes, "Let anyone be accursed who had no love for the Lord." While in 2 Corinthians, Paul expresses deep concern, he warns them: "So I write these things while I am away from you, so that when I come, I may not have to be severe in using" authority (2 Cor 13:10). Of course, in the other letters directly attributed to him, Paul's tone is more moderate and loving. However, the contrast between Peter and Paul is obvious. Peter is at peace.

Peter's five character traits are an alternative to secular solipsism. The twenty-first-century human most often is an anxious and restless creature, a flitting bug droning from saccharine values to hollow belief in a weed-choked garden of trite apothegms. On the other hand, those rooted in Petrine traits embody stability and steadfastness. They can navigate the tumultuous seas of angst to calm harbors, alee from capricious cultural winds. Those embodying Peter-like traits are starkly different from their neighbors, friends, and family. The peace of God does that. Embodied belief in God is like a lamp in a dark room (Mark 4:21).

The Petrine God

The twentieth-century religious wars pitted monotheism against atheism. Judeo-Christian democracies fought fascism, Nazism, and Communism throughout the century. Islamic conservative cultures battled perceived atheistic Western cultures, culminating with terrorist attacks and subsequent Middle Eastern wars that bled into the twenty-first century's opening decades. As the century continues, these wars will be replaced by a clash between monotheism and irrelevant-ism, a belief that disregards the existence of God by merely rejecting the relevance of any conceptions of the Other. Divine irrelevancy is the logical outcome of the Enlightenment's desire to wall off private beliefs from public discourse. Its clearest aphorism is "You do you."

The Petrine mystical theology regarding God opposes irrelevant-ism. The consideration of an imminent or transcendent God is no longer germane. God is the one who acts. God activity continues as a measure of God's mercy, spanning across the millennia and drawing new generations into the parental relationship initiated by Jesus Christ. God rebegets Christians and instills in them a living hope that will continue.

By God's mercy, God brought people out of darkness to light and, by that wondrous gift, gives people a new way of being. However, one may wonder about the continuation of God's mercy. As open rejection and harassment against Christians increase, will God change his actions? God retains autonomy and freedom of action, especially in matters of judgment and punishment. God is judge. God is patient and desires people to come to repentance. However, the twenty-first century's increasing secularism and divine irrelevancy may cause a shadow of divine judgment to increase.

God's actions also include a divine gift. People can share in the divine nature. Those moored to solipsism will struggle to accept that sharing in the divine nature is possible. They may eagerly delight in its idea, thinking it an even higher *raison d'être*; but accepting the gift means humans are not the universe's telos. Accepting the gift requires faith and humility.

The human potential to embody the divine nature is found in the eight links of the chain of Christian living. Starting with faith, the chain removes all notion of human pride and hubris before the *aretē* may be internalized. Knowledge of God and the divine nature would also be corrupted without faith. So, too, would be the others in the chain. Even love is defiled without faith in God, the one who calls people to holiness.

Another competing force will arise in the years to come. The metaverse will increase in its scope and influence. Within it, humans will craft a virtual cosmos that will entice many. The allure of an ego-created self, free of all physical diminishments and disadvantages, will cause many to forgo natural life and community for a neatly packaged realm of delightful but fabricated interactions. Within this realm, any sense of the divine nature will be absent or corrupted, though religious institutions will grab virtual real estate. The institutions will battle against irrelevance in the virtual cosmos. Metaverse interactions will lack the moral guidance created by the monotheistic religions. Instead, governed by paid conduct guardians and overseen by corporate trustees, the metaverse will remain a godless dimension based on transaction and use, lacking the precepts of authentic Christian community.

Instead of forming a capricious virtual realm, God forms communities in rebegottenness, holiness, and *metanoia*. Petrine mysticism deemphasizes human tendencies toward religious individualism. Yes, the whole does not exist without the individual, but the individual Christian does not exist without the community—the spiritual house, the holy priesthood, and the chosen kin. The individual is not primary. Relationship is. The connections to others and God are rooted in piety, brotherly love, and *agapē*. Petrine mystical theology insists on an authentic Christian community where *agapē* infuses all actions, interactions, and every relationship.

Not all humans will desire authentic Christian community. For some, authentic community will demand too much, leading to godless communities on Earth or on other planets. Others will dabble in the metaverse, only to discover its falsehoods. But belief in God will continue. The brooding angst hanging over humanity caused by the barrenness of twenty-first century secular life will cause many to seek God's movements and acts. God will convert them, lead them to authentic Christian community, and rebeget them into a new generation of witnesses, entrusted with the divine nature.

Divine Communication

If he chooses so, God will continue to be a force and presence on the earth and among humanity. As the one who acts, God functions in perfect freedom, and humans cannot anticipate where and when God will act. Thus, humans must not think to limit or regulate divine agency or communication. As he did with Samuel, God may interact with a child (1 Sam 3), or he may fulfil promises as he did with Simeon and Anna the daughter of Phanuel (Luke 2:25–38). Simply, Christians must behold the works of God no matter where they appear.

The twenty-first-century Christian churches and their people ought to anticipate God's communication. Ever operating out of mercy, God continues to rebeget Christians. The church can guide those newly rebegotten souls, assisting them to discern God's interaction with them and the divine purposes and mission unfolding in their lives. So often, Jesus encouraged the ones he healed and gave them instructions. For example, to the woman who had been suffering from hemorrhages for twelve years, Jesus said, "Daughter, your faith has made you well; go in peace" (Luke 8:48). As he healed the ten lepers, Jesus told them, "Go and show yourselves to the priests" (Luke 17:14). Each instance of God's work is a chance for the church to behold, enter into *dianoia*, and aid its people in *metanoia*. God's living hope is ever-present and always lifting up people.

The twenty-first-century church must not worry about itself. The living word of God sustains and nourishes its gathered people. The word is good news—not the ecclesiastical institution or its buildings—and while it can always be discovered in the Scriptures, the living word extends far beyond the biblical text. The living word of God is mystical, fluid, dynamic, and robust. It still grows and flourishes, not encumbered by humans but alive unto itself. It is the force that converts sinners, causing *metanoia*, and opens all Christians to the word's mystical workings. The responsibility of the church, therefore, is to instruct its people in the eight facets of the chain of Christian living; interpret via *dianoia* God's actions in people, the world, and itself; remain a humble witness to God's works; and be living stones shaped by the divine architect and built into one spiritual house.

Divine communication is spiritual pure milk. The undiluted connection creates an intimate, nurturing relationship that was so valued by mystics. For instance, Julian of Norwich speaks of the relationship with God, writing, "And in this binding and union he is a real and true bridegroom, and we his loved bride and his fair maiden, a bride with whom he is never displeased; for he says, 'I love you and you love me, and our love shall never be divided.'"[6] Such intimacy grows through the communication between humans and God.

In Petrine mystical theology, the relationship is two-way. The verse 2 Pet 3:12 is paradoxical to normative Christian teaching and challenging to hear, but if taken literally, readers see that, by their lives, Christians can hasten the coming of the day of God. While this statement is perplexing, it lets Christians comprehend the intimacy of God as more complex and richer than otherwise conceived. As with Nineveh's remorse at Jonah's proclamation, God listens to humans and can change his mind. Thus, prayer in all its forms pleases God and, by respecting human agency, allows his actions to be shaped by human concern.

Divine communication blossoms in intimate and nurturing relationship between God and humans. People can never presume that God will not or does not interact with the world or humans. Instead of seeking answers from God, Petrine mystical theology demands that people behold the living word of God, deeply consider its effects, and witness to its freely re-begetting those around us. Neither Christians nor the church control access to the spiritual pure milk. That sustenance pours forth without mediators. God meets people's persistence, desires, and longings, drawing them into intimate and nourishing relationship. As partakers of the divine communication, the mission of Christians is to inform people of God's grace and help them grow in the knowledge of God and Jesus.

Self-Knowledge

Twenty-first-century cultures assert several views regarding human self-knowledge. The first one comes from the twentieth century, namely, that humans are consumers. Persons living in a Western-styled democracy and capitalistic economic system are fully self-actualized by their ability to

---

6. Julian of Norwich, *Revelations of Divine Love*, 137.

consume goods and services. The more one purchases, the more that person participates in the culture and thus is worth more respect. The epigram coined by Malcom Forbes, "The one who dies with the most toys, wins," best illustrates the viewpoint.[7]

However, times have changed. Consumers have been replaced by users. Until the middle of the twenty-first century's second decade, Facebook and Twitter called its customers "users," though now they prefer "people."[8] Even with the more "empathetic" attitude, the identification lacks individuality. The statement "the customer is always right" sounds odd when "customer" is replaced by "user"; and even worse for conglomerates and governments would be "the people are always right." God forbid! With either term, the humanizing aspect of interactions between a business and a person is lost.

The same holds true for government programs and largess distributed through social programs. Even though such programs deliver vital financial support to many, the sense of individuality and human self-worth is encumbered by an opaqueness of systematized and bureaucratic administration. The intent is to ameliorate human need, distress, and suffering, but often, rules and regulations encumber the assistance, creating stress to the recipient. Classification naturally arises. For instance, the language used during the COVID-19 pandemic illustrates the tendency to classify people. The terms vaccinated and unvaxed forced people to choose between groups, losing the more nuanced and complex nature of individual situations. Decisions to get the jab pitted individual concerns against the will of governments and public health regimens. The result was an unfading scarlet letter that dehumanized the socially aberrant. Suffice it to say, humans, especially those in power, gravitate toward categorizing people.

Metadata and algorithms attempt to offset the dehumanizing experiences of twenty-first-century technology. Through massive data collection, machine-learning systems provide personalized experiences, allowing people to feel more connected and experience greater self-actualization. Despite the temporary gratification that internet interactions provide, the shadow of reductionism looms over them. As machine learning become more sophisticated, big technology companies will likely "hack humans."[9] The resulting invasion will attempt to reduce human choice and free will to

---

7. Forbes, "My Father, Malcolm Forbes," para. 20.
8. O'Reilly, "Facebook," para. 1.
9. Tran, "Expert Warns," para. 1.

neural synaptic processes and its electrical or chemical signals. The impact will threaten human ontology.

However, Petrine mystical theology provides an alternative to the twenty-first-century cultural reductionism and dehumanization. Humans can be *living stones* (1 Pet 2:5). As the architect and builder of a spiritual house, God molds and shapes individual stones, laying them side by side and one atop another to create one spiritual house. God shows no preference or classification. No one is beholden to societal prescripts or conventions. All people are important and vital to each other. Within the spiritual house, individuality and social cohesiveness embrace.

Christians can also become a royal priesthood. Christians' willingness and ability to embody holiness directly affect the community's royal priesthood potential and realization. United by the living hope, Christians can realize the self-actualization they seek. Again, the royal priesthood is a community replete with individuals worthy of God's attention. They offer spiritual sacrifices together as a determinate force in the world and as individual moral actors who gain self-knowledge by their conduct. Both as a group and individuals, they can know themselves.

Petrine self-knowledge is established and matures in the mystical spiritual house. It answers the seekers and believers' question, "Whose am I?" The answer is no human is diminished or reduced to consumer, user, or brain process. As members of a holy nation and royal priesthood, each person was called by God to dwell in a wonderful light (1 Pet 2:9). The individual can thrive as a member of the chosen kin that reflects holiness to others and receives the spirit of God that rests on them (1 Pet 4:14).

Petrine self-knowledge also allows all Christians share in the divine nature. They grow and mature in the divine nature through their actions, which develop through the chain of Christian living. Each link gives insight into themselves and God, furthering the development of their authentic selves. They can be humans who are self-aware *and* aware of God. The higher thinking unleashed within the divine nature enables Christians to think beyond base needs, rational goals, and material goods. They are no longer subjected to consumerism, metadata, and secular cultural influences but transcend those to be spiritual creatures—fully human.

The twenty-first-century culture's diminishment of human self-knowledge is clearly happening. At the start of the 2020s, anxiety is a worldwide phenomenon affecting hundreds of millions of people and has been increasing in recent years.[10] While many causes for anxiety exist, most center around stressors such as loneliness, lack of community support, financial instability, and social media usage.[11] These factors can also arise from a distortion of self-knowledge. Without healthy connections to a wholesome community and an authentic relationship with God, humans become existentially anxious. The Petrine mystical theology presumes the necessity of community from which self-knowledge grows. Within the company of believers, all learn of God through Jesus, experience God's grace, and embody peace.

Petrine *Metanoia*

As previous stated, *metanoia* is a profound spiritual transformation that is not reductionist in quality but releases a desire to bring the holy to others and the world, making them more sacred. Whereas rebegetting is a divine act, *metanoia* is an act of complete human agency. God patiently awaits for it, knowing that *metanoia* needs the person's acceptance. God also fully accepts that *metanoia* can result in a positive or negative outcome.

Such patience is hardly known by many in the political environs of the first quarter of the twenty-first century. By no means limited to the American culture, people across the world have become more intolerant of differing opinions. Morgan Kelly of the High Meadows Environmental Institute at Princeton observes, "Much like an overexploited ecosystem, the increasingly polarized political landscape in the United States—and much of the world—is experiencing a catastrophic loss of diversity that threatens the resilience not only of democracy, but also of society, according to a series of new studies that examine political polarization as a collection of complex ever-evolving systems."[12] Polarization dampens people's ability to change their views, leading to entrenchment and increased strife within their communities. Rather than allowing for agency, those with differing outlooks intimidate and vilify others with dissenting opinions.

Metanoia is wholly different. Unlike humans, God tolerates opposition and permits resistance. The author of Second Peter states, "The Lord is not slow about his promise, as some think of slowness, but is patient with you, not wanting any to perish, but all to come to repentance" (2:9).

10. *Depression*, 10.
11. Goodwin et al., "Trends in Anxiety."
12. Kelly, "Political Polarization," para. 1.

Spiritual transformation is holy space, even for God, who does not violate human agency and autonomy. *Metanoia* demonstrates God's respect for humans, seeing each person as valuable, wholesome, and beloved. God does not polarize people but brings them to a living hope, creating a spiritual house. *Metanoia* is the great leveler of humanity, leaving no one behind, showing no preference, and uniting all Christians to grow in grace and the knowledge of Jesus Christ.

Summary

Petrine mystical theology demonstrates that God acts in freedom. God transformed Peter and opened for him a new mission, eventually taking him to the locus of the first century's world power. Peter is also an example of the God who acts even in unusual places, like a quiet, isolated rooftop. Peter shows that God communicates freely, interacting with people and spiritually transforming them. The mystical knowledge received through a transformative interaction gives humans increased self-knowledge to be treasured and shared. The Petrine understanding of *metanoia* can shift cultural and societal desires for classification of people. *Metanoia* shows that the beloved children of God are one and equal.

10

THE THREEFOLD ROSE

YELLOW ROSES REACHED SKYWARD along the stone path to the deanery front door at Canterbury Cathedral. The cathedral gardens have many kinds of roses, including the pink Rosa Canterbury bred by the renowned horticulturist David C. H. Austin. Before entering the deanery, I beheld a cluster of yellow rose blossoms and marveled at each bloom's luster. The shape and form of the rose petals seem perfect. The outer ones frame the blossom's center, drawing the eye to its center. Beaming with color, the smaller inner petals unfold in succession. The heart of the flower seems to hide a gateway to the infinite. Perhaps the rose's heart is what, in his previously mentioned poem, Rilke meant by "a supple word / framed by the text of things."[1]

The gateway, the supple word longs for the questions: what is the word, and what does it intend? It further asks, what is a person's experience of the word, and what is God saying through it? These questions also hold the gateway to the infinite, a space of knowledge that expands as the observer beholds the word, the flower, the created object. The space enthralls the curious and never disappoints. When one enters through the gateway, the threefold seeing commences. The process of beholding, *dianoia*, and *metanoia* unfold in succession.

The threefold seeing is more than the blossom. Each petal represents the triadic vision of the gaze. The creator, the object, and the observer enter a relationship and interaction. The rose's creator, the creator of all, has numerous intentions in mind when bringing flowers into being, procreation

---

1. Rilke, *Roses*, 37.

and beauty among them. The object, the lovely rose bloom, has its own purposes, expressing its beauty, for one. The observer, the one who beholds the flower, finds meaning and satisfaction but also an endless outflow of learning. If not these, why create a flower, why express beauty, and why notice?

Like the blossom's petals, which seem to endlessly emerge from the rose's heart, the threefold seeing creates ever unfolding triangles. With each view, the triadic vision broadens and deepens. Its source is active and alive and constantly forms new triangles. What is more, no one view is the same. There is always more to observe, and the relationship and interplay never ceases. Knowledge flows from the creator as a gift to the observer.

The Object Looks Back

When one beholds an object, the object also looks at the observer. The rose does not suddenly or magically become animated, but its presence affects its surroundings. The bee is drawn to the rose as the sound of its buzzing resonates off the concave petals back to the bee. The flower and the bee begin a harmonious symbiotic relationship. The gardener marvels at the flower's beauty and tends to its needs. Relationships form on many levels, with plants and animals benefiting one another.

The same is true on a spiritual level. As the observer beholds an object, the object looks back. It is a spiritual and mystical interaction. Be it a flower or biblical text, the observer or reader interpret the object. Meaning is given. When another person views the flower, more meaning is made. If the two people speak about the flower, then another triangle emerges, causing the flower to become more significant. The gift of the rose and its creator expands and continues.

The flower is not only interpreted, but the observer is, too. The interaction changes not just the way the object is known but the way the observer is known. For instance, Rilke is forever known as a lover of roses. His final words, his last poems, are about roses. What he writes speaks of the rose but also of himself, the poet and the human. His identity with the rose can never be shorn.

When the creator creates the object, the creator has one or more views; but as the object leaves the creator, it becomes open to others' views. The artist, poet, painter, musician, writer, or preacher own their work until it is viewed or heard. Once it is viewed by others, it is no longer a connection between the two but is a part of the threefold seeing. The observer will see the object in new ways and know it differently. These new interpretations can affect the creator. The relationship between the object and the creator is never static but active and alive.

Petrine Mystical Theology

Like the rose, a biblical text assumes a triadic relationship. God, the text, and the reader enter the space of knowledge. The threefold seeing shifts exegetical reading and interpretation. The reader is not a dispassionate observer but one who enters a relationship with the creator and the object—God and the biblical text. By observing the text, the reader leaves this world through the threefold seeing, the gateway to a new vision. Regarding the seeing that commences as one moves through the gateway, Dohna Schlobitten explains, "There is a complex relationship between perception and interpersonal and synthetic understanding, all of which contribute to seeing something in the image that goes beyond an objective analysis of the image, even if such analysis contributes to it."[2] Dohna Schlobitten notes Guardini's view of a work of art: "You want to really know what you have chosen, penetrate it and become a good friend, become a lover."[3] The observer enters the relationship with the text to honor what is written, the one who wrote it and God who is in and beyond the text.

Thus, the interaction emerging from the threefold seeing is not outward but inward. The inward movement is at the center of Petrine mysticism. Rebegetting shapes the inward nature of the Christian. The living hope informs the spirit of the believers, both individually and communally. Petrine mysticism calls the readers to holiness because God is holy, and its triadic interaction is what shapes the living stones. Through the living word of God, the readers know God, and God knows the readers. In and through the relationship, the biblical text is active and alive. The threefold seeing allows the readers not only to take from the word, but to be taken by the Spirit of God in a reciprocal "gesture of unprecedented acceptance."[4]

However, the inward work must move outward. The relationship demands a *metanoia*, a spirit shift in sight, a transformation of the soul, and outward moral action. The Petrine chain of Christian living shows how to

---

2. Dohna Schlobitten, "Artistic Contemplation and Prayer," 3.
3. Dohna Schlobitten, "Artistic Contemplation and Prayer," 3.
4. Dohna Schlobitten, "Art and Transcendence," 19.

live morally, embodied in three outward expressions, namely piety, brotherly love, and *agapē*. Also, when the Spirit of God rests on the believers of Jesus, they naturally express themselves in love—for themselves, each other, all of creation, and God.

Finally, the fullest expression of Petrine mysticism and the threefold seeing triadic relationship occurs when the reader becomes a work of art, the created object. The Triune God shapes the believers, giving them the capacity to see and the courage to be enmeshed in the struggle to become sharers in the divine nature as an act of love. The observer becomes the Christian community, the nonbelievers surrounding the community, and the world itself. Like the rose in full bloom, God's work of art resonates with beauty and grace.

Bibliography

Achtemeier, Paul J. *A Commentary on First Peter*. Minneapolis: Augsburg Fortress, 1996.
Andersen, Elizabeth A. *Mechthild of Magdeburg: Selections from the Flowing Light of the Godhead*. Rochester, NY: Brewer, 2003.
Augustine. *Confessions*. Translated by R. S. Pine-Coffin. New York: Penguin Books, 1961.
Balthasar, Hans Urs von. *Romano Guardini: Reform from the Source*. Translated by Albert K. Wimmer and D. C. Schindler. San Francisco: Ignatius, 2010.
Barrett, C. K. *Acts 1–14*. Vol. 1 of *A Critical and Exegetical Commentary on the Acts of the Apostles*. International Critical Commentary. Edinburgh: T&T Clark, 1994.
Barth, Karl. *The Doctrine of God*. Vol. 2/1 of *Church Dogmatics*. Translated by G. T. Thomson et al. Edinburgh: T&T Clark, 1957.
Behm, J. "Nous in the New Testament." In *Theological Dictionary of the New Testament*, edited by Gerhard Kittel, translated by Geoffrey W. Bromiley, 4:951–60. Reprint, Grand Rapids: Eerdmans, 1978.
Benedict. *The Rule of St. Benedict in English*. Edited by Timothy Fry. Collegeville, MN: Liturgical, 2019.
Bock, Darrell L. *Acts*. Baker Exegetical Commentary on the New Testament. Grand Rapids: Baker Academic, 2007.
Bockmuehl, Markus. *Seeing the Word: Refocusing New Testament Studies*. Grand Rapids: Baker Academic, 2006.
———. *Simon Peter in Scripture and Memory: The New Testament Apostle in the Early Church*. Grand Rapids: Baker Academic, 2012.
Brown, Sherri. "The Challenge of 2 Peter and the Call to Theosis." *Expository Times* 128 (2017) 583–92.
Brueggemann, Walter. *Genesis*. Edited by James L. Mays. Interpretation: A Bible Commentary for Teaching and Preaching. Atlanta: John Knox, 1982.
Catherine of Siena. *The Dialogue of the Seraphic Virgin Catherine of Siena*. Translated by Algar Thorold. London: Kegan Paul, Trench, Trübner & Co., 1907.
Caulley, Thomas Scott. "Rehabilitating a Theological Stepchild? Reconsidering the 'Priesthood of all Believers' and 1 Peter." *Restoration Quarterly* 61 (2019) 1–11.
Christensen, Sean. "Reborn Participants in Christ: Recovering the Importance of Union with Christ in 1 Peter." *Journal of the Evangelical Theological Society* 61 (2018) 339–54.
Craddock, Fred B. *First and Second Peter and Jude*. Louisville: Westminster John Knox, 1995.

Bibliography

Cross, F. L. and E. A. Livingstone. *The Oxford Dictionary of the Christian Church*. New York: Oxford University Press, 1997.

Cullman, Oscar. *Peter, Disciple-Apostle-Martyr: A Historical and Theological Study*. London: SCM, 1953.

Cunningham, Laurence S., and Keith J. Egan. *Christian Spirituality: Themes from the Tradition*. New York: Paulist, 1996.

Danker, Frederick William, ed. *A Greek-English Lexicon of the New Testament and Other Early Christian Literature*. 3rd ed. Chicago: University of Chicago Press, 2000.

Delacroix, Eugène. "Fragments du journal d'Eugène Delacroix." *Revue des Deux Mondes* 116 (1893) 922–44. https://fr.wikisource.org/wiki/Fragments_du_journal_d'Eugène_Delacroix.

Delio, Ilia. *Franciscan Prayer*. Cincinnati: Franciscan, 2004.

Depression and Other Common Mental Disorders: Global Health Estimates. Geneva: World Health Organization, 2017. https://apps.who.int/iris/bitstream/handle/10665/254610/WHO-MSD-MER-2017.2-eng.pdf.

Dickinson, Emily. *The Complete Poems of Emily Dickinson*. Edited by Thomas H. Johnson. Boston: Little, Brown 1976.

Dohna Schlobitten, Yvonne. "About Trees and Spaces." Unpublished manuscript.

———. "The Aesthetics of Metanoia: The *Lauterkeit des Blicks* (The Sincerity of the Look) of Romano Guardini as Methodological Basis for a Transdisciplinary Knowledge." Paper presented at the Deepening Veritatis Gaudium meeting, Center for Faith and Culture Alberto Hurtado, Pontifical Gregorian University, Rome, 4 June 2019.

———. "Art and Transcendence: Educating One's Spiritual Senses." Paper presented at the International Theological Conference of the University of Malta, Msidia, Malta, 10–11 May 2019.

———. "Artistic Contemplation and Prayer: Romano Guardini's Method of the Sincere Gaze (Purity of Look)." Paper presented at the Evolving Methodologies Conference of the Study of Christian Spirituality and the Teologia Spirituale, Rome, 25–28 Sept. 2019.

———. "Imparare ad abbandonarsi a occhi chiusi: Una fenomenologia dell'esperienza spirituale nell'arte di James Turrell." *Gregorianum* 97 (2016) 761–76.

———. "La forma dell'immagine. La formazione liturgica." *Ikon* 9 (2016) 375–84.

———. "Lasciarsi guardare: Antropologia filosofica e teologica dell'arte come preghiera." *Ignaziana* 21 (2016) 87–108.

———. "Romano Guardini and Van Gogh: Light as a Drama of the Logos or a Spiritual and Ecumenical Reception of the Image." In *Art and Theology in Ecumenical Perspective*, edited by Timothy Verdon, 120–42. Mount Tabor Books Series. Brewster, MA: Paraclete, 2019.

———. "Romano Guardini e la Weltanschauung nella creazione artistica: Verso un'antropologia estetica come trasformazione relazionale." *Humanitas* 74 (2019) 391–402.

———, and Albert Gerhards, eds. *La lotta di Giacobbe, paradigma della creazione artistica: Un'esperienza comunitaria di formazione integrale, su Chiesa, estetica e arte contemporanea, ispirata a Romano Guardini*. Assisi, It.: Cittadella, 2020.

Donelson, Lewis R. *I & II Peter and Jude: A Commentary*. Louisville: Westminster John Knox, 2010.

Bibliography

Edwards, Dennis R. "Hermeneutics and Exegesis." In *The State of New Testament Studies: A Survey of Recent Research*, edited by Scot McKnight and Nijay K. Gupta, 63–82. Grand Rapids: Baker Academics, 2019.

Egan, Harvey D. *Ignatius Loyola the Mystic*. Eugene, OR: Wipf and Stock, 2020.

———. *Soundings in the Christian Mystical Tradition*. Collegeville, MN: Liturgical, 2010.

Ehrman, Bart D. *Peter, Paul, and Mary Magdalene: The Followers of Jesus in History and Legend*. Oxford, UK: Oxford University Press, 2006.

English, John J. *Spiritual Freedom: From an Experience of the Ignatian Exercises to the Art of Spiritual Guidance*. 2nd ed. Chicago: Loyola Press, 1995.

Forbes, Robert. "My Father, Malcolm Forbes: A Never-Ending Adventure." *Forbes*, 19 Aug. 2019. https://www.forbes.com/sites/forbesdigitalcovers/2019/08/19/my-father-malcolm-forbes-a-never-ending-adventure/?sh=5b36949719fb.

Fox, Everett. *The Five Books of Moses: Genesis, Exodus, Leviticus, Numbers, and Deuteronomy*. Vol. 1 of *The Schocken Bible*. New York: Schocken, 1995.

Francis. "The Testament of St. Francis." OFM, 1226. https://ofm.org/about/st-francis/testament.

Frey, Jörg. *The Letter of Jude and the Second Letter of Peter*. Translated by Kathleen Ess. Waco, TX: Baylor University Press, 2018.

Gench, Frances Taylor. *Back to the Well: Women's Encounters with Jesus in the Gospels*. Louisville: Westminster John Knox, 2004.

Gerl-Falkovitz, Hanna-Barbara. "Auge und Licht: Annäherung an Romano Guardinis Wahrnehmung von Welt." *Trigon* 9 (2011) 27–36.

———. *Romano Guardini, 1885–1968: Life and Work*. Mainz: Grünewald, 1985.

Goodwin, Renee D., et al. "Trends in Anxiety among Adults in the United States, 2008–2018: Rapid Increases among Young Adults." *Journal of Psychiatric Research* 130 (Nov. 2020) 441–46. https://www.sciencedirect.com/science/article/pii/S0022395620309250?via%3Dihub.

Green, Joel B. *1 Peter*. Grand Rapids: Eerdmans, 2009.

———. *Luke as Narrative Theologian: Texts and Topics*. Tübingen, Germ.: Mohr Siebeck, 2020.

———. "Narrating the Gospel in 1 and 2 Peter." *Interpretation* 3 (2006) 262–77.

Guardini, Romano. *The Art of Praying: The Principles and Methods of Christian Prayer*. Translated by Prince Leopold of Loewenstein-Wertheim. Manchester, NH: Sophia Institute Press, 1994.

———. *Aus dem Bereich der Philosophie*. Vol. 1 of *Unterscheidung des Christlichen*. Paderborn, Germ.: Schöningh, 1994.

———. *Der Anfang aller Dinge; Meditationen über Genesis; Kapitel I–III*. Würzburg, Germ.: Werkbund, 1961.

———. *Freiheit, Gnade, Schicksal: Drei Kapitel zur Deutung des Daseins*. Munich: Kösel, 1948.

———. *Gestalten*. Vol. 3 of *Unterscheidung des Christlichen*. Mainz, Germ.: Grünewald, 1995.

———. *The Humanity of Christ*. Translated by Ronald Walls. New York: Pantheon, 1964.

———. *Il Signore*. Milano: Vita e Pensiero, 1949.

———. *La vita come opera d'arte: Scritti di estetica (1907–1960)*. Brescia, It.: Morcelliana, 2021.

———. *The Lord*. Translated by Elinor Castendyk Briefs. Washington, DC: Gateway, 2019.

Bibliography

———. "Report on My Life: Intellectual Development and Literary Work (3/7/45)." Unpublished manuscript, Guardini Archive of the Catholic Academy, Munich.

———. *Über das Wesen des Kunstwerks*. Tübingen, Germ.: Wunderlich, 1959.

———. *Über das Wesen des Kunstwerks*. Kevelaer, Germ.: Butzon & Bercker, 2005.

———. *Von heiligen Zeichen*. Mainz, Germ.: Grünewald, 1998.

———. *Wurzeln eines großen Lebenswerks: Aufsätze und kleine Schriften*. 4 vols. Mainz: Paderborn, 2000–2003.

Hanhart, Robert, ed. *Septuagint*. Stuttgart: Deutsche Bibelgesellschaft, 2006.

Harrington, Daniel J. *Jude and 2 Peter*. Collegeville, MN: Liturgical, 2003.

Heimlich, Russell. "Mystical Experiences." Pew Research Center, 29 Dec. 2009. https://www.pewresearch.org/fact-tank/2009/12/29/mystical-experiences.

Hengel, Martin. *Saint Peter: The Underestimated Apostle*. Grand Rapids: Eerdmans, 2010.

Hilton, Walter. *The Scale (or Ladder) of Perfection*. Memphis: General Books, 2012.

Hollywood, Amy, and Patricia Z. Beckman, eds. *The Cambridge Companion to Christian Mysticism*. New York: Cambridge University Press, 2012.

House, H. Wayne. "Tongues and the Mystery Religions of Corinth." *Bibliotheca Sacra* 140 (1983) 134–50.

Hughes, Graham. *Worship as Meaning: A Liturgical Theology for Late Modernity*. Cambridge: Cambridge University Press, 2003.

Ignatius. *The Spiritual Exercises of Saint Ignatius*. Translated by George E. Ganss. Chicago: Loyola, 1992.

Jennings, Willie James. *Acts*. Belief Theological Commentary. Louisville: Westminster John Knox, 2017.

John of the Cross. *The Collected Works of St. John of the Cross*. Translated by Kieran Kavanaugh and Otilio Rodriguez. Washington, DC: ICS, 1991.

Johnson, Luke Timothy. *Miracles: God's Presence and Power in Creation*. Louisville: John Knox, 2018.

———. *Scripture and Discernment: Decision Making in the Church*. Nashville: Abingdon, 1996.

Johnston, William, ed. *The Cloud of Unknowing and the Book of Privy Counseling*. New York: Doubleday, 1973.

Julian of Norwich. *Revelations of Divine Love*. Translated by Elizabeth Spearing. New York: Penguin, 1998.

———. *Showings*. Edited by Edmund Colledge and James Walsh. New York: Paulist, 1978.

Kandinsky, Wassily. *Über das Geistige in der Kunst: Insbesondere in der Malerei*. 3rd ed. Munich: Piper & Co., 1912. https://digi.ub.uni-heidelberg.de/diglit/kandinsky1912.

Keating, Thomas. *Manifesting God*. New York: Lantern, 2005.

Kelly, Morgan. "Political Polarization and Its Echo Chambers: Surprising New, Cross-Disciplinary Perspectives from Princeton." Princeton University, 9 Dec. 2021. https://www.princeton.edu/news/2021/12/09/political-polarization-and-its-echo-chambers-surprising-new-cross-disciplinary.

Kelsey, Morton. *Discernment: A Study in Ecstasy and Evil*. New York: Paulist, 1978.

Kittel, Gerhard. "Dianoia in the New Testament." In *Theological Dictionary of the New Testament*, edited by Gerhard Kittel, translated by Geoffrey W. Bromiley, 4:963–68. Reprint, Grand Rapids: Eerdmans, 1967.

Koskela, Douglas M. "Discernment." In *The Bloomsbury Handbook of Pneumatology*, edited by Daniel Castelo and Kenneth M. Loyer, 345–52. T&T Clark Handbooks. New York: T&T Clark, 2020.

Bibliography

Kraftchick, Steven J. *Jude and 2 Peter*. Nashville: Abingdon, 2002.

Kurtén, Tage. "Ecstasy—A Way to Religious Knowledge: Some Remarks on Paul Tillich as Theologian and Philosopher." *Scripta Instituti Donneriani Aboensis* 11 (1982) 253–62.

Lane, Belden C. "Writing in Spirituality as a Self-Implicating Act: Reflections on Authorial Disclosure and the Hiddenness of Self." In *Exploring Christian Spirituality: Essays in Honor of Sandra M. Schneiders, IHM*, edited by Bruce H. Lescher and Elizabeth Leibert, 53–69. New York: Paulist, 2006.

Lathrop, Gordon W. *Holy Things: A Liturgical Theology*. Minneapolis: Fortress, 1998.

Lockett, Darian. "The Use of Leviticus 19 in James and 1 Peter: A Neglected Parallel." *Catholic Biblical Quarterly* 82 (2020) 456–72.

Lossky, Vladimir. *The Mystical Theology of the Eastern Church*. Crestwood, NY: St. Vladimir's Seminary Press, 1976.

Madigan, Shawn, ed. *Mystics, Visionaries, and Prophets: A Historical Anthology of Women's Spiritual Writings*. Philadelphia: Fortress, 1998.

May, Gerald. *Care of Mind Care of Spirit: A Psychiatrist Explores Spiritual Direction*. New York: HarperCollins, 1992.

McDonald, Lee Martin. *The Biblical Canon: Its Origin, Transmission, and Authority*. Grand Rapids: Baker Academic, 2011.

McGiffert, Arthur C. "Mysticism in the Early Church." *American Journal of Theology* 11 (1907) 407–27.

McGinn, Bernard. *The Foundations of Mysticism: Origins to the Fifth Century*. Vol. 1 of *The Presence of God: A History of Western Christian Mysticism*. New York: Crossroad, 1992.

McIntosh, Mark A. *Discernment and Truth: The Spirituality and Theology of Knowledge*. New York: Crossroad, 2004.

———. "Mystical Theology at the Heart of Theology." In *The Oxford Handbook of Mystical Theology*, edited by Edward Howells and Mark A. McIntosh, 25–44. Oxford, UK: Oxford University Press, 2020.

Merleau-Ponty, Maurice. *Das Auge und der Geist: Philosophische Essays*. Edited by Christian Bermes. Philosophische Bibliothek 530. Hamburg: Meiner, 2003.

Merton, Thomas. *New Seeds of Contemplation*. New York: New Directions, 1961.

Mikoski, Gordon S. "Discerning Divine Direction." *Theology Today* 73 (2017) 307–11.

Miller, Chris A. "Did Peter's Vision in Acts 10 Pertain to Men or the Menu." *Bibliotheca Sacra* 159 (2002) 302–17.

Miller, John B. F. "Exploring the Function of Symbolic Dream-Visions in the Literature of Antiquity, with Another Look at IQapGen 19 and Acts 10." *Perspectives in Religious Studies* 37 (2010) 441–55.

Moberly, R. W. L. *Prophecy and Discernment*. Cambridge: Cambridge University Press, 2006.

Mounce, Robert H. *A Living Hope: A Commentary on 1 and 2 Peter*. Eugene, OR: Wipf and Stock, 1982.

Newberg, Andrew. *Neurotheology: How Science Can Enlighten Us about Spirituality*. New York: Columbia University Press, 2018.

———, and Mark Robert Waldman. *How God Changes Your Brain: Breakthrough Findings from a Leading Neuroscientist*. New York: Ballantine, 2010.

Nicholas of Cusa. *On Learned Ignorance*. Translated by H. Lawrence Bond. New York: Paulist, 1997.

Bibliography

Nizon, Paul, ed. *Van Gogh in seinen Briefen.* Frankfurt: Insel, 1977.

Nogueira, Paulo Augusto de Souza. "Celestial Worship and Ecstatic-Visionary Experience." *Journal for the Study of the New Testament* 25 (2002) 165–84. https://doi.org/10.1177/0142064X0202500204.

O'Reilly, Lara. "Facebook: We Don't Call Them 'Users' Any More, We Call Them 'People,.'" *Business Insider*, 11 Dec. 2014. https://www.businessinsider.com/facebook-says-it-has-dropped-the-term-users-and-has-an-empathy-team-2014-12.

Orsy, Ladislas, SJ. *Discernment: Theology and Practice, Communal and Personal.* Collegeville: Liturgical, 2020.

Palamas, Gregory. *The Triads.* Edited by John Meyendorff. Translated by Nicholas Gendle. New York: Paulist, 1983.

Pelikan, Jaroslav. *Acts.* Brazos Theological Commentary on the Bible. Grand Rapids: Brazos, 2005.

Perrin, David B. "Mysticism." In *The Blackwell Companion to Spirituality*, edited by Arthur Holder, 442–58. New York: Wiley and Sons, 2005.

Petersen, Gerlac. *The Fiery Soliloquy with God.* New York: Richardson, 1872.

Peterson, Eugene H. *Eat This Book: A Conversation in the Art of Spiritual Reading.* Grand Rapids: Eerdmans, 2006.

Rahner, Karl. "Christian Living Formerly and Today." In *Further Theology of the Spiritual Life 1*, translated by David Bourke, 3–24. Theological Investigations 7. New York: Seabury, 1971.

Rilke, Rainer Maria. *Roses: The Late French Poetry of Rainer Maria Rilke.* Translated by David Need. 2nd ed. Durham: Horse and Buggy, 2015.

Ritchie, Angus. "The Role of the Church in Discerning the Testimony of the Spirit." In *Testimony of the Spirit: New Essays*, edited by R. Douglas Geivett and Paul K. Moser, 244–62. Oxford, UK: Oxford University Press, 2017.

Robinson, Daniel. *The Shepherd of Hermas: Updated to Modern Language.* N.p.: CreateSpace, 2013.

Rohr, Richard. *The Naked Now: Learning to See as the Mystics See.* New York: Crossroad, 2015.

Rorem, Paul. *Pseudo-Dionysius: A Commentary on the Texts and an Introduction to Their Influence.* New York: Oxford University Press, 1993.

Rosales-Acosta, Dempsey. "Jesus and the Demons: Portraits of the Spiritual Seeing in Mark's Gospel; Origen, Bonaventure and Ignatius as Hermeneutic Reading Key of the Gospel." *Teología y Vida* 54 (2013) 307–37.

Ross, Maggie. *Process.* Vol. 1 of *Silence: A User's Guide.* Eugene, OR: Cascade, 2014.

Schleicher, Marianne. "Mystical Midrash." *Nordisk Judaistik/Scandinavian Jewish Studies* 24 (2005) 149–66. https://doi.org/10.30752/nj.69604.

Schneiders, Sandra M. *The Revelatory Text: Interpreting the New Testament as Sacred Scripture.* 2nd ed. Collegeville, MN: Liturgical, 1999.

Schweitzer, Albert. *The Mysticism of Paul the Apostle.* Translated by William Montgomery. Baltimore: Johns Hopkins University Press, 1998.

Senior, Donald P. *1 Peter.* Sacra Pagina 15. Collegeville, MN: Liturgical, 2003.

Siegel, Daniel J. *The Mindful Brain: Reflection and Attunement in the Cultivation of Well-Being.* New York: Norton, 2007.

Smith, Hannah Whitall. *My Spiritual Autobiography: Or How I Discovered the Unselfishness of God.* New York: Revell, 1903.

Stace, Walter Terence. *Mysticism and Philosophy.* London: Macmillan, 1961.

BIBLIOGRAPHY

Staples, Jason A. "'Rise, Kill, and Eat': Animals as Nations in Early Jewish Visionary Literature and Acts 10." *Journal for the Study of the New Testament* 42 (2019) 3–17.

Steinke, Peter L. *Uproar: Calm Leadership in Anxious Times.* Lanham, MD: Rowman & Littlefield, 2019.

Tamfu, Dieudonné. *2 Peter and Jude.* African Bible Commentary. Buruku, Nga.: Hippo Books, 2018.

Teresa of Avila. *The Collected Works of St. Teresa of Avila.* Translated by Kieran Kavanaugh and Otilio Rodriguez. 3 vols. 2nd ed. Washington, DC: ICS, 1987.

Tran, Tony. "Expert Warns That Human Beings Are Going to Start Getting Hacked." Byte, 29 Oct. 2021. https://futurism.com/the-byte/yuval-harari-human-hack.

Underhill, Evelyn. *Mysticism: A Study in the Nature and Development of Man's Spiritual Consciousness.* 12th ed. Scotts Valley, CA: CreateSpace, 2015.

Van der Horst, Pieter W. "Hellenistic Parallels to the Acts of the Apostles." *Journal for the Study of the New Testament* 8 (1985) 49–60.

Van Engen, Charles E. "Peter's Conversion: A Culinary Disaster Launches the Gentile Mission; Acts 10:1—11:18." In *Mission in Acts: Ancient Narratives in Contemporary Context*, edited by Robert D. Gallagher and Paul Hertig, 133–43. American Society of Missiology Series. Maryknoll, NY: Orbis, 2004.

Vanhoozer, Kevin J., ed. *Dictionary for Theological Interpretation of the Bible.* Grand Rapids: Baker Academic, 2006.

Van Inwagen, Peter, and Meghan Sullivan. "Metaphysics." Stanford Encyclopedia of Philosophy, 10 Sept. 2007; revised 31 Oct. 2014. https://plato.stanford.edu/archives/spr2020/entries/metaphysics.

Villegas, Diana L. "Discernment in Catherine of Siena." *Theological Studies* 58 (1997) 19–39.

Wahlen, Clinton. "Peter's Vision and Conflicting Definitions of Purity." *New Testament Studies* 51 (2005) 505–18.

Wainwright, Geoffrey. *Eucharist and Eschatology.* Oxford, UK: Oxford University Press, 1981.

Wall, Robert W. "The Canonical Function of 2 Peter." *Biblical Interpretation* 9 (2001) 64–81.

Watson, Duane F., and Terrance Callan. *First and Second Peter.* Grand Rapids: Baker Academic, 2012.

Wesley, John. *The Journal of John Wesley.* Edited by Percy Livingstone Parker. Chicago: Moody Press, 1951. https://www.ccel.org/ccel/wesley/journal.vi.ii.xvi.html.

Westerholm, Martin. "On Christian Discernment and the Problem of the Theological." *International Journal of Systematic Theology* 16 (2014) 454–69.

Williams, Rowan. "Mystical Theology and Christian Self-Understanding." In *The Oxford Handbook of Mystical Theology*, edited by Edward Howells and Mark A. McIntosh, 9–24. Oxford, UK: Oxford University Press, 2018.

Williams, Travis B. "Delivering Oracles from God: The Nature of Christian Communication in 1 Peter 4:11a." *Harvard Theological Review* 113 (2020) 334–53.

Woods, David B. "Interpreting Peter's Vision in Acts 10:9–16." *Conspectus* 13 (2012) 171–214.

Yuckman, Colin H. "Mission and the Book of Acts in a Pluralist Society." *Missiology* 47 (2019) 104–20.

Subject Index

Abraham, 4, 12
acceptance, of *metanoia,* 109
Achtemeier, Paul J., 61, 67, 68, 71, 79, 82–83
adoption, by God, 72
aesthetic cognition, 27–28
Agnus Dei, 66
algorithms, 147
amōmētos (blameless), 103, 105
Ananias, 46
"and the morning star rises in your hearts," 97–99, 131
angels, 33
animals, 55–56, 105
Anschauung, 28, 29
Anselm of Canterbury, xix–xx
anxiety, 148–49
aretē, 91–92, 95, 135
Aristotle, 101–2
art, work of, ix–x, xii–xiv, xviii–xix
artist, xi–xii, 24
ascent, 4, 11–12
aspilos (spotless), 103, 105
audience, point of view of, 31–32
Augustine of Hippo, 5–6, 122
Augusto de Souza Nogueira, Paulo, 57
Austin, David C. H., 151

baking, process of, 26
baptism, 31–33, 108
Barnabas, 113
Barth, Karl, 10, 59, 123, 124
Beatitudes, 83
Beelzebul, 38, 39

beginning, power of, xviii
behavior, 71–72, 75
Behm, J., 101–2
beholder *(Betrachter),* xiv–xxi
beholding stage of threefold seeing, 30–34, 51, 52–53, 62–86
Benedict, St., 23
The Biblical Canon (McDonald), 90
biblical text, transformation of, xiii
blameless *(amōmētos),* 103, 105
blessings, 64, 66, 85, 126–27
Bock, Darrell, 48
Bockmuehl, Markus, 16, 45, 46, 60, 61, 115
Branch Davidian, 39
breastmilk, 75
Brock, Darrell, 56–57
Brown, Sherri, 96
Brueggemann, Walter, 138–39
Brunner, Emil, 10
Bunyan, John, 12

Callan, Terrance, 61, 66, 68, 74, 76–77, 84–85, 96, 100, 105
The Cambridge Companion to Christian Mysticism (Stang), 8
Catherine of Siena, 6–7, 48
catholic comprehension of the world (*katholische Weltanschauung*), xi, xx
Caulley, Scott, 71, 82
chain of Christian living, 94–97, 135
children, attentiveness of, 69–70, 71
Christensen, Sean, 76, 79

Subject Index

Christians/Christianity
  as blessed, 83
  call of, 79
  characteristics of, 132–33
  as chosen people, 82
  circumcised, 113
  communal nature of, 136
  community of, 144–45
  divine kinship of, 134
  exclusion of, 125–26
  gift and response within, 96–97
  God's calling of, 91
  God's favor of, 126
  God's work within, 81
  growth of, 131
  holiness and, 132–33
  as holy priesthood, 78, 79–80
  inheritance of, 132
  Jewish comparison to, 82
  lifestyle of, 94–97, 105, 135
  as living stones, 77–79, 133, 134
  moral behaviors of, 75
  mystical, 140
  peace (*eirēnē*) of, 103
  Peter's commands to, 103–4
  Peter's description of, 103
  as royal priesthood, 133, 134, 148
  salvation and, 132
  self-knowledge of, 133, 148
  self-understanding of, 122–23, 132–37
  as spiritual house, 133
  spiritual pure milk and, 133
  spiritual sacrifices of, 78, 133–34
  suffering of, 84
Christian Spirituality (Cunningham and Egan), 3
circumcised believers, 113
classification, 147
Climacus, John, 12, 40
communication from God, 121, 128–32, 145–46
community, 42–43, 144–45
compulsion to write, as mystic characteristic, 8
Confessions (Augustine), 6
consumers, 147
contemplation, 23, 120

conversion, foundational knowledge from, 93
Cook, Stephen, 20–21
Cornelius, 29, 57, 112–13, 141
cornerstone, Jesus as, 77–78
covenants, God and, 64–65
COVID-19 pandemic, 147
Craddock, Fred, 66, 81
critical-method tools, 25, 26
culture, as world of second degree, x
Cunningham, Lawrence S., 3, 23

dancing, as mystical experience expression, 14
Daniel, 48
darkness, 81, 83
The Dark Night (John of the Cross), 109
Dasein (new being), x, xiv, xix
Day of Our Lady of Guadalupe, 14
Delio, Ilia, 120
Delphi, oracle at, 39
Deluge, 138
demand, *metanoia* and, 114
democracy, 139, 140
dianoia
  defined, 36, 38
  example of, 111
  of 1 Peter, 62–86
  overview of, 101–2
  of Peter, 53–54
  process of, 43
  pure, 100–102, 127, 131, 135–36
  spiritual discernment and, 39
Dickinson, Emily, 26–27
dietary laws, 22
discernment, spiritual, 38–44
divine communication
  human growth and, 131
  knowing as form of, 130
  morning star *(phōsphoros)* as, 131
  overview of, 128–32, 145–46
  Petrine, 131–32
  pure *dianoia* as, 131
  rebegetting and, 128–29
  spiritual pure milk as, 130
  word of God as, 129
divine encounter, 119–23
divine knowledge, 40

Subject Index

divine revelation, 28
The Doctrine of God (Barth), 123
Donelson, Lewis R., 89, 92, 95, 96, 98, 105, 106
doxa (glory), 91

ecstasy, 52
Edwards, Dennis, 15
Egan, Keith J., 3, 23, 42
Ehrman, Bart, 45
ekstāsis, 49–50, 58
Elijah, 12, 129
English, John J., 24
epignōsis, 92–94, 130
eschatological theology, 57–58
Esther, 48
Eucharist, 57
evil, 65, 124–25
experience, as an approach, xx–xxi
exploration, 139–40
extrovertive mysticism, 4
eye, function of, xv–xvi
Ezekiel, 37

faithfulness, 141
false teachers, 99–100, 103
fasting, 48
Festugière, A. J., 4
The Fiery Soliloquy with God (Petersen), 119
figure *(Gestalt),* within a work of art, xiv
food, unclean, 53
"for whom the gloom of the darkness has been kept," 99–100
Fox, Everett, 138
Francis of Assisi, 35, 41, 110
Frey, Jörg, 89, 92, 98–99, 100, 102, 104
Frohlich, Mary, 8
fruit, of mystical experiences, 13

Gench, Frances Taylor, 47
gentiles, pagan, 32
Gestalt (figure), within a work of art, xiv
glory *(doxa),* 91
glory of God, 84, 85

gnōsis, 93–94
gnosticism, 4
God
  actions of, 81, 144
  activity of, 65–66
  authority of, 57
  blessing from, 126–27
  blessings to, 64, 66
  as builder, 77
  characteristics of, 120, 124, 128
  communication from, 121, 128–32, 145–46
  detachment from, 138–39
  direct communication with, 50
  faithfulness of, 64
  favor of, 126
  gender of, 75
  glory of, 84
  knowledge of, 119, 120, 123–28, 132, 136
  light from, 107–8
  mercy of, 64, 65–66, 68, 124, 143
  milk from, 75–76
  mystical action of, 54–55
  as *nous,* 102
  patience of, 143, 149
  personal interaction by, 21, 50
  Petrine, 143–45
  point of view of, 33
  power of, 91, 126
  presence of, 84, 97–99, 125
  promise of, 64
  revealing by, 27, 121
  shaping by, 154
  spiritual ascent to, 11–12
  spiritual house of, 126, 128
  standards of, 80
  as trustworthy, 64
  understanding of, 123
  values of, 127
grace, 86, 105–6, 127, 131
gratitude, 127
Greek language, 61
Green, Joel, 54, 65–66, 67, 74, 81–82
Guardini, Romano, ix–xxii, 24, 28, 116–17, 120, 121

Subject Index

Harrington, Daniel, 89, 90, 93, 95, 98, 105
heavens, opening of, 54, 57
hell, 99–100
hermits, 7
Hilton, Walter, 119
holiness, 70, 71–72, 78, 132–33
holy priesthood, 78, 79–80
Holy Spirit, 61
hope, 68, 124, 125, 141–42
How God Changes Your Brain (Newberg and Waldman), 12–13
Hughes, Graham, 55
human agency, 124–25, 127
human brain, 136
human knowledge, 40
humility, 40–41, 85–86, 127, 142

identity, 88–89
Ignatius, 24, 42
illuminative state of mysticism, 5, 12
Inge, William Ralph, 10
inheritance, from God, 68
intermittent fasting, 48
introvertive mysticism, 4
Israelites, 20, 71

Jacob, 4, 59
Jairus's daughter, 47
James (brother of Jesus), 46
James, William, 2
Jeanrond, Werner, 21
Jennings, Willie James, 56
Jeremiah, 73
Jesus
  arrest of, 36
  as cornerstone, 77–78
  fasting by, 48
  following, 73
  as foundation, 2
  John the Baptist and, 34
  knowledge of, 38–39
  presence of, 97–99
  quote of, 29, 38, 83, 86, 103, 136, 145
  rejection of, 79
  as revelation source, 121
  spiritual discernment role of, 43
  Zacchaeus and, 32
John, 37
John of the Cross, 48, 109, 122, 124, 130, 132
Johnson, Luke Timothy, 39, 53
Johnson, William, 120, 132
John the Baptist, 34
Jonah, 111–12, 113
Joppa, 47
Joseph, 33
Julian of Norwich, 120, 146

Keating, Thomas, 121
Kelly, Morgan, 149
Kelsey, Morton, 39
kingdom of heaven, 57
kinship, divine, 134
Kirk, Kenneth Escott, 10
knowledge
  as act of an encounter in love, xi
  divine communication as, 130
  divine *versus* human, 40
  epignōsis as, 92–94
  gnōsis as, 93–94
  of God, 119, 120, 123–28, 132, 136
  growth of, 104, 105–6
  interpretations through, 116
  origin of, ix–x
Koskela, Douglas, 42
Kraftchick, Steven, 94, 96–97, 104
Kurtén, Tage, 52

The Ladder of Divine Ascent, 12
lambs, 105
Lane, Belden C., 31
Lathrop, Gordon, 55
law, internalization of, 37
Lazarus, 47
lectio divina, 23
lepers, 35–36, 41
light, 81, 83, 107–8
liturgy, 54–56
living hope, 67
living stones, 77–79, 133, 134
Lockett, Darian, 71
Lossky, Vladimir, 11
Lot's wife, 112

Subject Index

Luke, 22

machine learning, 147–48
Madigan, Shawn, 6–7
Martini, Carlo, 23
Mauch, Theodor, 20
May, Gerald, 39
McCartney, Dan, 76
McDonald, Lee Martin, 90
McGiffert, Arthur, 15
McGinn, Bernard, 4, 10, 11–12, 119
McIntosh, Mark, 40, 119
mechanics, 26
Mechthild of Magdeburg, 5, 13–14
mental wrestling, 59–60
mercy, 64, 65–66, 68, 124–25, 143
Merton, Thomas, 7, 120
metadata, 147
metanoia
  acceptance within, 109
  action from, 111
  defined, 108, 149
  demand and, 114
  example of, 108
  goal of, 116–17
  negative side of, 110, 111–12
  overview of, 108–9
  patience within, 113–14
  Petrine, 149–50
  positive side of, 110
  testing of, 112–14
  types of, 110–12
metaverse, 144
Mexico, 14
Mikoski, Gordon, 39, 43
milk, spiritual pure, 75–76, 130, 133, 146
Miller, Chris, 47
Miller, John B. F., 57
mind, 37–38
Miriam, 14
Moberly, R. W. L., 42
morning star *(phōsphoros)*, 97–99, 131
Moses, 4, 12, 48, 55, 84, 85
Mounce, Robert, 112
mystic
  characteristics of, 3
  Christian, 7–9

communication by, 8
compulsion to write characteristic of, 8
defined, 3, 5, 7
identification of, 5
overview of, 3–7
writings of, 13
mystical experiences, 4, 10–11, 13
mystical liturgy, 54–56
mystical theology
  branches of, 11–14
  fruit of mystical experiences branch of, 13
  importance of, 60
  overview of, 9–11
  Petrine, 14–15, 153–54
  as theological question anchor, 119
mysticism, 1, 4
Mysticism and Philosophy (Stace), 4
The Mysticism of Paul the Apostle (Schweitzer), 10

The Naked Now (Rohr), 3
nature, as world of first degree, x
neurotheology, 12–13
new being *(Dasein)*, x, xiv, xix
Newberg, Andrew, 12–13, 49, 136
new birth concept, 67
New Testament, methodology regarding, 16–18
Nicholas of Cusa, 120
Nicodemus, 66, 74
nous, 101

obedience, 71
omnipotence under God *(sub Deo omnipotentia)*, xx
On Learned Ignorance (Nicholas of Cusa), 120
openness, xx, 23, 41–42
Origen, 4
Orsy, Ladislas, 40
Orthodox Church, 11
The Oxford Dictionary of the Christian Church, 12

Packard, George, 118

Subject Index

pagan gentiles, 32
Palamas, Gregory, 48, 120
patience, 41, 113–14, 141, 143, 149
Paul, 66–67, 68, 113
peace, 103, 104–5, 142
Pelikan, Jaroslav, 49
Perrin, David, 2, 5
persecution, 65
perspective, within spiritual
  discernment, 40
Peter
  within Acts of the Apostles, 46
  audience of, 31–32
  authorship of, 60–62
  background of, 60
  characteristics of, 45–46
  denial by, 36, 86
  education of, 60–61
  ekstāsis of, 49–50
  emotional state of, 47, 63
  faithfulness of, 141
  God of, 143–45
  healings by, 61
  hope of, 141–42
  humility of, 142
  imagery regarding, 2–3
  isolation by, 47
  within Joppa, 47
  miracles of, 46, 47
  mystical theology of, 14–15, 153–54
  New Testament references to, 45
  as outsider, 55
  overview of, 2–3, 140–43
  paradigm shift regarding, 14–15
  patience of, 141
  peacefulness of, 142
  point of view of, 32
  rebuke to, 86
  as the rock, 2
  rooftop experience of, 22, 29, 48,
    49–58, 70
  as student, 2
  travels of, 46–47
  vision of, 29, 48, 49–58
2nd Peter
  "and the morning star rises in your
    hearts" within, 97–99
  aretē within, 91–92, 135

authorship of, 89–90
canonical inclusion of, 89–90
chain of Christian living within,
  94–97, 135
dianoia within, 131
epignōsis within, 92–94, 130
"for whom the gloom of the
  darkness has been kept," 99–100
Petersen, Gerlac, 119
Peterson, Eugene, 21, 121
Pharisees, 38, 42
pilgrimage, 12
The Pilgrim's Progress, 12
Plato, 4
poetry, 26–27
polarization, 149
polyhedral seeing, 22, 29, 31–33
Poor, Sara, 8
post-flood, 138–39
postmodernism, 139
postmodern mind, 37–38
power of God, 91
prayer, 30, 48, 54–55, 120
prayerful reading, 23–24, 30
presence of God, 84, 97–99, 125
pride, 112
priests, duties of, 78
Pseudo-Dionysius the Areopagite,
  4–5, 9
pure mind, 101
purgative state of mysticism, 5, 12
purification, 29

Rahner, Karl, 10, 140
rebegetting, 63, 66–67, 72, 73, 128–29,
  141
Red Sea, 20
regeneration, 66–67
religion, changes regarding, 139–40
religious artwork, xiii
resurrection of Jesus, 68, 124
revelation, 27, 28, 121, 122–23
The Revelatory Text (Schneiders), 17
rich young man, 112
Rilke, Rainer Maria, 27
Ritchie, Angus, 43
Ritschl, Albrecht, 10
Rohr, Richard, 3

Subject Index

rooftop experience of Peter, 22, 29, 48, 49–58, 70
Rosales-Acosta, Dempsey, 102
rose, 26, 151–54
Ross, Maggie, 30
royal priesthood, 133, 134, 148

sacrifices, 78, 105
Sadducees, 42
Salem witch trials, 39
salvation
    Christians and, 132
    in community, 69
    guarding of, 127
    hope through, 65
    Paul's concept of, 66–67, 68
    peace within, 104
    Peter's concept of, 67, 68–69
    power within, 64
Sapphira, 46
The Scale of Perfection (Hilton), 119
Schleicher, Marianne, 49–50
Schlobitten, Dohna, 24, 25, 27, 28, 116, 153
Schneiders, Sandra, 17, 121
Schweitzer, Albert, 10
Scripture
    as divine communication, 129
    divine reading of, 23
    interpretive approach to, 15
    as living, 73–75, 125, 129, 145
    presence of God through, 125
    as revelation, 121
seeds, imperishable, 72–73, 74
seeing, process of, xv–xvi
Seeing the Word (Bockmuehl), 16
self-implication, 31, 51
self-interest, 51
self-knowledge, 133, 146–49
self-understanding, 122–23, 132–37
Senior, Donald, 67, 68–69, 79, 83, 84
Sermon on the Mount, 24, 29
The Shepherd of Hermas, 40–41
Siegel, Daniel, 37
Silence (Ross), 30
Smith, Hannah Whitall, 97–98, 110–11
socialism, 139
Sodom and Gomorrah, 112

solipsism, 143
Sonderegger, Katherine, 59
spiritual ascent, 11–12
spiritual discernment, 38–44
spiritual exercises, 23, 24
spiritual experiences, 48
Spiritual Freedom (English), 24
spiritual house, 77–78, 126, 128, 133
spiritual life, 116
spiritual process, 12
spiritual pure milk, 75–76, 130, 133, 146
spiritual sacrifices, 78, 133–34
spiritual seeing, 21
spotless *(aspilos)*, 103, 105
Stace, Walter Terence, 4
Stang, Charles, 8, 13
Staples, Jason, 53, 57
sub Deo omnipotentia (omnipotence under God), xx
suffering, 84–85

Tabitha, 47
Tamfu, Dieudonné, 104
temple, destruction of, 50
Teresa of Avila, 13–14, 122, 124
textual seeing, 21–22
theology, ethics within, 96
threefold seeing (gaze) *(Blick Christi)*
    analogies of, 26–27
    defined, x
    description of, 24–25
    encounter of, 27–29
    goal of, 115–17
    interaction from, 153
    object looking back within, 152–53
    overview of, xxi–xxii, 21–24
    process of, xi–xii, 29
    purpose of, 25
    remaining with created object within, 115
    rose as, 151–54
    struggle to engage with God's demand within, 115–16
Tillich, Paul, 52
trance, 49
trustworthiness of God, 64
unclean food, 53, 56

Subject Index

Underhill, Evelyn, 5–6, 7, 10, 12
union, within mystical theology, 9–10
unitive state of mysticism, 5, 6, 7, 12–13
users, defined, 147
utensil, symbolism of, 55

van der Horst, Pieter, 50
Van Engen, Charles, 55–56
Van Gogh, Vincent, xii–xiii, xix
Venus, 98
vessel, symbolism of, 55
Villegas, Diana, 40
vision, 28, 29, 37, 48, 49–58, 116
von Balthasar, Urs, 116–17

Wahlen, Clinton, 53
Wainwright, Geoffrey, 57
Waldman, Mark Robert, 12–13, 49, 136

Wall, Robert, 100
Watson, Duane, 61, 66, 68, 74, 76–77, 84–85, 96, 100, 105
Wesley, John, 97, 110
Westerholm, Martin, 41
whole of being, xii
widow of Nain, 47
Williams, Rowan, 60, 122, 123
Williams, Travis, 76
wisdom, 8, 13
Woods, David, 53
word, quantitative value of, xvii
word of God. *See* Scripture
world, conceptions of, x
wrestling, 115–16

Yuckman, Colin, 53–54

Zacchaeus, 32, 114

Scripture Index

OLD TESTAMENT

Genesis

7	138
19:24	112
19:26	112
32:24–32	59

Exodus

15:20	14
19:5–6	80
24:5–8	85
34:28	48
34:29	84
40:10	55

Leviticus

19:2	71

Deuteronomy

6:5 LXX	36
16:16	12

1 Samuel

3	145

1 Kings

19:13	129

Esther

4:16–17	48

Psalms

1:2	36–37
8:3–4	122, 127
8:4	132
11:4–7	12
22	116
38:2b–3a	116

Proverbs

3:34	86

Isaiah

40:8b	73
43:19	55
45:8	54

Jeremiah

1:4	73

Ezekiel

1:1	54
3:1	37
3:3	37
4:1	37

Scripture Index

Jonah

1:1–3	111
2:2	111
4:1	112

Malachi

3:10b	54

NEW TESTAMENT

Matthew

1:20	33
1:29	34
3:16	54
4:1–11	48
5:8	24, 29
5:11	83
5:23–24	56
12:24	38
12:25b–26	38
13:33	55
14:28–31	86
16:13–23	142
16:16	73
16:19	2
16:21–23	86
19:16	112
19:21	112
22:37	36
26:69–75	86

Mark

4:21	143
4:39	129
12:30	36n3

Luke

2:25–38	145
4:1–13	48
8:48	145
10:27	36n3
17:14	145
19:8	114
22:32	70
22:61–62	36

John

1:12–13	72
3:3	66
3:4	74
4:35	30
14:6	121
14:27	103

Acts

3:2–9	86
4:13	61
8	46
8:39	61
9	46
9:1	46–47
9:32–35	86
9:40–43	86
10	1, 18, 22
10:1–48	53
10:9	48
10:9–20	44
10:10	49
10:11	55
10:11–16	51
10:12–13	29
10:17–20	52
10:36	53
11	46
11:4	142
11:18	113
15	46
15:7–11	142
21	46

Romans

1:9	73

1:16	68
6:4	66
10:9	66–67
14:14	56

1 Corinthians

3:11	2
4:14	142
10:19	57
13:12	31

2 Corinthians

3:18	31
6:6–8	94
13:10	142

Galatians

1:6	142
4:5–7	72
5:22–23	94, 110n3

Ephesians

2:19–22	2
4:32	95

Philippians

1:12	73

Colossians

3:12	95

1 Thessalonians

1:5	73

1 Timothy

4:3–4	56
4:12	95

1 Peter

1:1–2	142
1:2	10–12, 17–22, 68
1:3	77, 141

1:3–5	63–69, 124–125, 128–129, 132–133, 141
1:5	9–10, 68
1:6	78
1:8	86
1:9	68
1:12	21
1:13	36
1:14	142
1:14–16	69–72, 129, 132–133
1:23	72–75, 77, 125, 129, 133
1:25	73
2:2	68, 75–77, 130, 133, 142
2:5	77–80, 125–126, 133–134, 148
2:9	80–83, 126, 134, 148
2:11	142
3:8	86
3:21	68
3:21–22	31
4:8	86
4:12	142
4:14	21, 83–85, 126–127, 134–135, 148
5:5b	85–87, 127, 130, 134–135

2 Peter

1:2	92, 104–105
1:2	3, 8, 92–94, 130
1:3	91, 92, 96, 103
1:3	4, 5, 91–92, 135
1:3–4	92, 96
1:3–7	96
1:4	89, 91, 92
1:5	91
1:5–7	94–97, 96, 135
1:16–19	97
1:19	97–99, 131
1:20	112
1:20–21	42, 115–116
2	100
2:9	149
2:13	105
2:17	99–100, 127
2:20	92–94, 93, 130
3	100

(2 Peter continued)

3:1	36, 100–102, 127–128, 131, 135–136
3:8–9	104
3:9	104
3:10–13	103
3:12	146
3:14	17-18, 102–106, 131, 135–136

Revelation

4:1	54
22:16	99

www.ingramcontent.com/pod-product-compliance
Lightning Source LLC
Chambersburg PA
CBHW062041220426
43662CB00010B/1601